Public Enemies

Also by John Walsh
in Large Print:

Tears of Rage

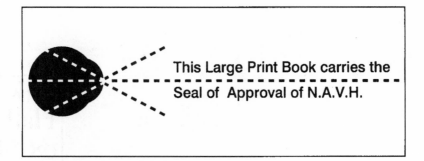

This Large Print Book carries the
Seal of Approval of N.A.V.H.

Public Enemies

THE HOST OF
AMERICA'S MOST WANTED
TARGETS THE NATION'S MOST
NOTORIOUS CRIMINALS

JOHN WALSH
WITH PHILIP LERMAN

G.K. Hall & Co • Waterville, Maine

Published in 2001 by arrangement with Pocket Books, a division of Simon & Schuster.

G.K. Hall Large Print Nonfiction Series.

The text of this Large Print edition is unabridged.
Other aspects of the book may vary from the original edition.

Set in 16 pt. Plantin.

Printed in the United States on permanent paper.

Library of Congress Cataloging-in-Publication Data

Walsh, John, 1945–
    Public enemies : the host of America's most wanted targets the nation's most notorious criminals / John Walsh with Philip Lerman.
        p. cm.
    ISBN 0-7838-9730-8 (lg. print : hc : alk. paper)
    1. Criminals — United States. 2. Crime — United States.
3. Violent crimes — United States — Case studies. 4. Criminal investigation — United States — Case studies. 5. America's most wanted (Television program). I. Lerman, Philip. II. Title.
HV6789.W33 2001b
    364.973—dc21   2001054363

To OUR PARTNERS IN LAW ENFORCEMENT,
who put their lives on the line every day;

To THE DEDICATED STAFF MEMBERS OF
America's Most Wanted, who work countless
hours to get the show on the air each
week, and who make such a difference
in the lives of crime victims;

AND TO OUR LOYAL VIEWERS, who have
kept *America's Most Wanted* on the air for
more than thirteen years, and who have
brought closure and justice to countless
suffering victims of crime.

Acknowledgments

My partner, Lance Heflin, is the creative vision behind *America's Most Wanted*, and I will always be grateful to him for the drive and passion he brings to all the projects he spearheads, including this one.

Once again, Phil Lerman and his team have melded their meticulous research and their compassion for the victims of crime to help bring this book to life. Leading that team is Lydia Strohl, whose writing and research are impeccable, and whose contribution was essential; my sincere thanks also to David Braxton and Eleanor Lerman, who helped us put together several of the chapters.

Thanks also to Cheri Nolan, whose patience and guidance are an essential grounding force; to Emily Bestler at Pocket Books, whose counsel we rely on; and to Shelly Perron and Felice Javit at Pocket Books, whose careful readings of our earlier drafts were a key component in the creation of an accurate accounting of the stories we wanted to tell.

Thanks to all the current and former members of the *America's Most Wanted* family who gave of their memories, their time, their files, and their hearts, and on whose work these stories were built: including Ashleigh Banfield, Tom DeVries, Joann Donnellan, Neal Freundlich, Anne Garofalo, Sharon Greene, Avery Mann, Ed Miller, Tom Morris Jr., Lena Nozizwe, Margaret Roberts, Cindy Smith, and the irrepressible Tony Zanelotti.

Were it not for David Hill, the man responsible for resurrecting *America's Most Wanted* after it was cancelled, we would not be here at all. Our gratitude goes to him, and to all those at Fox who have helped to support and sustain us: You have proved that television can, indeed, be used as a positive force.

As always, my thanks go to all the law enforcement officers who have allowed us to be part of their efforts, and helped us in ours; and, mostly, to all the crime victims who have let us into your lives and trusted us to tell your stories honestly, and caringly, and with dignity. I hope we have lived up to your trust.

Contents

1

Public Enemy Number One

I remember the first time I felt true fear.

It was just before dark on Monday, July 27, 1981, in the parking lot outside a shopping mall in Hollywood, Florida. It was the day my son Adam disappeared.

The fear did not come right away. I had spent all day in desperate but controlled activity, questioning police, demanding answers, rushing around, trying to find anyone who'd seen anything that day. The frantic activity of a father whose son has disappeared is fueled by adrenaline and panic; you do everything you can to try to will that little boy back into your arms. You are moving so fast and so furiously that you do not notice the hole in your stomach, the gaping hole growing larger and larger.

But just before dark, the lights began to be turned off at the mall, and they were locking up; most of the cars were gone, and suddenly there was nothing to do but leave this place, leave without Adam, go home without my little boy. And then, for the first time, I felt that hole, the gaping hole in my stomach, that felt like the wind was blowing through it, that my life was blowing through it, as though I were so much sand in the wind and only by force of will could I keep myself from disintegrating. It is an all-consuming fear: your child is gone, and, God forbid, is it possible that there is nothing you can do?

You push the fear down, and you move forward, resolutely: of course there are things you can do. You will find that child. Let's go. Let's get the flyers out, let's muster the troops, let's sound the call to battle. My child is somewhere and he needs me and by all that is holy I will do what my child needs and bring him back to me.

But late at night the fear creeps back as you lie silently in your bed, knowing that you will not sleep tonight, wondering if your wife is asleep and knowing she is not, feeling like you are falling, feeling consumed by an awful, nauseating, dizzying, overwhelming loneliness. As indescribably painful as it has been, all these years, to deal with the death of that lovely boy, those days when we did not know where in the universe he was, whether he was in the hands of some madman, suffering God-knows-what pain, those days of not knowing were the worst.

In those days I understood true, blinding, paralyzing fear.

It is now twenty years since I died the thousand deaths that a parent of a missing child suffers, and in those twenty years I have seen the look of that fear in the faces of so many other parents, ravenous for information, desperate to find their missing children.

I know it's not right, and I know it's not fair, but I will admit this to you now: there are some cases that affect me more than others. I don't know why that is — something in a mother's plea as she holds your hand and tells you little things she remembers about her daughter: how she laughed, how she smelled, where she liked to Rollerblade. Something in a father's down-turned eyes as he sits before you, afraid to look at you directly, afraid to start crying because he fears he'll never stop, feeling he has to be inhumanly strong for his child. Something in that first photo you see of a missing child, a photo hurriedly pulled from a family album or ripped from a frame on the mantel, a photo of a child who by all rights should be driving her parents crazy right now because she refuses to turn off the TV and go to sleep.

There are some cases that affect you more than others. At those moments, you freeze in your tracks and say, we have got to find this child. Now, here, this is where I draw the line. This time, the kidnapper is not going to get away with it. The son of a bitch will pay. This time, we will stop him. Enough is enough.

This was one of those cases.

Because this time, we would go to battle with evil itself.

The missing-child stories that reach the public's consciousness seem to come in waves. The summer and fall of 1993 was one of those times. It seemed every time you picked up the paper, another child had been abducted. In Northern California the abduction of eleven-year-old Polly Klaas — a man had actually snuck into her home, into a slumber party she was having with her friends, and dragged her away while her mother slept down the hall — sent a chill through every parent's heart everywhere. The fact that the case was trumpeted by a parade of celebrities, including Winona Rider and Robin Williams, kept it high in the public consciousness.

This was also the summer when twelve-year-old Sara Wood disappeared in upstate New York. She was last seen bike-riding home from vacation Bible school, and that afternoon police found her bike and papers strewn by the side of the road, another image that cast an indelible imprint. The proximity to New York meant that the parents had access to the morning talk shows, which picked up the case and ran with it. Being from upstate New York myself, I also knew some of the cops involved in the case, and I was drawn into it as well.

The summer had started with a case of an adorable six-year-old, whom I'll call Nancy. (We named her at the time she was missing, of course, but her parents have asked that we stop using her real name publicly, so I'll leave it out here.) Nancy and two friends were sitting in a driveway when a man approached and — I swear to God — offered them candy. He then grabbed Nancy and drove away with her. The cops, the National Center for Missing and Exploited Children, and *America's Most Wanted* launched a massive search. We broadcast satellite alerts out to cover the region, blanketing the state with media coverage.

After fifty-one hours, the kidnapper felt the heat and dropped Nancy off at a public phone booth.

She called her mom, and we joined that rare celebration, that wonderful moment when a stranger abduction ends in a tearful, loving homecoming.

A few days later, I sat down with Nancy for a little talk.

"What did the man say to you?" I asked her.

"He said, 'Do you want some candy?' " Nancy replied.

"And what did you say?"

"Yes." An embarrassed smile crossed her beautiful little face.

"Oooh," I said, trying not to sound mean. "Big mistake, huh?"

"Yeah!" she said with a nervous laugh.

"Then what happened?"

"I come with him, and he dragged me and tossed me into the car."

"Bet you were scared, huh. Then what happened?"

"I had to go down on the floor."

"And he drove away?"

"Uh-huh."

"What did you think was happening to you?"

Nancy fell silent. "Being kidnapped," she said, finally.

"He told you what?"

"Don't move a muscle."

"Don't move a muscle?"

"Not even one."

"Not even one," I repeated. "Bet you were scared. You know, other kids are going to be watching this. If you could say something to those kids about strangers who come up to you, what would you say to those kids?"

"Don't listen to them."

"And what if they want to give you candy?"

"Say no."

"And then what?"

"Go to the house what you're close to."

"Good advice. And what do you think should happen to the man?"

Her little face brightened. "I think he should go to jail for a hundred years!"

I thought, from your mouth to God's ear, little darling. From your mouth to God's ear.

It will haunt me to my dying day that, at the same moment I was sitting and talking with Nancy — having the wonderful joy of knowing that we had helped bring a missing child home safely — at that same moment, a thousand miles away, a woman named Sue North was walking over to a friend's home to get her daughter

Jeanna and bring her home.

But Jeanna was not there.

And the nightmare was about to begin again.

She was a tiny baby, weighing just a little more than six pounds. The hair that would later turn to beautiful, fluffy waves of auburn started out jet black. That tiny head was peeking out of the yellow blanket they wrapped her in the day she came home from the hospital, and Sue North and her husband, John, had the same thought at the same time: she looks just like a little corn on the cob! Jeanna Dale North took on the nickname "Cobbie" that day, and in affectionate moments she was Cobbie to her mother ever after.

Almost from the time she could walk, Jeanna was running: a bundle of happy energy who never seemed to stop moving. "She just goes from dawn till dusk," Sue North told us later. "You have to lay her down on your lap and hold her head still for her to go to sleep."

Sue North's three daughters were very different from one another. Jessica, the oldest, was the brainy kid in the family: tested early on with an IQ at genius levels, she developed more into a right-brain teenager, loving her painting the most. Jennifer, the middle child, was the quiet and passive one: in the tumult of the household, Sue sometimes turned around, surprised to see Jennifer sitting there quietly, just watching the chaos unfold. And at the center of the chaos, usually, was Jeanna; "my little hyper-bug," Sue called her.

As they got older, Jeanna got on her sisters' nerves, as only hyper little sisters can. But with Dad and Mom both out working construction, they also had charge of Jeanna and were as protective of her as two little momma lions with a tiny cub. She knew how to annoy them, but they could not stay angry at Jeanna for very long: her bright, devilish eyes and coy smile would come bouncing at you, she would scrunch her little features into a funny face, and you were helpless to keep from grinning and going along with whatever little game she would think up next. She loved being the little clown of the house, as though the assignment given her by God was to keep her family laughing, to make sure they didn't take themselves too seriously, to fill every little moment with as much fun as she could. It seemed at times as though she was trying to pack an entire lifetime into every day; little girls do not have the philosophical bent to live each day as though it were your last, but the energy that abounded in Jeanna Dale North certainly made it seem as though she were doing just that.

As though any given day could be her last day on earth.

By the time she turned eleven, Jeanna was still tiny — just a few inches over four feet, she could get the scale over fifty pounds only by jumping up and down on it, which was not outside her realm of mischief. And if she "didn't like to mind so much," as Sue put it, she certainly had a way of getting you to forgive her. The trail of sneakers and socks and jacket and books and candy wrappers from the front door to her room told you that Jeanna had come home; the fact that her beloved Rollerblades were gone told you she was out again.

She was a whiz on the Rollerblades, as though they were the one mechanism for channeling all that abundant energy in a single direction. Once, at the local roller arena, she got going so fast that the crowd spontaneously cleared the rink for her, and she flew, around and around, again and again, smiling child-wide, in her favorite place — the center of the spotlight. As she flew by she caught her mom's eye, saw her mother beaming with approval and pride, and Jeanna's smile grew just that much wider.

Little accomplishments mean a lot to a kid who doesn't do all that well in school; Sue North instinctively knew this and encouraged Jeanna as best she could. The first time she came home with a 100 on a spelling test, Sue framed it and put it on the wall.

"She wasn't a straight-A student," said her dad, John, "but she was easy to love, and she gave a lot of love away."

At eleven, Jeanna was still her daddy and mommy's little girl. The only time she stopped moving was to climb in her dad's lap and cuddle in his arms, and she still slept in her parents' bed whenever she was allowed. But now she was becoming more adventurous: one day she decided to climb to the top of the water tower, just to see if she could do it.

Sue had to punish her for that, and had to punish her again on the afternoon of June 27, 1993, when Jeanna came home from summer school. It was a bad moment to have to chastise her daughter: Jeanna, uncharacteristically, had been a little sad and sullen the last few days. But as she burst through the door, she announced, "I don't know nothin' about it" — Sue had no idea what she was talking about but understood it to be a preemptive strike against the inevitable. Sue, of course, soon had the story out of her daughter: some silliness about someone taking someone's colored pencil had gotten a little out of hand, the way things can with hyperactive eleven-year-olds. She sternly told Jeanna exactly what she thought of her bad behavior.

Later that afternoon, a sad-faced Jeanna came up to her mom in the kitchen.

"Are you mad at me?" she asked her mom.

"Oh," she told her daughter, cuddling her in her arms, "I guess I'll keep you around for a while."

Sue was at work the next evening, around 10:30 P.M., when Jeanna and her friend Clarice were out Rollerblading around town. The town of Fargo, North Dakota, where Jeanna grew up, is still the kind of place where people watch out

20

for one another, so when they stopped at a local Dairy Queen around 10:30 P.M., for a snack, then left, a police officer noticed. "A little late for those two to be out alone," he said to the clerk at the store. "I hope they're headed home."

They headed directly to Clarice's house, where Jeanna planned to spend the night. Although she was eleven, Jeanna had only just started having sleepovers — she preferred the security of home. When she got to Clarice's, she chickened out, and decided to go back and sleep in her own bed instead.

Clarice watched Jeanna skate down the street, toward her home, a block away. Then Clarice turned and went inside.

But Jeanna was still being watched . . . by a predator.

A second set of eyes, charming and sinister, followed her as she skated up the street.

In the darkness, they moved toward her.

The man approached, and she stopped.

She knew this man; he lived right across the street. So she had, she believed, no reason to fear.

Had she known the secrets that lurked in Kyle Bell's dark past, she would have understood: this man was as fearsome and dangerous as the panther tattooed on his left arm, as deadly as the Grim Reaper tattooed on his right.

From the time Kyle Bell was three years old, there was something strange about him. Once, while his mother was neglecting him, he gnawed through the wooden bars of his crib. Soon after, Kyle and his father went to live with Kyle's grandparents, hardworking farmers outside Aberdeen, South Dakota. The Bells had lots of family around — Kyle's Uncle Tom and Aunt Kim lived nearby with their children, and Grandma Bell ran an old-fashioned household ("three banquets a day, complete with home-made pies," remembered Kim Bell).

But into this big, loving extended family, Kyle Bell came like a virus, disrupting the peace and respect of the household with his bizarre behavior. Grandma and Grandpa Bell didn't know what to do with a three-year-old who put his cousin's Barbie dolls in sexual positions — this was a household in which you didn't even joke about sex — but the doctors they sought out said there was nothing wrong with Kyle, that he would grow out of the weird behavior.

Instead, he grew into it.

In the fifth grade, a puppy followed him home from school. For some reason, this enraged young Kyle.

So he killed the puppy by impaling it on a sharp stick.

A few years later, Grandma saw something strange on the side of the house. When she investigated, she could hardly believe what it was.

Kyle had been masturbating out a second-story window.

Again and again, the family tried to get help

22

for Kyle — through the schools, through counseling, through the church. But in the 1950s, in Washburn, North Dakota, no one really knew how to deal with these sorts of things.

So it just got worse.

Uncle Tom and Aunt Kim had moved away, but every summer Kim Bell's young children came to stay with Grandma. This started when the daughter was about five years old and continued until she was about ten.

And in ways too unspeakable to describe, again and again, day in and day out, year after year, relatives later told us Kyle Bell forced one of his little cousins to have sex with him.

Again and again, this poor child was subjected to the most horrible, disgusting, vile whims of Kyle Bell — who told her, again and again, that if she ever breathed a word of this, he would kill Grandma. And so this poor terrified child kept her silence.

It was the first time he preyed on a family member. It would not be the last.

As he grew to adulthood, his tastes ran to boyish-looking young women. After moving to Fargo, he moved in with his then-girlfriend, a young woman named Kim Engelstad, whom he soon married. Kyle was older than she — he was 25, she was only 18 — and her family didn't like the situation one bit. "He liked young girls, that was his thing," Tom DeVries, one of our producers on the case, explained to me later. "His wife told me that when he met her she was in high school. She was a slender, boyish girl. That's what he liked. He married someone who was as close to his sexual ideal as he legally could.

"She told me that when she got pregnant he lost interest in her. Why? Because she developed breasts."

And so his eyes began to wander, looking around the neighborhood.

And they settled on a little girl who lived across the street.

Little eleven-year-old Jeanna North.

I can't tell you how many hundreds of times I've spoken to groups of kids and asked them what child molesters look like. And the kids, no matter what age, always tell me the same things: they're dirty. They're smelly. They have big foreheads, and dark eyebrows, and weird eyes, and raincoats. Or, as in the case of little Nancy, they are strangers who pull up in strange cars. And it is so hard, so hard to reach out to these kids and tell them: it's not like that. Molesters don't look like the boogeyman. They look like that nice guy next door, that man with the easy smile and the soft brown hair and the nice truck that he gives you a ride in and lets you sit in his lap and pretend you're driving. But somehow, kids can't make that connection. We can teach them the lesson "don't talk to strangers" — we were about to air the Nancy story as just such a reminder — but they can't keep their guard up when the stranger is no stranger, when it's that nice friendly man from across the street.

And Bell was so charming, so friendly, that none of the kids in the neighborhood worried about him.

So on the night of June 28 little Jeanna had no reason to fear when the nice man from across the street stepped out of the shadows as she Roller-bladed home from her friend's house, Roller-blading home because at heart she was still a little girl who felt safer sleeping under the same roof as her mommy, and she was just a stone's throw from her home, where she could sleep safe and warm. But now the man from across the street approached her. Children are by nature innocent and trusting, and, without a moment's hesitation or fear, she stopped.

And she could not know it, but in that moment, a chasm was opening between her and the safety of her home, a chasm she would never cross.

The next morning, Sue North walked over to Jeanna's friend's house, the house where she assumed her daughter had spent the night. She was feeling lousy about yelling at Jeanna over the trouble at school and was looking forward to making everything okay.

When she heard Jeanna's friend say that no, Jeanna hadn't stayed there, that she had decided to go home, her heart sank into her stomach.

The thought ran through her like an electric

shock: a whole night has gone by. I don't know where my child has been for a whole night.

Slowly at first, then faster, she went to one house in the neighborhood, then another, and another, knocking on doors and saying the words no parent ever wants to utter: my daughter is missing. Have you seen her?

And at each door, the answer was no.

John North got in his car and drove around the neighborhood, asking everyone he saw if they had seen Jeanna. He even ran into Kyle Bell and asked him if he knew anything about where Jeanna might be.

Cool and calm, Kyle Bell stared him straight in the eye. "No, John, I don't," he said.

A frantic Sue North called the police and was told to give it some time, that they were sure Jeanna would show up. Maybe she just ran away, they said. Maybe she's just letting off some steam.

"The hell she ran away," Sue North told us. "A mother knows her child. I knew she didn't run away. She was always right where I could find her."

But as darkness fell that night in Fargo, the panic was replaced by that deep, aching fear that any parent of a missing child knows all too well, the engulfing fear, your mind trying to imagine what could have possibly happened to your child, and then snapping shut immediately, because you do not want to imagine what has possibly happened to your child.

For me, that fear has crystallized and hardened over the last twenty years into pure, white-hot rage — rage that surfaces whenever I hear that a parent has called a police department and said their child is missing, and is told to wait.

Because the only thing we do *not* have in a missing-child case is time.

There are just too many police departments in this country that still do not know how to react when a child goes missing. The first thing they want to do is assume that the child is a runaway, and to question the parents, to see if there is something hidden in the family dynamic that will lead to the answers about where the child might be. I will grant you that many, many times the family is responsible — but in the same breath I will say that I don't give a damn if it's one in a hundred or one in a thousand times that a child's disappearance turns out to be a stranger abduction. When that call comes in, it's essential that the police launch a dual investigation. Question the parents until you are blue in the face, hope that the child is just a runaway, and keep your fingers crossed — but at that same time, alert the FBI, *America's Most Wanted*, the local media, the radio stations. Call 1-800-THE-LOST, the twenty-four-hour hotline at the National Center for Missing and Exploited Children. Call the sheriff, and the state police, and everyone else you can find who will listen. Get the word out within twenty-four hours, because if you don't, and that child has been abducted, that's about all the time you've got. There is a myth in this country that you have to wait twenty-four hours before you start a full-scale missing persons investigation, and quite frankly it is a myth that too many police departments help perpetuate, because it means that they don't have to spend too much of their strained resources chasing after children who turn out to have just gone to the mall without permission. And it is also a myth that is fatal: because of it, children wind up dead, and how in God's name can you ever, ever forgive yourself for not launching the one investigation that could have saved a child's life?

But nothing happened that day. No missing child alerts went out. No state police were notified. No posters of Jeanna Dale North, with her auburn hair and beautiful blue eyes and devilish smile, graced the lampposts and 7-Eleven windows of Fargo that night.

And through that night, a mother lay collapsed on a couch, tears streaming down her face, rocking slowly, trying, as every parent of a missing child has done, to communicate psychically with her darling baby — to send her the words, don't be afraid, Daddy and I will find you. To call out to her through the universe, to will her back into her arms, thinking to herself, I love you, Cobbie, I love you, Cobbie, as though that love that a mother has for her child is enough to will her back into Momma's arms, as though the love that is stronger than the force that holds atoms together is somehow strong enough to bring her home.

But as the night began to ease away under the light of a false dawn, Sue North was still on that couch. Her daughters and her husband were with her, were trying to comfort her, but in that moment, without her Cobbie, Sue North felt cold, and frightened, and terribly alone.

The next day, word had spread through town about the little girl who didn't make it home; the news somehow made it to the mayor's office, and a call went from there to the police department — and I will say this: once they got involved, they put their heart and soul into the case.

I first met Detective Dennis Peterson that Friday afternoon, when we were finishing the taping of that week's show. We had already put out a satellite alert to all the TV stations within a few hundred miles of Fargo, and now we were breaking open the show to include Jeanna's story.

Peterson may have been handicapped by being given a late start on the case, but he made up for it fast. By the time he had boarded a plane for Washington, to hook up with our team at *America's Most Wanted*, Fargo was a beehive of activity. The local printing press was churning out posters, and hundreds of volunteers were pasting them up all over town. A team of police and search dogs were combing the woods and fields, and a second team was scouring the neighborhood, trying to find anyone who had seen something that night. Three hundred volunteers showed up to help stuff envelopes with Jeanna's picture.

That Saturday we aired the story of Nancy, the little girl who was brought home safely because of all the media attention to her case, and all we could do was pray that we could make lightning strike twice.

Normally, on a Saturday night, the Crime Center is a very busy place; from the moment we go on the air, the phones are ringing nonstop. Our twenty-four trained operators, handling forty-eight incoming lines, have their hands full. While they're answering the phones, that night's episode runs on a big screen on the set. But most of the operators have already studied the case files and are so engrossed in the incoming calls, they rarely watch the broadcast, their attention taken by the hundreds of tipsters trying to help out on that night's cases.

That's how it usually is.

But when Jeanna's case came on, you could hear a pin drop.

The juxtaposition of happy, giggling Nancy, safe in her parents, arms, and the photos of Jeanna, who at this moment might be suffering terrible pain or torment or torture, was hard enough. But we had asked Sue to send us a video, so that people could get a better sense of Jeanna, and when the video came on, it was heart-stopping. The enormous energy and happy-go-lucky gait of this beautiful child, bounding across the screen, froze everyone in the Crime Center. For a moment, there was not a sound in that room, as everyone stared into the face of this delightful imp with the tousled hair, arms akimbo, moving in every direction at once, this little darling so full of life, and they all had but one thought:

Please, let the next call be the one to bring her home.

But the tip we needed did not come through that night.

On Monday morning, disappointed but determined, Lance Heflin, our executive producer, sent a team to Fargo to produce a longer story. Sometimes we are able to bring a child home just by showing a picture or some video; when that doesn't work, we know we need to find another way to break through.

Often it is the passion and pain of the victim's family that breaks through the screen, that opens a viewer's heart, that gets someone to pick up a phone and make that call. In this second story we aired, we began with Jeanna's father as he spoke on the radio, his tone measured and determined, almost stoic — but the catch in his throat, the tremble in his voice, told of the searing torment that he was barely holding in check.

"Jeanna," he said into the microphone in the

radio studio, "I love you. Your mother and I miss you very much. Please, call home, or 911, or somebody, please, try to get word back to us, if you can."

Our camera crew was invited into the North home, to chronicle the desperate search. But when they returned, we were faced with a dilemma.

Because Sue North could not speak without crying.

This is the fine line we walk at *America's Most Wanted*. I have seen too many reporters shove a microphone in a mother's face, asking that terrible question: "Your daughter is missing. How do you feel?" What stupidity! How do they think a mother is going to feel?

Reporters and producers for *America's Most Wanted* are trained to be respectful of victims, which is why the victims trust us, why they let us into their homes and their hearts. Now here we were, with the kind of videotape that most news organizations lust after — only, I wasn't sure we should run it.

I saw the first cut of the segment that we had put together, and I thought it was just too much. As the father of a murdered child, I felt that putting Sue North's agony on public display would be a step over the line. We are not a tabloid show and we never have been, and we take the time to make sure that we are not taking advantage of people in horrible situations.

The argument raged around the room among

our missing child producers, our executives, and me: what is the point of showing this mother crying her eyes out? Are we helping to find a child or are we exploiting her pain?

There is no easy answer here. I wanted to spare Sue North the humiliation of baring her terrible pain to the world. But the producers argued that this was the element of the story that brought the reality of the moment through the screen — that made the disappearance of Jeanna North real, tangible, and painful to every viewer who saw it.

In the end, we compromised, cutting the scene down, leaving just a little of the tape in the piece, but removing the most painful moments, trying to allow Sue whatever privacy and dignity the mother of a missing child is allowed. I know, I have been there: the media wants to see you cry, every day. They come out with their cameras and they roll until you cry and they go home and put the tape on the news, and God bless them for keeping your child's face before the public, but you have no more privacy, no more dignity. You have traded those away for the desperate chance of bringing your child home, and you would suffer a million more indignities, a million times worse, to see that child one more time.

So if there is ever a way to give a family a shred of control, a shred of dignity, a shred of privacy, then that is what we will try to do. We will turn away and give them a moment to compose themselves, and then begin again, begin the real work:

not the work of making television, but the work of bringing an adorable eleven-year-old home safely.

But the weeks turned into months, and there was no sign of Jeanna.

Now the investigation went into phase two: the frantic search, the race against time, is over. There is no chance of finding the kidnapper red-handed before he has a chance to cover his tracks. The second phase of a missing-child investigation is a slower, more plodding one, as the police follow the hundreds of leads that have been generated by *America's Most Wanted*, and by their own interviews, and, one by one, focus on or eliminate suspects.

And the suspect that they were focusing on was Kyle Bell.

He hadn't told us at the time, but Detective Peterson had been suspicious of Bell from the start. A good detective works from the gut, and there was something just not right about the guy.

"I interviewed him right away," Peterson later told us, "and there were some inconsistencies in his story."

Peterson was keeping his suspicions of Bell close to the vest for two reasons: one, if you've got the right guy, you want to keep the media off of Bell's door, so that he is less likely to behave in a careful manner, more likely to make a mistake that will give him away. Two, if you've got the wrong guy, then you haven't tarnished an innocent man — although, in this case, Peterson wasn't too worried about that possibility.

But the news did leak out — and oddly, it was Bell himself who leaked the news to the press that the police were looking at him in the North disappearance.

He told a local reporter that he knew he was a suspect — and when asked why, he dropped this bombshell: "I was one of the last ones to see her, I lived on the corner of her block, I refused to take a lie detector test, and basically, she was in my truck, I suppose." Bell admitted seeing Jeanna the night she disappeared, before she went to the Dairy Queen; samples of Jeanna's hair had been found in his truck, and he said they had gotten there innocently, from a ride on another day.

With the cat out of the bag, there was less reason for discretion, so Peterson decided to take a trip down to Aberdeen, South Dakota, where Bell had grown up, to do some sniffing around. The case was beginning to obsess him: he worked on it constantly, his beeper was always going off. Peterson's daughter wrote a school essay about the case — and how much it took her daddy away from the family — and he felt awful about it. But he could not give up. He had to solve this case.

What he learned about Bell down in Aberdeen made him all the more suspicious: the strange tales of Bell's aberrant behavior came out, as did stories of him getting in trouble in junior high school for molesting a classmate on a bus, as did the startling information that when he was eighteen, he was convicted of statutory rape for getting a fifteen-year-old girl pregnant.

My dad always said, if you want to know a guy, look at his track record. And this guy was already compiling a hell of a track record.

But all that was nothing compared to what we all learned about Kyle Bell that October, after a freak accident.

Kyle had asked his seven-months-pregnant girlfriend, Kim, to marry him — even though, as we now know, he was already losing interest in her, and as we learned later, he was already turning his attention to the little girls in the neighborhood. Kyle's father and grandmother were headed to the wedding, making the drive up from Aberdeen to Fargo in their van. But on the way, a truck driver coming in the opposite direction fell asleep at the wheel — and in the fiery crash that followed, both of Kyle's relatives were killed.

In a disgusting show of self-absorption, Kyle had the funeral held up so that the wedding would not have to be postponed — and when he did show up at the funeral home, his first question was whether his presents had been burned up in the van as well.

His Aunt Kim, of course, was at the funeral, with her children. After the funeral, the words Kim heard shocked her to her very soul. It was a conversation between her son and daughter.

"Why," her son asked, "does my blood run cold whenever I see Kyle?"

"Because," his sister said, matter-of-factly, "he molested you as a child."

Their mom broke in: "How do you know this?"

"Because, Mom," her daughter said, bravely shattering the silence of a dozen years, "he molested me, too."

This opened the floodgates of emotion for Kim's daughter, and she fell to pieces, all the pain of all those years finally washing through her, a torrent of pain and tears.

What caused her to open up in this moment? Perhaps it was all those threats from Kyle, all those years ago, that if she ever told what happened he would kill Grandma; perhaps the shock of Grandma's death brought back that terror, reopened those wounds.

But for whatever reason, Kim's daughter had finally broken her silence. She had a terrible ordeal ahead: "My daughter was on Social Security disability for post-traumatic stress disorder," Kim said later, "and she never served in a war."

After her daughter's confession, Kim had summoned the FBI to interview the children about Kyle Bell. "After they talked to the children," Kim said, "they said to me, 'because of the situation I can't tell you the details, but in twenty-five years of service it's the worst I have ever seen.'

"The hardest thing was, I counseled how to recognize it, but I never saw it," Kim Bell told us just recently, saying she and her husband, Tom, still haven't come to terms with what that bastard Kyle Bell did to their family. "Tom and I just Friday night sat down across from one another. I said, I need to tell you something. I carry so much guilt for allowing this to happen to our children. And Tom said, 'So do I.' Where do we go with that? We have no place to go. Our kids come over every Saturday — our kids don't blame us, we do. The pain is still there: where was I when that was happening to our kids?"

Well, I want to say this to you right now, Kim Bell — to you and to all the parents out there whose children have been preyed upon by monsters like your nephew Kyle. You need to know, and understand in your heart, that this is not your fault. The vile, deranged psychotics like Kyle Bell do not just harm the children that they prey upon; their evil spreads throughout the families of their victims. It can tear them apart, destroy them, leave them shattered and empty. But you have been strong, and God bless you for your courage: you have counseled and helped your daughter back to health, you have held your family together. And most of all, when you learned what had happened, you did everything in your power to make sure that Kyle Bell did not get away with it. The actions you took speak volumes about the strength of your character and the depth of your heart. "We hate Kyle," you once told us, "for what he's done and the hell he's brought on our family. But above all, we never want molestation swept under the rug — there are animals out there and they have to be stopped."

Kim, you have nothing to feel guilty about. There is only one guilty person here, and that's Kyle Bell.

When you learned what happened, you spoke out. And for that you are my hero.

Kyle Bell's world was growing progressively smaller. In addition to the ugly stories of his past and the horrible tales that were told by his cousins, more stories of molestations started to surface — most importantly from his new wife's family.

It had all started a few months before the wedding, just after Jeanna North disappeared. That summer Kyle was searching for more little girls — and among his victims were two young relatives of his wife.

He touched them, he fondled them, he violated them, he stripped off their clothes and masturbated on them. He got a Polaroid camera for Christmas and took lewd photographs of them, starting that very day.

One of these innocent little girls was just seven years old.

The other was only three.

When I think about that, all I can say is: hell would be too easy for this guy.

Those stories came out in the spring of 1994, a few months after Bell's child was born, when a packet of Polaroid pictures was found in Kyle Bell's home. The first was taken on Christmas Day, the day he got the camera, showing him holding the box the camera came in.

The rest ranged from disgusting to horrifying.

The film made its way to the police, and by the time they had gotten to the end of the roll, Bell's fate was sealed. Things moved quickly — and on Wednesday, April 20, 1994, the bastard was thrown in jail.

Thank God.

It seemed like justice was finally catching up with Kyle Bell.

Now, you have to understand how desperately conniving, self-centered, and devious these child predators are. They maintain two lives — their public, charming selves masking their private, deranged selves. As a result, they become masters of manipulation — even getting themselves to believe their own lies in order to better lie to the people around them. Ever wonder why these guys sometimes are able to pass lie detector tests when the rest of the general public can't? It's because they actually convince themselves of their own innocence long enough to tell whatever story they must to get out of whatever scrape they're in.

That's why Kyle Bell — who up until this point had basically abandoned his wife and baby

— was able to muster up tears when his wife came to visit him in jail.

"When I got there, he was sitting in a chair," she told us. "He had a paper in front of him, and it was upside down. He pushed it over to me. I looked at it, and read it, and it said what he was charged with, and I just sat there.

"He looked right at me. He grabbed my hand, held my hand, and he cried, and we just sat there, not even saying a word. He wanted me to be there for him, you know, to be on his side. He wanted me to help him because he admitted he was sick, and he needed help.

"I just pulled my hand away. I had to get out of there. I didn't want to be in the same room with him."

And so, for a moment in time, Kyle Bell was all alone, tapped, his dark secrets exposed.

How honest was his cry for help?

About as honest as it usually is with these guys.

It took the police only one day to find that out.

Remember the car crash that took the life of Bell's father and grandmother? Well, as a result of that crash, Kyle got an insurance check — about $80,000 — and it was his ticket to freedom.

And the poor, penitent man asking for help because he was sick decided he didn't need help after all — except for help in escaping.

At 2:45 P.M. on Wednesday, Bell paid his $20,000 bail and checked into a motel. He started calling around to motorcycle shops, seeing if he could buy a motorcycle by phone — and if they could bring it to him at the motel.

Clearly, he didn't want anyone to know he was trying to buy a vehicle.

He went to a local beauty salon to try to get his hair permed and dyed, but the shop was closing, and they didn't have time to dye his hair.

His wife had moved back in with her father, and at 4 A.M. the next morning, she woke up her dad in a panic: someone, she said, was trying to break into the house.

Her dad grabbed a loaded pistol and went to the back door.

He saw a ladder propped up against the house and heard noises on the roof.

He went inside, turned on the outside lights, and stepped back outside the house.

And he saw Kyle Bell, ladder in hand, running toward the river. After a few moments, Bell dropped the ladder and kept on running.

And that was the last they saw of him.

Bell decided to hang around town for a few days. In his arrogant, cold, and calculating way, I'm sure he was trying to give the impression that he had no intention of fleeing. He did cut and dye his hair and bought a car from a local dealership, which he paid for in cash. That Friday night, he went to a local bar, had a couple of drinks, danced with a woman he met, and went out with her the next night. The last photo we have of him is when he was sitting in that bar, hanging out, apparently having the time of his life.

"On Monday," one of the cops on the case told us, "he withdraws the rest of his money, and we haven't seen or heard from him since."

At first, the sheriff's department was optimistic that they'd be able to track down Kyle Bell, but as the weeks went by with no sign of him, they realized they needed help.

So they came to us.

And we jumped at the chance to go after the slime bucket.

Remember, Bell was not charged in the Jeanna North case, but I had been champing at the bit to go after this guy. The more I heard, the more I was certain that he was at the bottom of her disappearance.

And now, in my mind it was time to act. His own family is saying he's a slimeball. More disgusting details keep emerging. Now we know his past, and in the present he's a bail-jumping pedophile, and I know we gotta take him off the streets, because the next thing he's gonna do is find some other little girl to molest.

And we're not gonna let that happen.

I do not rush to judgment. But I believed he was as guilty as sin in the North case. Obviously we couldn't say that on the air, although we did start to report that he was a suspect. But I knew that at least we had him on the molestation charges involving his family members, and hopefully the cops could use that as leverage to squeeze some information out of him on Jeanna North.

So we went to work on both ends of the story — the update on Jeanna North, naming Bell as the prime suspect, and the hunt for Bell on the separate molestation charges.

But a strange thing started happening.

As the news began to surface about Bell molesting his nieces, a lot of people had the same reaction.

They didn't want to believe it.

Why, they asked, would he be a child molester when he's such a good-looking, charming, nice young man who could probably attract a lot of nice women?

Well, let me tell you. I gave up asking those kinds of questions nineteen years ago. As I said earlier, I've learned one thing: the average child molester doesn't have a hump on his back, isn't the troll under the bridge with a trench coat and no pants on. There is only one difference between child molesters and normal, decent human beings: they do not think like we do. And I don't care whether it's genetic or whether it's upbringing. Whatever it is, he has a preference for children, and he uses his good looks to lure them, to ingratiate himself to them, and then to take terrible advantage of them. Kyle Bell is nothing but a selfish, spoiled, rotten, self-absorbed lowlife who can only satisfy his deepest, dark desires by having sex with children and then hurting them. When people ask me why, I will tell you that after twenty years of chasing these pedophiles, I don't really give a damn what makes them do it. I am of the school that says, catch his butt, throw him in jail, make him pay, and then study him all you want. Dissect him, take a piece of his brain, put his blood under a microscope.

At this moment, I don't have any patience with the theories and questions about Bell's past, and I wouldn't give two cents for his future.

At this moment, all I know is, we gotta take him off the street.

We sent Tom DeVries, a freelance producer from the West Coast, to handle the story in Fargo. Tom works for a lot of shows but he understands that *America's Most Wanted* is different: while working at other shows you're expected to remain objective, but at *America's Most Wanted* it's not only allowed but expected that you will let your emotions show. And so Tom's heart immediately went out to Sue North, a simple woman with a simple desire to see her daughter again.

Television production is often more a matter of logistics than journalism: where can I get a camera person, a sound person, where can I get a place to stay, does the camera guy have lights, who has a van, where are we gonna hook up, how long is it gonna take to haul all this equipment into this little house, and by the time we haul it in will that sunlight still be coming through that window, and would this shot look better if the subject is sitting against that other wall, and excuse me but would you mind if we moved that dining room table into the kitchen so we can switch the sofa to the other wall, and what is that buzz that the cameraman is picking up — oh, it's the refrigerator motor, it's too loud, do you mind if we turn off your fridge for a little while — now can I get a sound check, Sue, would you please say and spell your first and last name, so we have that on the top of the tape?

These are the little details that let other journalists remain objective, the thousand logistical decisions that put an emotional barrier between you and the person you are here to interview. But Sue North waited, patiently, as these three big men hauled all this equipment around her small home, rearranging the furniture and tweaking the lighting — and then, finally, Tom sat down in front of her and asked her a few simple questions, and she gave him a few simple answers — telling, for the one thousandth time, the story of the night Jeanna disappeared.

"At first," she said, echoing the words I'd heard from so many parents of missing children, "I was hopefully thinking that some nice lady just picked her up that wanted a little girl.

"But after that, well, I've been almost insane thinking of all the things that could be happening to her now. I want to think it's Kyle, and I don't want to think it's Kyle, you know,

46

because it was right there at the corner where he lived."

And then Tom asked her about Kyle Bell, and she said, "I remember the kids used to watch him work on his cars . . ." And she stopped, and felt the enormity of it, of talking about this monster whom she believed had taken her darling daughter; and in that silent moment, Sue North and Tom DeVries looked into each other's eyes, and both of them started to cry.

"It's been a year," Tom said, finally. "What has this done to you?"

"There's no way to describe it, Tom," Sue said. "It rips your soul out every morning when you have to get up and she's not there.

"And the longer she's gone, the scareder you get."

Toward the end of the interview, Tom handed her his handkerchief.

The cameraman handed Tom a tissue.

The sound man handed the cameraman a tissue.

And these grown men, who have probably done a thousand stories among them, sat in a small room with a small, frightened woman, and for just a tiny moment, they understood what it feels like, every hour, every day, to live the life of a parent of a missing child.

"How," said Tom, "do you get through it?"

"One minute at a time, bud," Sue said, trying to smile through her tears. "One minute at a time."

It hurt to watch the footage that Tom brought back: Sue North, appearing so much older than she had a year ago, seeming so tired and lost. Kyle Bell's wife, still looking like a teenager, terrified by the maelstrom she had found herself inside. Detective Peterson, standing in Jeanna's room — a room that looked exactly like it did the night she disappeared, filled with all the happy and frilly accoutrements of the world of an eleven-year-old, from the poster of teen-idol wrestler Bret Hart on the wall to the little plastic rose in a vase next to a big stuffed panda bear — Peterson, standing in that room, admitting that he felt helpless in this case, looking for all the world like he was about to break down and cry himself.

That Friday as we were getting ready to tape the show, I watched our update on the North case, and then talked with Peterson's teammate, detective Steve Gabrielson, to get caught up on the latest on the case.

I realized something was missing.

I told Lance, the executive producer, that I didn't feel the ending was strong enough. I wanted to make a personal plea to the audience, to let them know how much this case had affected me, to beg with them, to plead for one clue that could bring Jeanna home. I also wanted to make a personal plea for them to be on the lookout for Kyle Bell, because for me this had become very personal, and I knew he was a dangerous monster. And even though I knew I couldn't say this part on the air, we were certain he was the key to solving the disappearance of Jeanna North.

That was the ending of the story that I wanted to air anyway.

By late that morning, though, a smart rookie cop in Englewood, Colorado, would give us a better ending.

Officer Steve Kunst was riding with his mentor, officer Mark McCann, when they pulled into an alley and spotted a red Buick with North Dakota license plates.

"There had never been any cars there before," McCann told reporters later. "In my mind, it didn't belong there. Then I saw the out-of-state plate. I thought it might be a burglary. There's a Jim Paris tire store across the alley, and it had been burglarized before."

The rookie cop decided to run a routine check on the vehicle — and it came back with the information that the car was registered to a fugitive on the run from child molestation charges in Fargo.

Kunst called the hit in to the office, and soon police and FBI agents were staking out the alley. A few hours later, a man approached the car, along with a woman and two small children. The computer readout said he had long brown hair, not short blond hair, and he was traveling under an alias — but there was no mistaking the tattoos, the panther on his left arm, the Grim

Reaper on his right, along with a rose and an angel on his chest.

It was, indeed, Kyle Bell.

Amazing.

The manhunt was finally, finally over.

Back in Fargo, the trial of Kyle Bell was painful, but brief. The jury convicted him of molesting his nieces. I was so thankful that this scumbag didn't manage to wriggle out of the charges, as so many others have.

But now came the question of sentencing — and you never know what a judge is going to do in these cases — so we all waited nervously as January 25 approached, and the sentencing hearing began.

But no one was as nervous as Sue North.

We didn't know it at the time, but the pain, and the anger, and the hurt, and the frustration were building inside Sue North.

And as she sat, listening to prosecutors remind the judge of how horrible were the acts Kyle Bell had been convicted of, she started to shake.

The prosecutors were telling about how Bell would take his little victims into the bedroom of his mobile home, and what happened to them there, and suddenly, the year and a half of torment erupted from deep within Sue North's soul. She rose to her feet, shaking violently.

"You bastard!" she screamed, and from behind a three-foot high railing, she lunged at Kyle Bell. "Bastard!"

Bell turned to look at her, and then looked down.

Sue tried to leap the railing but was restrained by her family members. She seemed to calm down for a moment but then erupted again, words failing her now, tears streaming from her eyes, her mouth twisted into a furious grimace, her hands grasping for the low wooden railing that was all that kept her from reaching the monster, from putting her hands around his throat and sending him to the hell he belonged in, but now hands came at her from everywhere, all her family members holding her back, at first, and then, as her feet slipped out from under her, holding her up. She strained with all her might against them and then relaxed into their arms, understanding that there was nothing she could do to release her pain, whispering, "Okay, okay," and letting them guide her from the courtroom.

I have thought about this moment many, many times. I know it's wrong, and I know that we are not vigilantes, and I know that it is only through the justice system that we can control these monsters.

But I also know something else, and I will admit it to you now.

In the hidden center of my soul, there is a part of me that wishes Sue North had made it over that railing and wrung Kyle Bell's worthless neck.

She didn't, of course, and the hearing went on.

The judge gave Kyle Bell forty years, the maximum sentence.

And that night, something unbelievable happened.

First verbally, and then in writing, he made a confession.

A confession about Jeanna North.

There are those who think he did it because his stone-cold heart was touched by the pain of Sue North. I'd like to believe that's true, but in honesty, I don't think he had a second's worth of remorse. I think he had something else in mind — maybe he wanted to make a deal. Maybe, in his sick way, he wanted to get more attention, more publicity.

But for whatever reason, he finally let out the secret we had been trying to unravel since that evening nineteen months ago, when a little corncob of a girl was Rollerblading home, and a man appeared from the shadows.

This is what Kyle Bell said happened that night.

He said he managed to lure the little girl into his trailer.

He took her into the back room.

And molested her.

Later, he says, she threatened to tell her mother about the despicable acts he had forced upon her, and he slapped her, and she fell backward and hit her head.

He said it was an accident.

But if it were an accident, you might speculate that Bell might have tried to help her. He might have called 911, he might have called her mother, he might have done something — at least deposited her out on the street and made an anonymous call to the cops.

But he did none of those things.

This is what he did:

He got a rope. He got a fifteen-pound concrete cinder block.

He took the rope, and the cinder block, and the young unconscious girl, and drove to a bridge over a river.

We do not know if Jeanna was alive at the time. We do not know if Kyle Bell knew.

Or cared.

But in the gloomy light of his prison cell, he calmly told detectives that on the night she disappeared, he tied Jeanna North's tiny body to the cinder block.

And threw it into the river.

Sue and John North were inconsolable when they heard of the confession — inconsolable and yet, in some way, at peace. I have always said that the not-knowing is the worst. But after the pain and shock and horror of learning what happened to their little girl there was the understanding that they would now, at least, be able to say their good-byes to Jeanna, to send her to heaven with their love, to let her rest in peace.

"The one thing that hurt us the most was that

we never knew," John North told reporters then. "We don't accept the fact that she is dead, but at least we've got a good idea what happened to her. Hopefully, we'll be able to find her body."

I understand this as well. Although it is the most difficult and painful moment in the entire, miserable, never-ending experience of being the parent of a murdered child, all of the parents I have worked with and counseled have the need to put a true end to their search, to finally put that young person to rest.

The desire to disbelieve, the need to keep hope alive, is so powerful when you are talking about the loss of a child, that only the reality of burying your child's body, or in some way being given the actual knowledge of her final resting place, can get you past the self-denial, can let the grieving and healing process begin.

So I understood that until the body was found, John and Sue would still wonder if, for some incomprehensible sick reason, Kyle Bell had made the whole story up. We had a good idea, of course, that Bell was telling the truth. In addition to what we knew about Bell, and what we had reported, there was another piece of information that the police had asked us not to air. On the night we first broadcast the interview with a local reporter, in which Bell admitted being a suspect, we got a call from an anonymous tipster.

She said that she had seen Bell on the night of

the disappearance of Jeanna North.

She had run into him, by chance, and talked to him.

The place where she had run into him, she said, was on the bridge over the river in Cass County, the river which now, most likely, served as the final resting place of Jeanna Dale North.

Fargo was covered with a thick blanket of snow, and on the morning after Kyle Bell's confession, the river was frozen over, as it had been for some time. At first authorities decided that the weather conditions made it impossible to begin the search for Jeanna's body.

But there was not a soul in Fargo who did not grieve for that child, and not a single person could walk by that river and not pause, and think of Jeanna, and feel in their heart that the child deserved a proper burial. The question — is there a child tied to a cinder block at the bottom of this river? — was too much for this caring, loving populace to bear.

And so, a few days later, as a brilliant sun rose over the frigid river, Sue North stood by the banks of that river, chain-smoking cigarettes and witnessing a truly remarkable sight.

A hundred volunteers, their breaths curling in white clouds above them, were beginning the doleful but angelic task of searching the river.

First, huge corkscrew drills were brought out to break through the ice on the river, which was more than a foot thick. Then backhoes and bulldozers were driven out onto the ice, to widen the openings. Finally, divers in blue-and-orange wet suits braved the frigid, murky waters. They could barely see their hands in front of their scuba masks once they submerged, and no wet suit can keep out the bone-chilling cold when you are diving in a frozen river; no diver wants to risk the dangerous plunge into a frozen lake, but again and again they went in as the crowd around grew bigger and bigger, volunteers passing out coffee, assisting the divers, and just waiting, waiting for an answer, waiting for a sign.

But the sun crossed the sky, and then sank below the trees, and now it was too dark and cold to continue.

And no sign ever came.

It was a scene that would be repeated more than a dozen times in the coming weeks. Again and again, these brave and dedicated divers searched the river. On one heartbreaking day, a diver came up with what appeared to be a rib bone. It turned out to be the bone of an animal. On another day, they retrieved a bit of cinder block, which may have matched a sample taken from Kyle Bell's home.

But to this day, the divers have never found that one piece of evidence that says, yes, Jeanna North died here, and now we can put her memory to rest.

And to make matters worse, the one thing we did have to hang on to — Kyle Bell's confession

— soon disappeared as suddenly as Jeanna herself.

Because, without warning, Kyle Bell recanted.

It doesn't surprise me, really. The moment of compassion that Kyle Bell may have felt when he was confronted with Sue North's rage was out of keeping with his selfish, self-centered, self-preserving character. As soon as he got together with a lawyer, I'm sure he was convinced that compassion was not within his self-interest, and he reverted right to form.

The state charged Kyle Bell with the murder of Jeanna North, but a judge ruled that during the course of the confession Bell asked to speak with an attorney and that the request was ignored; as a result, the entire confession was thrown out.

That means the district attorney could not use it in court — and with no confession, and no body, and no murder witness, there wasn't much of a case.

I know from experience that most D.A.'s would give up at this point. People don't realize that since the district attorney is an elected position, there's much more politics than crime-fighting going on in the average district attorney's office. They are out to get themselves reelected, like any politician, and like any politician, they will avoid anything that makes them look bad. A great won-lost record is good for the career of a major league pitcher, and good for the career of a major league district attorney, too. And so if there's a case with little chance of success — even if the perp is a dangerous child molester like Kyle Bell, who if let out on the street is certain to attack other children; even if the mother in the case has become distraught and stretched to the breaking point, aching for justice and for answers — it is likely that the district attorney will decide not to prosecute, making the excuse that the case is too flimsy, and never giving a jury a chance to hear all the facts and decide for themselves.

And that's exactly what I expected the district attorney to do in this case.

And I am pleased to report that I was dead wrong.

John Goff, the state's attorney for Cass County, North Dakota, made the decision to try the case. It was a gutsy call, one made from the heart, and I have to commend him for his courage. He put the safety of children and the desire for justice ahead of the concerns of his career, and that's what the system is supposed to be about. Try a murder case with this little to go on? Not one prosecutor in a hundred would take the chance.

But when a victim's family cries out for justice, it's the only right thing to do.

It took forever for the case to come to trial, but in August of 1999, it was finally on the docket, and right from the start, prosecutors caught a big break.

The day after Kyle Bell made his confession — the one he recanted — he made some comments to a detective named Jim LeDoux and a sergeant named Rollie Rust. The judge ruled that while the confession was off limits, LeDoux and Rust could testify about those comments.

It was still a long shot — trying to prosecute a man for murder when the victim's body hadn't been found. I can't remember another case like it in the history of *AMW*. But the testimony of LeDoux and Rust would be huge.

The opening statements outlined the strange circumstances of this case — the case against Bell that seemed so obvious and yet so unwinnable.

"We know straight from the horse's mouth. We know directly from Kyle Bell what happened," Assistant Cass County State's Attorney Mark Boening said in opening arguments.

"We are truly convinced the state . . . will not be able to meet the required burden of proof," Bell's attorney, Steve Mottinger, said and added, regarding Jeanna North: "They will not even be able to prove she is dead."

But when the two detectives took the stand to talk about their conversation with Bell, you could tell the jury was being swayed.

LeDoux testified: "Mr. Bell said to me, 'Jim, she was gonna tell what happened in the garage, so I just backhanded her, she fell and hit her head."

He and Rust said that in their conversation

with Bell, he admitted tying her to a cinder block and throwing her in the river. They said he even admitted going back to make sure she hadn't resurfaced.

And our anonymous tipster decided to come forward. Mary Hoglund, who lives near a bridge on the river, testified that she saw Bell on the bridge on June 28. She's sure it was him, because later he came up to her farmhouse, saying he had run out of gas; she gave him a five-gallon can of gasoline — and he gave her his name and phone number, saying he'd later return and pay for the gas.

The jury deliberated for four hours, and when they returned, Sue and John North sat in the last row in the courtroom, his arm around his wife's shoulder; tears welled up in her eyes as she waited for what seemed to be an interminably long time for the courtroom to come to order.

Finally, it was silent. And then she heard the word she had waited all these years to hear.

Guilty.

Kyle Bell was guilty.

Her fist went into the air, shaking, a fist of defiance: the bastard that killed her daughter would not get away with it. Soon he would be sentenced to life in prison.

After the trial, John and Sue, and Jeanna's sisters Jessica and Jennifer stood shoulder to shoulder, arm in arm, united, in the hallway outside the courtroom. All were in tears, barely able to speak; but from John came a quiet, controlled baritone, speaking the words they all were feeling:

"Finally," he said, "this nightmare is over."

Oh, John.

How could we know?

How could any of us know that the nightmare wasn't over?

That it was going to begin all over again?

As soon as Kyle Bell was sentenced, North Dakota decided to get rid of him. Kick him out of the state, send him to a Supermax prison, and forget the whole sordid mess. North Dakota averages only seven homicides a year, and five of those are usually domestics — so the Bell case stirred up more publicity, more emotion, and more anxiety than any case had in recent memory. There was a certain catharsis that would come in sending him out of state — almost as though his continued presence, even behind bars, was a continued threat to the populace.

Besides, there was the threat of a breakout.

Bell had tried to escape from jail once before — in 1995, while awaiting trial — and less than a week after his conviction, he made another attempt.

On August 26, 1999, guards found a makeshift knife in Bell's cell in the Cass County jail. That landed Bell in solitary. Then guards found out he'd written to a woman he knew, asking her

61

to help him break out of jail.

So when it came time to move Bell from the county jail to a more secure prison, the authorities selected a Supermax prison in Oregon.

That's how it came to pass that on October 13, 1999, Bell was on a private prisoner transport bus — having private companies handle prisoner transfers is more and more common; the feds and a lot of states figure it's cheaper to farm the job out rather than do it themselves — and on this particular day, one of those buses was hauling a dozen inmates to a variety of locations, pinballing all around the country to drop off each of their charges.

At about 4 A.M. that Wednesday morning, although he was bound from North Dakota to Oregon, Kyle Bell found himself pulling into a rest stop in Santa Rosa, New Mexico. As the bus pulled into the stop, Bell looked around.

He sat quietly with eleven other inmates.

And four guards.

And a bent paper clip taped to the bottom of his shoe.

Two of the guards were asleep, and a third was buying gas. That left just one guard watching all twelve inmates.

And then this guard, in charge of one of the most dangerous fugitives to ever leave the state of North Dakota, made the excellent decision to get off the bus and get a cup of coffee.

Leaving Kyle Bell and the other inmates unguarded.

It was just for a few minutes.

But that was all Bell needed.

Quickly he pulled the bent paper clip off the bottom of his shoe. It's not a difficult magic trick: if you bend a paper clip just so, you can open the average pair of handcuffs. Bell was uncuffed in moments, and with the help of another inmate, boosted himself through a roof hatch on the bus.

But he did not make a break for it.

He lay on top of the bus, not making a sound.

And he waited.

Soon the guards returned, and — not bothering to count the prisoners — headed back out toward the highway.

And just before they turned and sped off, Bell slipped off the back.

And the slimy, slippery fugitive, the man we all thought we were done with, was back out on the street.

It's incredible to me that this even happened in the first place — why such a dangerous fugitive would be entrusted to some private company, why the prisoners weren't searched thoroughly before they boarded the bus, why the hell they had to take him through New Mexico to get to Oregon, why on earth they didn't follow some sort of procedure to make sure at least one guard was watching the prisoners, and why they didn't follow the obvious and simple procedure of counting the convicts after each stop.

But here's the most unbelievable part of the story:

All morning, the guards drove on, not realizing Bell was gone.

They didn't notice, in fact, until 2 P.M. the next afternoon.

Ten hours after the escape.

Finally, these bright bulbs counted their prisoners and came up one short. Within hours, the news of this got all the way to the top. North Dakota Governor Ed Schaefer was walking down the hall in the capitol, leaving his office, when his chief of staff stuck his head out into the hallway and said, "We've got bad news."

Governor Schaefer was incredulous. "I thought, 'Oh, no, anybody but this guy,'" Schaefer told us later. "He's the worst of the worst. Then it was disbelief that the company took ten hours to notify us. Then that one guard was sleeping and the other getting coffee — it was like a movie."

Governor Schaefer hooked up with the governor of New Mexico, and all through the night the top officials in both states manned the phones, put a battle plan in place, and hoped for the best. In a jailbreak situation, you need to seal off a perimeter as quickly as you can; then it's just a matter of doing a meticulous search within that perimeter. The size of the perimeter depends on how quickly you get your people in place after the escape. But police dogs had picked up Bell's scent, and it ended at a highway in Santa Rosa — and from there, with a ten-hour lead, Bell could be anywhere, the governors realized.

There was no perimeter to set.

The manhunt would have to go national. Immediately.

And so we were back on the case.

Big time.

Evan Marshall, the young associate producer who covered the Midwest, was, as usual, one of the first ones in the office the next morning. Evan is not a morning person. He likes to have his coffee and read the paper so he'll be somewhat civilized by the time the rest of the office rolls in.

He was through the front pages of *USA Today*, and was getting ready to check out his beat in the news-from-every-state page, when his phone rang. It was one of his sources in North Dakota, telling him that a guy named Kyle Bell had escaped, and he might want to check it out. Evan didn't recognize the name Kyle Bell, since the whole story had gone down before he joined our staff.

And he didn't get particularly excited about the call — you get a call like that just about every day at *America's Most Wanted*. But the caller did mention that we had profiled the case before. So, still feeling a bit grumpy, Evan looked up the case and started watching the pieces we had aired.

When he realized it was a child-killer who had escaped, he snapped into full alert; and when he saw how much we had done on the story, he realized that this had been one of our top fugitives and that this was going to be very, very big.

He ran quickly to the wire terminal and called up the early wire story on the escape. He then started calling around North Dakota — and the moment the cops heard it was *America's Most Wanted* on the line, he got transferred to Drew Helms, the FBI agent in charge of a special task force that was already up and running.

Evan's next call was to the governor's office in North Dakota, where he expected to get the runaround: while law enforcement always welcomes *AMW*, politicians tend to be more publicity conscious, and there was no question this was going to be a publicity disaster for Governor Schaefer.

"Look," Evan started, ready to give them a good dose of reality, "we are going to need a lot of help if we're going to catch this guy, and you're going to have to give it to us."

"Come on down," the governor's aide told him. "You have an open door to the state."

I got the call later that morning, and I cannot remember being more furious about any story we'd done. My first thought was: this is going to wreak emotional and psychological havoc with the family. They've been through so much. I had heard that Sue and John had separated, and it didn't surprise me. So few families remain intact through the loss of a child. I have seen so many families torn apart by the pain, and the guilt, and the recriminations. John and Sue North were still good friends, still talked every week, still both actively participated in raising their other children, but the pain of having a child murdered was too much for them — and I knew that the agony of this escape would be unbearable.

I can't even begin to tell you what I thought about the private transport company. In the old days, if you had to move a prisoner, two sheriffs would put him in leg shackles, buy three plane tickets — two round-trips and a one-way — and stick him in prison. Good riddance. Now, as a false economy, we've decided to privatize these jobs because it saves a few bucks, so a guy who in two days isn't going to be allowed to go to the bathroom without two guards watching him is suddenly sitting on a bus, being guarded by a couple of guys who are sleeping and another who decides he needs a cup of coffee and then forgets how to count.

It's infuriating.

That day, I come into the office loaded for bear. The producers have put together a short little piece, just to get Bell's picture on the air, and I'm thinking: this isn't enough.

We need to unleash all the power and the fury we can muster and go after this guy like we've never gone after anyone before.

I go into a sound booth and record the voice-overs for the minute-and-a-half piece.

And then I call a meeting.

I tell everyone that I really hope we get Kyle Bell this weekend. But if we don't, I want to make a personal request.

It's a request I'd never made before.

I want everyone in this room to make a commitment: we put Kyle Bell on the air every single week until we catch him. We make him our Public Enemy Number One, and we throw every resource we have at this case. If we don't catch him this week, he leads next week. And the week after that. And the week after that. This guy is the worst scumbag out there, and if *America's Most Wanted* has a mission, it's to catch Kyle Bell.

No one in the room disagreed — in fact, no one in the room said a thing.

I realized I'd been yelling for about ten minutes.

Suddenly, things got very quiet, and I realized why I had been yelling.

I knew that in this moment, I had come to hate Kyle Bell.

I hated him for all that he stood for, for all that he had done, for the unspeakable acts I imagined he was committing right now, because pedophiles can't ever stop being pedophiles, and because this particular pedophile had absolutely nothing to lose; I hated him for what I've seen a hundred guys like him do to a thousand innocent little children.

I hated him for what he had done to Jeanna North's family.

I hated him for what he had done to Jeanna North.

But this one wasn't just for Sue North.

This one wasn't just for Jeanna.

This one was for Adam.

As I feared, the minute-and-a-half piece didn't catch him, so we went into Public Enemy mode like we'd never gone before.

It began with Evan and his team on the ground in North Dakota. The first stop was the governor's office, and I gotta hand it to Governor Schaefer: he didn't try to soft-pedal this, or cover his butt. He was honest and open and took responsibility: he admitted that the authorities in his state had screwed up big-time.

"If you know how to bend a paper clip, you can open a handcuff," Governor Schaefer said. "I did it myself, because I didn't believe it, so I had a meeting where they brought in a pre-bent paper clip to show me how to do it. The lesson learned there is, they put a little black box around the handcuffs, a second locking system — and needless to say, our dangerous criminals are going to wear those lock boxes now."

The governor told Evan that he was putting up a $50,000 reward for Bell's capture, to send the signal to everyone that he was taking this case seriously.

He also told Evan about his first action — and his hardest — after hearing of the escape: telling Jeanna's parents.

Sue North was a puddle of tears when Evan arrived at her home; she tried her best but could barely speak without raging or sobbing. John North was his stoic self, serious and sad: "It was almost as bad as the night that we lost her and woke up that morning and found out she was gone," he said. "It was very heartbreaking, a complete shock, and just disbelief that something so simple to do could be botched so bad."

As he was wrapping up, Evan asked John for a recent family picture. John admitted that he didn't have one — and hadn't taken one, in fact, since Jeanna went missing. "We just haven't gotten around to taking a family picture anymore, because there's one person missing."

The FBI is usually pretty hinky about letting anyone inside a task force center, but Evan was given the run of the place. FBI agent Drew Helms and Colonel Jim Hughes of the state police were running the task force. They were both candid and emotional. "We need closure on this case," Hughes told us, "and the closure's gonna come . . ." His voice trailed off for a moment, and then, his voice tight with emotion, his jaw set, he continued: "The closure's gonna come when we catch his ass and put him in jail, that's when the closure's gonna come."

Evan got help from one other source on this story, a rather surprising one. Again and again, in the case of child molesters, we run into families who say, I don't believe it, I won't believe it, it couldn't have happened. They don't coop-

70

erate with the police, they don't cooperate with *America's Most Wanted*, they spend all their time in denial. Even if the victims were members of their own family, they still try to protect the fugitive, concealing the family photos so the cops can't create good posters, lying about where the scumbags might be, doing everything they can to hinder the investigation and hide their shame.

But Kyle Bell's family was not hiding and not defensive. I am so proud of these people. They overcame their fear, and the stigma, and the ties that bind a family together no matter what, and they stood up and said: Kyle Bell is a menace to society. He is sick, and we must stop him before another child is hurt.

Among those who stepped forward was Kyle's aunt, Kim, and his uncle, Tom Bell.

"I feel it's time that we prove that the Bell family is not the same as our nephew," he said. "The crime that he did is so heinous to me that I — I can't see protecting somebody that does that, no matter that he is family. He may be sick, and he may need help, but that's no excuse for what he's done.

"If I could talk to Kyle," he continued, "I would tell him, 'Kyle, be a man about the things you've done, things you shouldn't have. My advice is, turn yourself in and get it over with. There's nothing you can do to change what you've done. Pay for it. You've done the crime. You have to do the time.'"

Evan learned that Tom Bell's wife had gone so

far as to contact the North family, to try to apologize for what Kyle had done.

"We've had sympathy for the North family for the last seven years," Tom told Evan, "but we didn't know how to contact them, or — I mean, we didn't know how to approach them without being, you know, looking, I don't know how to say it . . ."

Evan offered, "That you'd feel like a guilty party as well?"

"Yeah, yeah," Tom replied. "We didn't want to be known as that, I guess. But after he escaped, the wife finally made contact with John North."

John, solid soul that he is, was kind to the Bell family, but the conversation was brief; Sue was not doing very well after the news of the escape hit, and he had to take her to the hospital.

Evan had an idea — partly as a TV producer, and partly as a nice guy who saw two families in pain, and thought they both could help each other heal.

"I have to go back to the North's tomorrow," he told Tom Bell. "Would you like to come with me?"

The next day, Evan and the Bells made the long drive from Bismark to Fargo.

A producer waited with Sue North for the arrival of the Bismark crowd — but Sue's mind was elsewhere. She was nervous, holding back tears. "I'm trying hard not to fall apart," she admitted. "I'm doing this because I want to help keep Kyle Bell's picture out there. But whenever we do these things, I always get visuals of Jeanna. She's right there up front for me. So it's very hard."

John was more focused on the events of the day: "I hold no animosity toward the Bell family," he said. "This is the black sheep of their family. He's done his damage to their family, and sexually assaulted members of their family, so I'm sure they want to get him off the streets as much as we do."

A little while later, there was a knock at the door. Tom and Kim Bell walked in.

Tom, a good foot taller than Sue, carried a single white rose. He handed it to her. Instinctively, pulled together by the forces that bind all crime victims together, they put their arms around each other, and stood, without a word. Sue choked back tears; Tom caught a quiet sob in his throat, then let it go.

They relaxed and looked at each other, a mixture of sadness and relief in their faces brought by the deep feeling that crime victims desperately need to feel, that sense of: I know, I know.

You are not alone.

A few moments later, John North came into the room. He shook Tom's hand, and then Kim's.

She burst into tears.

"I'm so sorry," she said, releasing all the pain of knowing what her nephew had done. She put her arms around John, sobbing into his shoulder: "I'm so sorry."

He patted her back, softly.

"It's not your fault," he whispered. "It's not your fault."

They sat down for one of the most brutally honest conversations four people can have.

"I have to tell you," Sue said, "I believe in capital punishment in cases like this. Because these guys are not ever going to get better." Here was a mother of a murdered child, talking to the woman who helped raise her child's killer, telling her that her nephew should be put to death.

"I'll tell you something," Kim replied. "I asked Tom, on the drive up here. You know, they might come to a point, in apprehending Kyle, that they have to shoot him. How are you going to feel about that?

"And Tom said to me, 'I'll feel: Thank God.' "

At the same time as Evan was producing the North Dakota end of the story, we had another crew reenacting the crime. We were able to gear up quickly because, by chance, another fugitive we were profiling — Claude Dean Hull — was captured on the day we began filming. So the big Claude Dean Hull film team became the big Kyle Bell film team.

I spent hours on the phone with the director, going over every shot, how we would light it, everything. I wanted this to be perfect. I wanted to grip the audience like we never had before. I

74

wanted to mesmerize them with this piece, hypnotize them into hating Kyle Bell as much as I did, so that they would walk the streets with their eyes wide open and a mission in their hearts.

When it was all over, Evan edited the piece and it was everything I was hoping for: it was powerful, and emotional, and it showed Kyle Bell for the dangerous, dangerous fugitive we knew he was.

When we got down to taping that week's show, I looked at the script, and there was nothing there. It just said "Kyle Bell Update III Intro" with a lot of blank space.

Lance told me he wanted the viewers to hear what he heard in that meeting we'd had, so he didn't want to give me a script. He said, wing it.

I looked back at the tape of that show a little while ago, and I didn't recognize myself. I was shaking, and I was not exactly thinking like a network news anchor: the first words out of my mouth were, "I hate Kyle Bell and I hate him with a passion."

Frankly, I thought we'd catch him the first week. Why? Because this is not a mobster with an underground organization to hide him out. Nobody's going to provide him with a passport. Nobody is going to provide him with running money. He wasn't a white-collar criminal who had money stashed. He didn't belong to the Crips or Bloods or some gang that had secret hideouts. He didn't belong to some white supremacist group that's going to take him to

Montana and hide him in the woods, or some anti-abortion group with a ton of dough, or some militia group that's expert at creating new identities. The only chance he has is finding some vulnerable woman to prey on, and the best chance we have is to catch him before he can set up house.

The problem was, Kyle Bell was a little too much of an everyman — a little too average-looking — so we were overwhelmed with sightings of look-alikes. And sometimes, with a segment like this, the power of the producing works against us: people shared our hatred of Kyle Bell so much that they *wanted* to believe they had spotted him, so some very well-meaning calls sent us on a few wild-goose chases.

In all there were more than six hundred tips, both to us and the cops, but by the end of the week, nothing had panned out. I couldn't believe it. He had eluded the manhunt again.

We were preempted over the holidays, and that drove me nuts, too. Somebody took my son and killed him and destroyed Christmases for me for years. Even now, I look at Christmas pictures and they're not complete — there should be a twenty-five-year-old son towering over my other three kids. That's the family, that's the Christmas pose we will never see. And I kept calling Lance and saying, can't we kill this preemption? Every year the network preempts us at Christmas because they don't feel like *America's Most Wanted* makes for happy holiday viewing.

But I'm thinking, what if he kills somebody's child over the holidays? How horrible would that be? How could we live with that? We are the avenging angels, what right do we have to take off the holidays?

But our pleas fell on deaf ears at the network, and Fox preempted us over the holidays. I was left with the haunting questions:

Would we ever catch Kyle Bell? Would we find him before he killed again?

After our first broadcast back on the air — January 8, 2000 — I would get my answer.

Rick and Mattie Wilson managed a small apartment complex in Dallas. They knew all their tenants pretty well, and knew what was going on in their lives.

So when they saw a good-looking young man named Christopher Larson move in with one of their tenants, just before Thanksgiving, they were pretty pleased at first. The tenant had a hard time making ends meet — she had just come from a homeless shelter, and as a single mom with five kids, she needed all the help she could get. Once in a while, when she was having trouble scratching up the rent, the Wilsons let her slide. So they were happy to see this charming, polite, good-looking man eagerly move in to take care of her. He was working temporary jobs, as a plumber and parking attendant, while helping her pay the bills and feed the family.

But then they started noticing strange things

— just slightly out of the ordinary. For example, Christopher would put the little girls on his knee and let them suck his thumb. Or they'd go up and find the thirteen-year-old sitting on his lap. It made them feel creepy.

They weren't sure if they should say anything to the girls' mom. But through the holidays, everything seemed pretty peaceful.

Then on Saturday night, January 8, they sat down to watch TV. They weren't die-hard *America's Most Wanted* fans and were just channel surfing. But they did trip across our show.

"I don't know what triggered it," Rick Wilson said, "if it was God or something, but it was meant for me to watch *America's Most Wanted* on Saturday night — especially at 8:22. I've never been more alive in my life than I was in that moment."

Because 8:22 Central Time was the moment we aired the picture of Kyle Bell.

And they got the shock of their lives.

"You know how sometimes you see someone on TV, and they don't look like they do in person?" Rick Wilson said later. "Well, there was no question here.

"The picture of Kyle Bell looked just like Chris Larson. He had a mustache and beard — but it was him."

Rick started calling the 1-800-CRIME-TV hotline. It took him ten minutes to get through, but when he did, he sounded so certain that the agents in the studio immediately called the FBI in Dallas and asked them to check out the tip.

Along with the Dallas police, four FBI agents cautiously staked out the apartment complex. When they got there, Chris Larson wasn't around. So they waited. And about 12:30 A.M., he came home.

The agents had to be extremely cautious. They knew there might be children inside, and things could go bad. This was a convicted child killer with nothing to lose.

Two agents stood on either side of the door to Apartment 206; a third, between them, knocked on the door.

Larson was surrounded: the FBI were coming in the front door, and when Larson looked out his back balcony, he saw that the Dallas police had sealed off that end of the building.

When he let the FBI in, he told them he'd never heard of Kyle Bell.

What's more, he produced an ID card showing that he was, in fact, Christopher Larson.

Could the Wilsons have been wrong? Could they have the wrong man?

After a moment, one of the FBI agents asked Larson to remove his shirt.

After a moment, he complied.

And there they were.

The panther tattooed on his left arm.

The Grim Reaper tattooed on his right.

The rose appeared, and the angel, and finally,

finally, it was over.

They had their man.

We had captured Kyle Bell.

This time there would be no prison transport bus. They did it the old-fashioned way: the cops from North Dakota went to Dallas and flew him home, shackled and manacled.

But while that plane was headed from Dallas to North Dakota, another plane was leaving the Fargo airport, headed in the opposite direction.

Because there was somebody who needed, with all her heart and soul, to meet the man who had caught the child killer.

We had become so used to seeing a somber, tearful Sue North, trembling, holding back tears, that we were not prepared for the woman who appeared in Dallas. It was as though the incredible weight that made her shoulders sag, made her head droop, made her eyes puffy and her legs weak, had dissolved in the brilliant morning sunshine. She was dressed in a colorful sweater and came bounding up to meet Rick Wilson, her smile a mile wide, and when a woman whom you have not seen smile in many years smiles at you like that, the universe feels, just for a moment, very safe and sweet and easy.

They hugged, and talked, and Rick told Sue all about Chris Larson, and how he had pulled the wool over everyone's eyes. Sue just ate it all up — so happy not to be talking about a fugitive, not to be pleading with anyone for anything, not a thing, not anymore.

After a while, and a few more hugs, she started to leave. "Thank you, so much, for what you did," she said to Rick. "Take care of your girls."

And as she walked lightly away, she had one more parting thought for the girls themselves. "Take a lesson from your father," she said with a giggle. "You watch *America's Most Wanted*, you never know who you're going to catch."

When I got the word, I was over the moon.

I had spent so many nights staring out the windows of airplanes as I crisscrossed the country, gazing into the darkness, lonely, mad, frustrated, thinking about how little justice there really is for kids. But now I was so proud of our team. The reason I first got involved with *America's Most Wanted* was to catch a child killer who was on the run — not Adam's killer, but a predator who we knew would keep killing until we found him — and now it had all come full circle. And how sweet, and appropriate, that Bell was caught by a kind, gentle, middle-American couple, just like the Norths themselves.

Sweet justice.

I couldn't wait to meet Rick and Mattie. We were flying them up to Washington that Friday, to be on the set as we were taping the show — and we had a little surprise for them.

We hadn't mentioned the $50,000 reward on the broadcast that Rick and Mattie saw. The night they made the call they knew absolutely nothing about any reward. They made their call out of a sense of righteous justice, not out of any hope of personal gain.

But now, we were gonna make damn sure they got the reward.

We called Governor Schaefer's office and asked his press secretary, Julie Liffrig, if we could cut through all the red tape that usually surrounds rewards and speed things along. She agreed wholeheartedly. In fact, the governor even volunteered to come to Washington — unbeknownst to the Wilsons — to be on the set with them and give them the $50,000 reward.

That Friday, we were in the middle of taping, a thousand things going on, and everyone who'd been involved in this story was on the set — including Drew Helms of the FBI and Colonel Hughes of the state highway patrol, along with a caravan of media from North Dakota — when I spotted them off in a corner. I could tell in a moment that they were shy, unassuming people: Rick, a tall, slim guy with a long ponytail and bushy beard, and Mattie, holding his arm, looking frightened and nervous.

As soon as we took a break, I went over and chatted with them for a while, just to thank them, privately, for their courage.

A few minutes later, it came time to interview them. "You knew it was him," I said. "You made the call — but you also knew he was a convicted child killer on the run. Were you concerned for your own safety?"

"No, my own safety didn't enter into it," Rick said, his flat and unemotional midwestern tone belying the weight of his words. "What I was thinking about was the kids. It was the only thing that entered my mind. And it was a chill that ran through me."

Governor Schaefer was very gracious, thanking them and giving them the check on behalf of the people of North Dakota.

And then the Wilsons told us what they planned to do with some of the money. And we couldn't believe it.

They felt bad, they said, for one thing: the woman Kyle Bell was living with had, after all, come to count on Bell's paycheck. She wasn't angry at the Wilsons for making the call — she understood that her children were in danger — but now came the practical question of making ends meet.

So the Wilsons decided to share part of the reward money with her. "She doesn't want to go back to the homeless shelter," Mattie told us. "We don't want her to go back to the homeless shelter. She's a victim, too, very much. So we're going to do everything we can to help her."

Just a simple act of human kindness. And it touched us all.

We finished the interview then, the decency and the caring of these two simple, dear people filling the room. I get jaded, sometimes, dealing with so much crime and violence, but meeting people like these two really restores your faith, reminds you that people are basically good at heart. For one beautiful moment, nobody spoke, nobody moved; we just basked in the knowledge that we had all, through the grace of God, been allowed to do something so perfectly right. The silence was shattered a moment later by the voice of the stage manager, on cue from the director in the control room, shouting, "Okay, moving on to act two," and the camera people and lighting people and stagehands and hotline operators all started bustling around us, and the governor got up to go, and I hugged Mattie and shook Rick's hand one more time.

And then, as the crew set up for the next act of the show, I stepped outside, to be alone for a moment. It was a chilly January day, and my breath curled out in front of me as I looked up at a sky the color of slate. I thought about Sue North and hoped that this would set her on a road of healing. I thought about that woman in Dallas, and her five kids, and knew in my heart that we had saved them from a life of torment — or worse.

I thought about Jeanna, and said a little prayer.

And then, as I always do in moments like these, I thought about Adam.

My son, I was never able to bring your killer to justice.

I'm so sorry for that.

But I have tried, in my way, to make it up to you.

You are the force that guides my hand, that

teaches me right from wrong.

You are the one who set me on this path.

And so it is you, not I, who has saved all these other little boys and girls.

I know that you are in a better place now.

And when I remember all that, I am not afraid, anymore.

2

Never Too Late

America's Most Wanted has reached back in time to make some pretty amazing captures. There was William White Graham, a revolutionary hijacker and cop-killer who had spent twenty years on the run but finally turned himself in to authorities after we featured him on our show. And then there was the case of John List, who had been a fugitive from justice for eighteen years after murdering his wife, mother, and three teenage children in New Jersey. We caught him by having a forensic artist create an age-progressed bust that turned out to be such a good likeness that it took only eleven days for viewer tips to lead to List's takedown.

I'd always thought that helping to track down those two guys would be the oldest — and coldest — cases we would get involved in, but I was wrong. In March of 1999, the FBI, along with the Los Angeles Police Department, asked us to help them with a case that would not only send us back more than two decades in time, but would also create one of the biggest debates among *AMW*'s own staff — about whether

Kathleen Soliah, the fugitive we were tracking, really needed to be found.

Lots of people remember 1967 as the summer of love, but just a few years later, the good vibrations were waning: the Vietnam War was raging, demonstrations against the war were becoming violent and were being met with strong resistance from law enforcement, and some political activists were turning to more radical measures to express their rage and frustration. And it wasn't just Vietnam they were angry about. A whole host of social and political causes were turning up on the agendas of all kinds of groups who wanted to create a revolution of one sort or another.

Many, many positive things came out of the anger of the time. Many young people embraced nonviolence and tried to work toward bringing about equality for all, to help the poor, to right racial injustices.

But others couldn't wait around for the rest of the country to adopt their sometimes twisted ideas of how things should be run. So they decided to force the issue — with pipe bombs and murder.

In the early 1970s, an inmate named Donald DeFreeze started to attend black liberation meetings in California's Vacaville Prison.

Doing five years to life for robbery and a shootout with police, DeFreeze lapped up the radical ideas of defiance.

During these meetings, DeFreeze — who soon took on the counterculture name Cinque — apparently talked about planning bombings that would bring down the prison walls, and of political kidnappings to further his agenda. One of the people his group reportedly targeted for kidnapping was the granddaughter of publishing baron William Randolph Hearst, and daughter of Randolph Hearst, who was then president and editor of the *Examiner*, one of San Francisco's most influential newspapers. Few people outside the Bay area at that time knew the name of heiress Patricia Hearst.

Soon, the whole world would know her.

In 1972, Cinque was transferred to Soledad prison. He was assigned to a work detail, and shortly thereafter he managed to escape by walking away from his landscaping assignment. He made his way to the San Francisco Bay area, where he found refuge in the local underground community, and he soon began to connect with some of the more radical and dangerous members of certain groups who were now calling themselves urban terrorists. Cinque soon formed his own small band of radicals, and even came up with a name for his group: the Symbionese Liberation Army, or SLA (the name seems to have been derived from someone's idea of "symbiosis," a merging of disparate elements into a cohesive whole). They also created a flag for their fledgling terror cell that bore the likeness of a seven-headed snake. And they had a motto: "Death to the fascist insect."

But the more Cinque tried to spread his vague and sometimes shifting militant ideas around the San Francisco underground, the less support he seemed to gather. Other leaders in the alternative movement viewed him as paranoid and lacking any real political viewpoint. And they didn't like the ultraviolent tactics he espoused.

So maybe it was the need to prove himself as an important underground leader. Or maybe it was just to get attention. But whatever the motivation, Cinque came up with a plan designed to grab the lead spot on the nightly news. As their first "act of revolution," Cinque decided that the SLA would carry out the cold-blooded murder of Marcus Foster, superintendent of schools for Oakland, California, right across the bay from San Francisco.

Marcus Foster was a hero to many in the predominantly black, low-income community of Oakland because he had reformed and revitalized the city's school system.

Foster wanted to involve parents and others concerned with the welfare of young kids by getting them to patrol Oakland schools, but Cinque and the other SLA members decided, through their own twisted logic, that the superintendent's real motivation was to impose a fascist police state on Oakland schoolchildren. Their response was delivered on Tuesday, November 6, 1973, when Marcus Foster was gunned down in cold blood after leaving work. The next day, the SLA delivered a communique to a local radio station, claiming responsibility for the murder and implying that there was more to come.

And there was. The SLA was about to carry out one of the most famous and confusing kidnappings in the history of the United States — the abduction of Patricia Hearst and her conversion from heiress to terrorist.

True to his long-stated intentions, Cinque, aided by Angel Atwood and Bill Harris, kidnapped Patty Hearst, dragging her kicking and screaming from her Berkeley, California, apartment on February 4, 1974. During the next two months, the SLA bombarded the press with rambling political "communiques," demanding they be published or the SLA would take the life of their "prisoner of war," Patty Hearst. At the same time, Patty herself was undergoing an extraordinary change. Today, Hearst maintains that her fifty-seven days of imprisonment, where she was kept bound and gagged in a dark closet, enduring mental and emotional torture, turned her into a brainwashed robot, willing to do anything her captors told her to do. (The courts later decided otherwise, holding Patty responsible for acts she carried out with the SLA, for which she served two years in prison.)

But whatever really happened to Patty Hearst during that time, she finally surfaced on April 15, 1974, toting a machine gun, taking part — apparently willingly — in an SLA robbery of the

Hibernia bank in the San Francisco Bay area.

The entire SLA gang now numbered nine people, including Bill and Emily Harris, Cinque, and Patty Hearst. Deciding it was time to get out of town and lay low for a while, the SLA sent Patty and the Harrises to stock up on clothing by robbing a Los Angeles sporting goods store called Mel's. But Bill Harris got into a scuffle with one of the security guards, and Patty covered him by shooting up the front of the store. The three SLA members got away but remained separated from the rest of their group, who were hiding out in a house in Compton, a low-income Los Angeles neighborhood. The bungled robbery at Mel's raised the SLA's profile again, and tips eventually led the Los Angeles Police Department to the SLA's hideout.

On May 17, 1974, the LAPD surrounded and barricaded the SLA house. And before long the situation turned ugly.

The cops knew the SLA members inside this house were heavily armed. This was a residential neighborhood, where gunfire was sure to put innocent neighbors and bystanders in peril.

LAPD Police Captain Mervin King was on the scene. He pleaded through the bullhorn, again and again, for the SLA members to come out and surrender.

They did not.

The police lobbed tear gas into the house, hoping it would flush out the armed encampment before anyone got hurt.

91

The next thing King heard was the sound of gunfire.

Lots of it.

He ducked for cover.

"I didn't anticipate, when the bullhorns went off, that automatic weapons would be coming out through the curtains in the front window and putting holes in the buildings across the street," King told us later.

"It was just random gunfire," said LAPD Detective David Reyes. "They were just shooting. There were homes, there were apartments. It was a residential area, and they didn't mind. It was, 'This is where we're going to make our stand, and we don't care who gets in our way.'"

In the homes around them, there were women who would later come to be known as "soccer moms," there were innocent children, there were fathers just trying to make a living. And the SLA members chose not to surrender but to shoot it out, and the neighbors be damned.

Make no mistake: these were urban terrorists, as dangerous as any threat that comes from a foreign shore. Only more insidious. Because they attack from within, and they attack with the cold hand of the zealot who believes he is killing for a cause and therefore justified in the murderous acts he commits, even if the people he kills are innocents.

Over the next hour, the silence of that quiet neighborhood would be shattered by the sounds of incessant gunfire. A reported nine thousand rounds of ammunition would be fired — that's right, nine *thousand* — and still the SLA held fast. The house caught fire — apparently a result of a tear gas bomb — but the SLA refused to surrender.

"I couldn't understand how people in their right mind would stay in a place and know there's no escaping other than surrendering," said King. "And I just couldn't visualize why someone didn't say, 'Okay, we're done,' and come out."

I remember seeing the videotape of the gunfight and subsequent fire on television later that night. It was an awful and terrifying sight, hammering home to me how desperate and, in my mind, absolutely crazy these radicals could be, willing to sacrifice not only their own lives, but also the lives of everyone around them to serve some confused and often barely articulated cause.

When it was all over, all six members of the Symbionese Liberation Army inside the house were dead, including leader Donald DeFreeze.

That left only the three who happened to be out of town — Bill and Emily Harris, along with Patty Hearst — to carry on the SLA mission of mayhem.

So it was time to recruit some new members.

Most of the radicals of the time didn't want anything to do with these violent, misdirected terrorists.

But two did.

The radical left and underground movements in San Francisco — indeed, across the United States — were by and large disgusted with the SLA. Most had been horrified by the senseless murder of Marcus Foster and further put off by the bizarre aftermath of the Patty Hearst kidnapping, including her metamorphosis into "Tania" (the name she took as a member of the SLA), and by the violent Compton shoot-out. When Emily Harris, hiding out with Bill and Patty in Oakland, tried to reach out to the Bay Area underground for help, she was rebuffed at every turn. Rebuffed by everyone, that is, except Kathy Soliah and her boyfriend, house painter Jim Kilgore.

Soliah hadn't started out as a radical-chic kind of kid: her dad says she was a conservative teen ("a Republican too, like me"), and in high school was a member of the pep club, played powder puff football, and was a member of Future Teachers of America.

But when she entered the University of California at Santa Barbara in 1965, things changed, and she started becoming more political. That's where she met her boyfriend, James Kilgore; after college, they wound up in Berkeley, the center of the West Coast hippie movement.

She worked as a waitress at the Electric Underground restaurant in San Francisco, where she became close friends with another waitress — a waitress who happened to be

Angela Atwood, a secret member of the SLA.

Angela was one of those who would meet their death in the conflagration at the SLA's house in Compton.

Two weeks after the shoot-out, at an ad hoc memorial service/protest in what had become known as Ho Chi Minh Park in Berkeley, she stood up and gave a eulogy to the six who were killed in that showdown: "I am with you," she said, raising a clenched fist in the air. "We are with you."

Apparently, the SLA noticed.

When Emily Harris got in touch with Kathy and asked for help, Kathy was reportedly ecstatic at being singled out by the remaining members of the SLA as a worthy contact, and she and Jim immediately set about trying to help the fugitives in any way they could, including raising money. Kathy also introduced the Harrises and Patty to her brother, Steven, who later became Patty's lover for a time; to her sister, Josephine; and to a sportswriter named Jack Scott who had radical sympathies. Scott also agreed to help the tattered SLA cadre, and so began a strange "lost year" where Patty and the Harrises traveled to the East Coast, staying in various hideouts, including an apartment in Manhattan, a farm house in Pennsylvania (where their "baby-sitter" was Wendy Yoshimura, another wanted fugitive, sought in connection with SLA-related crimes), and a cabin in the rural Catskill mountains of New York. (While others went to the Catskills to enjoy the skiing and the many famous resort hotels, the SLA members were apparently running around the back country with their weapons, training for the revolution they still expected to instigate sometime in the unspecified future.) During this time, Kathy Soliah and Jim Kilgore remained in the Bay area, but they stayed in touch with their SLA friends.

Eventually, the Harrises and Patty returned to the West Coast, Patty reuniting with the rest of the SLA in Sacramento.

For the next few weeks, Kathy Soliah and her brother and sister, as well as Jim Kilgore and Patty Hearst, all stayed in Sacramento, in a house rented by Kathy. Apparently, Kathy provided food and clothing by shoplifting whatever anyone needed.

In her memoir, *Every Secret Thing*, Patty Hearst says that when it came to shoplifting, Soliah and one of the other SLA members were "masters. They came back with steaks and chops and fancy desserts; according to them, such a diet was all part of the counter culture. It was perfectly appropriate for them to rip off the establishment supermarkets."

Soon, though, the Harrises arrived at the house, and the SLA members started to get back in the revolutionary swing of things. After robbing a mail truck, which netted them only about a thousand dollars, the new SLA upped the ante. Police say they held up the Guild Bank in Sacramento, getting away with a slightly large haul of $3,700. Police believe James Kilgore led the robbery, along with a new associate, Mike Bortin — who later married Kathy Soliah's younger sister, Josephine. Police say Kathy was the lookout and Steven Soliah drove the getaway car.

According to Patty Hearst's memoirs — and an allegation still under investigation by the Sacramento sheriff's department — the SLA next robbed the Crocker National Bank in suburban Sacramento.

This one turned out to be a much more serious mistake.

Kathleen Soliah denies being involved in this crime.

But Patty Hearst, who admits driving the getaway car, alleges that Kathleen Soliah and Jim Kilgore were in the bank, actively participating in the April 1975 robbery.

During the robbery; a forty-two-year-old woman named Myrna Opsahl walked into the bank, unaware of what was going on. The wife of a surgeon and a mother of three, she was depositing the collection money from her church.

A shot rang out.

And, with her three children waiting for her in the car outside, Myrna Opsahl fell to the floor of the bank — dead.

I'll tell you this right now — I don't care if Kathleen Soliah was in that bank that day or not. She was part of that group, she housed them, she

97

fed them, she sat in on their planning, and she could have come forward after that day. She could have said: that woman's three children have a right to know who killed their mommy.

She could have said: maybe I'll be a mommy myself someday, living a nice life in a nice suburb someplace, and I'll have children of my own. And maybe then I'll be able to imagine the unspeakable heartbreak they would suffer if someone shot their mommy to death, and how unbearable it would be for them to live their whole lives knowing somebody got away with that, that no one was ever punished for that.

But you know what?

Kathleen Soliah made no phone call.

To this day, she has never said, "I'm sorry that woman got killed."

Her lawyer talks about how those times were different. But guess what. Losing your mother is losing your mother, whether it's the 1960s or the 1990s or the new millennium.

Roy Opsahl, now a doctor in Sacramento, was a seventh grader when his mother was murdered.

"We've adjusted," he told reporters recently. "We've dealt with it. And life goes on.

"But you wonder why they get off."

They get off, Roy, because no one has the guts to come forward. I'll give Patty Hearst credit: she tried to right this injustice. She contends that the shooter was Emily Harris. So far, the lack of corroborating evidence and testimony from backup witnesses have left Mrs. Opsahl's murder unsolved and Emily Harris unindicted. The only person who was ever charged in the crime was Steven Soliah, but the evidence against him was weak, and he was eventually acquitted.

I know that no one else has been charged in this case. But I also know that Patty Hearst has no reason to make up a story about robbing that bank. She has no motive for saying her group committed the crime if, in fact, they did not. Put aside the legal questions for a second. The moral question here is overwhelming: how can anyone call herself a good, Christian, God-fearing woman, as Kathleen Soliah does, and keep whatever information she has about this case to herself all these years?

But, as I said, Kathleen Soliah apparently never felt any more compunction about the woman lying in a pool of blood on the floor of a bank with her church's collection money in the purse lying next to her. None at all.

After that botched robbery, the Symbionese Liberation Army with Kathleen Soliah along, went on their merry way, never looking back.

The SLA members and their friends soon decided that they had to get out of Sacramento, so they returned to San Francisco to spread more fear and destruction. Before long, the group members apparently began arguing among themselves about what actions to take next. It seems to have been Kathy's boyfriend, Jim Kilgore who suggested the next course of action.

Bombs.

He first proposed that they blow up a cop car in front of the Mission District police station, a popular target of bombs and bomb scares for local revolutionary groups. Jim Kilgore seems to have become the SLA's chief bomb-maker, experimenting with different devices and detonators to see which ones would pack the biggest punch.

In August 1975, Patty Hearst, along with Kathy's sister Josephine Soliah, allegedly placed the Mission District bomb as planned. Fortunately, it failed to go off.

Later that month, infuriated by their failure, and using the rationale that they wanted to get revenge for a 1973 police shooting of a black teenager, Emily Harris and Steven Soliah reportedly planted another bomb under a cop car parked outside the Emeryville police station, also in San Francisco. Kathy Soliah and Jim Kilgore reportedly watched from a nearby restaurant.

This time, the bomb went off.

The explosion was huge, the sound echoing off the nearby buildings.

By the grace of God, no one was injured.

The SLA planted two more bombs that same month of August, blowing up police vehicles at the Marin County Civic Center. Though the SLA had tried to use the bombs to bring about maximum destruction — the first explosion was supposed to bring deputies running to investigate, allowing the second bomb to kill as many law enforcement personnel as possible — the thankfully incompetent terrorists again only managed to destroy squad cars and did not harm any human beings.

Do not for a second make the mistake of thinking that this was part of some humane plan. These bombs were planted in places where police, where innocent people, where children, where anyone could have been standing when they went off. And as we would soon learn, protecting innocent people was the last thing on the SLA's mind.

The group now moved their terror campaign to Los Angeles.

It was time to pay back the LAPD for the death of the six original SLA members.

Time for revenge.

On August 20, 1975, according to police records, Kathy Soliah and a male companion — either Jim Kilgore or Bill Harris — went to the Larsen Pipe Supply Company and bought two three-by-twelve-inch sections of U Brand pipe. The Larsen Supply salesman later told police he vividly recalled the transaction because the customers were not regulars, they didn't make the purchase under a business name, and the size of the pipe bought by the man and woman was not commonly requested.

The salesman later identified the woman as Kathy Soliah.

The SLA bomb makers took their purchases home and this time made sure to pack the pipe bombs with concrete nails to make them even more lethal.

They completed the construction of their bombs and included a crude triggering device they had dreamed up, using a magnet and fishing line to attach the device to the police car and a clothespin with electrical contacts for the wiring.

Late on the night of August 21, 1975, police say Bill Harris, Kathy Soliah, and Jim Kilgore first planted one bomb under a police car parked at the Hollenbeck station and then another under the car of young officers John Hall and James J. Bryan, parked outside an International House of Pancakes on Sunset Boulevard in Hollywood.

The two patrolmen had run into the restaurant for a quick bite to eat. It was a hot summer night in Southern California. "The movies where just letting out," officer Hall told us. "There were a lot of men, women, their children, coming into this restaurant, eating. The tables were full."

None of them knew how close they were to being blown to bits.

Later, our producers set up a camera at the spot where the bomb lay and just let the tape run. I remember looking at that tape later, seeing all those innocent people, sitting in the restaurant, and walking by, women with strollers, an old man with a cane, delivery kids on bikes, teenagers on Rollerblades, and thought, if a bomb went off on that spot, a bomb filled with big thick nails you could hammer into cement, they wouldn't stand a chance.

"You would die, definitely," Detective Reyes said later. "The bomb would kill you. Also, loss of limbs, it would rip your arms off, and tear off your legs. It could almost cut your torso in half. That's the force of these bombs."

It was enormously painful to watch that tape, to imagine these things happening to innocent passersby.

But this is what the police say Kathleen Soliah was imagining.

This is what she was plotting.

This is what she had in mind that day.

Officers Hall and Bryan ate quickly and headed back to their car.

"As we left the restaurant, we received a call of a man with a gun, shots being fired. My partner and I ran down to the car."

Speeding off, they did not notice the device lying under their car.

Once again, thanks to the grace of God or the incompetence of the bomb-makers, or both, the bomb did not go off. Its firing mechanism missed by a fraction of an inch.

A few minutes later, another restaurant patron

noticed the suspicious-looking device in the parking lot. He alerted a beat cop on Sunset Boulevard, who immediately identified the device as a bomb and summoned help. Officers Hall and Bryan heard the call, and when they returned they realized the bomb was lying in the exact spot where their car had been parked. Checking under their vehicle, they found the magnet and fishing line still attached, pieces of the nail-packed pipe bomb that had failed to detonate.

John Hall, who is still a member of the LAPD, still has a vivid recollection of that night and what would have happened not only to him and his partner but also to the restaurant full of people where his car was parked. "We would have been gone for good," he told reporters. "So would a lot of innocent people in that restaurant. The impact would have brought down the restaurant as far as I am concerned. There's no doubt that it would have caused death."

Hall and Bryan both still bear the emotional scars of the attempted bombing: Bryan was so devastated by the incident that he quit the force; Hall says that for years afterward, he had to get down on his knees and look under any car he was about to get into.

The LAPD quickly issued an alert to all area police cars, and law enforcement officers all over the city went out into the night to check their vehicles.

The second bomb was soon found under a

police car at the Hollenbeck Station. This device, also packed with nails, was rigged to explode when the car was moved, which would have been early in the morning. Placed where it was, on a busy street next to the police station, it also could well have caused mass murder.

Fortunately, the FBI was starting to close in.

It started — not surprisingly, as we've learned more than six hundred times — with a tip. It came from the brother of sportswriter — and SLA sympathizer — Jack Scott. The brother told police in Pennsylvania near the farmhouse where the fugitives had hid out for part of the "missing year" that he knew the whereabouts of Patricia Hearst.

Acting on this tip, the FBI raided the farmhouse — and hit the jackpot. They found fingerprints, clothing, papers — all sorts of evidence that led them to an apartment where they believed Soliah was staying. They didn't find her — but who should be passing by at the end of an hour of jogging? Bill and Emily Harris.

They jogged right into the arms of the FBI — but that was just the beginning.

A short time later, an FBI agent found himself creeping up the back stairs of the apartment where the Harrises lived.

Through the window, he saw a woman in the kitchen.

He recognized the face instantly — but then again, who wouldn't. It was the most famous face in the nation, the face that had been on the cover of every news magazine, on every nightly news show, on every newspaper. The most famous victim-turned-fugitive in America.

Patty Hearst.

She was with Wendy Yoshimura, the SLA member wanted on explosives charges. The agent burst through the door. "Freeze!" he yelled.

The women froze.

And, according to reports, Patty Hearst promptly wet her pants.

Inside the apartment — which later turned out to have been rented by Kathleen Soliah — they found a considerable amount of bomb-making material that was almost identical to the two bombs placed under the police cars. Detonators, wire, and Plum Brand end caps found in the apartment also matched those used in the bombs. And, in a front bedroom, they found some other interesting items belonging to Kathleen Soliah, including a .38 caliber revolver in her dresser drawer.

While the agents were inside the apartment, Steven Soliah had the bad luck to walk up and was immediately arrested.

In one day, almost all the major players in the SLA drama were finally in custody.

But Kathy Soliah — who would later be indicted on charges of conspiracy to commit murder — and Jim Kilgore, who heard about the arrests on the radio, eluded capture.

On that September day, twenty-five years ago, Soliah and Kilgore slipped away into oblivion.

Or so they thought.

What they hadn't reckoned with was a young man's memory, and the determination of an FBI agent who believes that there's no such thing as a case that can't be solved.

The young man was Tom King, a rookie cop in 1975 when Kathy Soliah became a fugitive and now supervisor of the LAPD's detective support division. For King, the Soliah case was special because it was personal.

His father, Mervin King, was a police captain in 1975 and the officer in charge when the Symbionese Liberation Army had their bloody shoot-out with the Los Angeles Police Department.

Mervin King was also instrumental in the investigation that followed, helping to develop the evidence that pointed toward Kathy Soliah's involvement in the attempted bombings at the International House of Pancakes and the Hollenbeck police station. Mervin retired before the Soliah case was resolved, but his son Tom never forgot about the case or about his father's commitment to bringing the bombers to justice.

Tom King went to work in the detective support division around 1987. "I wanted to work the case then," King told the Associated Press, "but it was assigned to someone else. Now I'm the supervisor; I assign the cases." And that's just what he did, asking one of his best detectives, David Reyes, to track down Soliah and finish the job his father had started. From the very start, King says, he and Reyes — who was just thirteen years old when the Symbionese Liberation Army was terrorizing the citizens of California — recognized that the case could be a high-profile one that would generate a lot of publicity. "But that was not our purpose," he says. He had an outstanding arrest warrant for Kathleen Soliah, and he wasn't concerned about how old it was. "This is what we do," he says firmly. "We are under a legal and moral obligation to serve that warrant."

Reyes decided to get the FBI involved. He was put in touch with special agent Mary Hogan, who listened to Reyes's description of the events involving Kathleen Soliah and was intrigued. Besides, the twenty-fifth anniversary of the SLA shoot-out was coming up and it seemed like a good time to try to finally bring some closure to the long-ago events. "The case was historical in nature, which appeals to me," Hogan says. "I was also interested because of the SLA connection. I was just learning to drive when these people were placing bombs."

Hogan, who says she likes to read every document in the files relating to her cases, immediately went to work. "It was like a history lesson for me," Hogan explains. She had the FBI issue a warrant, called a UFAP, or unlawful flight to avoid prosecution, which allows them to get involved in cases that cross state lines. UFAPs were issued for both Kathleen Soliah and Jim Kilgore. But Hogan soon realized that the trail had gone cold.

Well, that's where we come in.

"I knew we needed national coverage for this story," Hogan says. "And, if we were lucky enough to get our case on the show, *AMW* could provide that for us."

Around the end of March 1999, Sharon Greene, the West Coast bureau chief of *AMW*, was alerted to the fact that the FBI and LAPD wanted some help with a case related to the Symbionese Liberation Army. They sent Sharon some basic background information on the SLA along with the wanted posters for Kathleen Soliah and Jim Kilgore, and asked for a meeting. Sharon, who isn't old enough to remember the SLA, was interested but not yet convinced that the case should be squeezed into *AMW*'s always crowded schedule. She agreed to a meeting, but because it was a particularly hectic week — Sharon was in the middle of coordinating pro-duction of twelve other segments for the show — it wasn't until she parked her Toyota 4-Runner in front of the FBI headquarters in Los Angeles that she had time to crawl into the back and dig out the file they'd sent her. Sharon read it quickly, then headed inside for the meeting.

The meeting moved Sharon closer to the idea that the Soliah case was one that *AMW had* to cover. But what really convinced her was talking to her family and friends who were old enough to have vivid memories of the SLA, the kidnapping of Patty Hearst, the Compton shoot-out, the Hearst trial.

"I asked my seventy-one-year-old neighbor, the woman I play mah-jongg with," said Sharon. "She remembered every day of the trial."

The people Sharon talked to also remembered the fear caused by the wave of bombings and attempted bombings, right there in Los Angeles, engineered by Kathleen Soliah and her fellow terrorists. Some remember how strange it was to walk the city streets on the days when the bombs were found. Today, when terrorists strike in America, when we all live through an Oklahoma City or a World Trade Center, we all feel a little less safe; this was, in many ways, the first time we experienced how a single act of urban terrorism can affect an entire country.

With the encouragement of her friends, Sharon decided to move the story forward.

Greene assigned freelance producer Margaret Roberts to do some further research and come back to her with a recommendation about airing the Soliah case on the show. Margaret brought in another local freelancer, Ray Mize.

They were the perfect team to reach back into the past.

Because in their pasts, they were on the team that started *America's Most Wanted*.

Roberts and Mize were the heart of the news

team that had caught John List. In fact, it was Roberts who first hired Sharon Greene as one of our early hotline supervisors.

Now the question was: could they catch lightning in a bottle again?

"This was something of a classic *AMW* story," Roberts explained. But she did have reservations. "At first," she said, "I kind of scratched my head and thought, yes, it was the SLA and it was interesting and there was the Patty Hearst angle; but like others, I thought, it kind of sounds like an old and cold case." Add to that the fact that, as events related specifically to Kathleen Soliah, the bomb she'd been responsible for hadn't gone off and hadn't caused physical injury to anyone. *Was* this, really, a case *AMW* should spotlight?

She wasn't sure.

So she spent the weekend reading Patty Hearst's memoir, *Every Secret Thing*.

It was a revelation.

"I was shocked and stunned," Roberts said. "And riveted by the account of the months preceding the conspiracy — the plot, the manufacturing of the bombs that would be placed under police cars in San Francisco and Los Angeles. To read about the unique characteristics of the bombs was really frightening. I was struck by the fact that the bombers had deliberately filled the devices with nails that would inflict particularly gruesome injuries on the cops that were in the cars, and in anyone who happened to be nearby." She credited the amount of detail in

Patty Hearst's book with really bringing the crimes into focus for her.

She had arranged to meet with Detective Reyes and his partner, Michael Fanning; they arrived at her office that Monday.

"Under his arm," Margaret remembered, "one of the detectives carried an exact replica of these bombs that were placed under the cars. When I saw this bomb after reading the account, I was stunned, again, by the physical reality of what would have happened if this bomb went off."

Then the officers also showed Roberts a video-taped re-creation of what the explosion would have been like if the bombs had, in fact, exploded. As she watched the video monitor and saw a police car and its dummy passenger being literally blown to bits, Roberts imagined what would have happened to the two young policemen — Officers Hall and Bryan — whose car had been targeted back in 1975.

It was obvious that if Kathleen Soliah had indeed been part of the crew creating and planting these bombs, then clearly she had intended to kill people. She hadn't cared who they were, who loved and needed them, whose brothers and sons they were. She wanted them dead simply because they wore a policeman's uniform. But the cops who were Soliah's intended victims *did* care about people, cared deeply and passionately: when Roberts later got the chance to talk with Officer John Hall, and

Marty Finemark, who found the bomb outside the Hollenbeck station, both spent more time talking about the gruesome injuries, even death, that would have been the fate of innocent passersby if Kathy Soliah's bombs had exploded than they did about the possibility of their own lives coming to an end.

After these interviews, Roberts believed she understood why the LAPD and their counterparts in the FBI were so deeply committed to reviving this case.

And soon she was just as committed as they.

Now the question was, could they convince *AMW* to air the case?

I always think about crime from the victim's perspective. What if it were you? What if someone pointed a gun at your child's head and fired? Would you forgive them just because they happened to be a bad shot and missed by a fraction of an inch? How is that any different from placing a bomb in a public place where any child could have been maimed or killed?

And what difference does it make if two years or twenty have passed since the crime? If your mother was killed in a bank while you waited outside, if that happened last week or twenty years ago, you still live your life without your mother. Do we want to live in society where people are allowed to say, well, I know I did these terrible things, but I've asked myself if I would ever do it again, and I said no, so I decided to give myself a full pardon?

So to me, the question of airing this case was cut and dried.

To the producers, however, it wasn't so clear.

My partner, the executive producer, Lance Heflin, was on the fence.

His number two, co-executive producer Phil Lerman, wasn't.

Lerman wanted to pass on the case.

Phil Lerman had been a young man of nineteen back in 1975, and he remembered the era well. While he hadn't completely heeded the call that was everywhere back then — *tune in, turn on, drop out* — he had been a supporter of the anti-Vietnam War movement and certainly wouldn't have argued with anyone who called him a hippie. He could recall the anger that many young people felt against the government during the time when Lyndon Johnson and later Richard Nixon were president and how, for many, law enforcement officers like the local cops on the beat came to represent a repressive system that wasn't listening to the younger generation's cry to give peace a chance.

Maybe, Phil suggested, we should think about those times. Maybe we should think about the social and political influences that drove Kathleen Soliah to plant those bombs. Maybe, Phil offered, by putting Kathleen Soliah in the same category as John List and William White Graham, we're going too far.

Greene and Roberts were astonished by Phil's

doubts. A hurried meeting was called, a hurried conference call was put together — Greene and Roberts on the West Coast, Lerman, Heflin, and the rest of us on the east.

And the fur started flying.

Greene, on the speakerphone, talking to Phil, was her usual, tactful self. "Phil," she asked, "are you out of your mind?"

Sharon's argument mounted quickly: was the cause of peace advanced when the Symbionese Liberation Army killed a school superintendent who wanted to make classrooms a safe place for kids? Was it a peaceful afternoon in Compton, California, when they shot thousands of rounds of ammunition into the neighborhood streets instead of letting the police take them into custody? And would the world have been a more peaceful place if Kathleen Soliah had managed to kill a few young policemen and some ordinary Americans eating pancakes in a restaurant on a beautiful summer night?

But the bombs didn't go off, Phil said. No one was hurt.

Sharon jumped right back. *No one was hurt?* she said. What about Officer James Bryan, who was so emotionally devastated by realizing that there had been a bomb planted under his car that he couldn't go on being a policeman, a career he had hoped and planned for his whole life? And what about Officer Hall, who still has trouble getting into a car without checking to see if someone wants to blow him up? And since

115

when, Sharon added, do we decide whether or not a criminal should face justice by the amount of pain and suffering he or she has caused? Would Soliah's actions still be forgivable if Officer Hall had lost only one arm or one leg? Or if only one child passing the Hollenbeck police station on the way to school had been killed?

Where, Sharon demanded, do you draw the line?

Phil was weakening. I could tell he didn't want us to get involved in this case, but he was realizing that, given the facts, we couldn't walk away from it.

I looked over at Lance. He had his arms folded across his chest. He was listening carefully but not saying anything.

You don't stay partners with someone for ten years and not know what he's thinking.

I knew he had already made up his mind.

We were going to take a lot of heat for it.

A lot of people would criticize us for doing it.

But we were going to get into the case.

It was time for Kathleen Soliah to answer for her actions.

And after twelve years, after William White Graham and John List and all the other "impossible" cases we'd broken, everyone in the room was thinking the same thing.

We've got a damn good shot at catching this one.

With the help of the Los Angeles Police

Department and the FBI, we had the segment about Kathleen Soliah, as well as her fellow fugitive Jim Kilgore, put together in just a few weeks. The FBI had given us old photos of Soliah and Kilgore that their lab had enhanced, along with some age-progressed sketches of what Soliah and Kilgore might look like now.

The show was broadcast on Saturday night, May 15, 1999, just two days before the anniversary of the shoot-out. FBI special agent Mary Hogan, the one with the encyclopedic mind for historical cases, was in the studio that evening when tips began to come in. Eventually, more than twenty leads were generated that night. People trust *AMW* and they trust our hotline operators — callers do sometimes feel wary about talking directly to a police officer, but they're more comfortable talking to us. That's how we developed that bond of trust with our callers — they know that cops don't answer our phones, and that we won't put a cop on the phone without their permission.

Hogan read the tip sheets filled out by the phone operators as they talked to citizens in different parts of the country who thought they had useful information about the whereabouts of Kathleen Soliah. And as she went through the leads, Hogan had a good feeling that her cold case had just heated up again.

Hogan took the information she got at our studio that night to LAPD Detective David Reyes. And back at *AMW*, we waited to see what would happen.

As things turned out, we didn't have to wait too long.

Just about a month later, on the night of June 15, 1999, Detective Reyes called producer Sharon Greene at her home. "I'm on my way," he told her. While Reyes wasn't going to give her any more details on the phone, Greene and Reyes had known each other a long time, and she understood what he meant: *America's Most Wanted* was about to chalk up capture number 570.

And it was going to be Kathleen Soliah.

"Where are you going?" Sharon asked.

"I can't say anything more," Reyes replied.

"Can we play the yes-and-no game? Is it in California?"

"No."

"Is it in the state I grew up in?"

"No."

"Is it in the Midwest?"

"Yes."

"Okay. Call me when it happens."

They hung up. Sharon was convinced that Soliah was going to be captured in Chicago.

She was wrong about the location.

But she was right about the capture.

We found out later that though Larry Hatfield, a reporter for the San Francisco *Examiner*, had been acting as an intermediary between the authorities and Kathleen Soliah, trying to cut a deal for her surrender, the negotiations did not result in Soliah coming forward on her own. She did not do the right thing.

So early on the morning of Wednesday, June 16, FBI special agent Mary Hogan, LAPD Detective David Reyes, and other law enforcement personnel, acting on a tip from one of our viewers, set up surveillance outside an ivy-covered house in an affluent neighborhood of St. Paul, Minnesota. They watched and waited as a slim, fifty-two-year-old woman who called herself Sara Jane Olson climbed into her gold minivan, setting off on a routine morning of running errands.

But Sara Jane Olson's routine day would not turn out as planned.

Mary Hogan was going to see to that.

"It was one of the most stressful days of my life," agent Hogan admits. "And one of the most rewarding.

"I didn't sleep at all the night before. I was concerned about the safety of the officers who would be involved in the arrest, and I wanted to be absolutely sure we had the right woman, because the name she was using — Sara Jane Olson — had never come up in any of the information developed about the case before.

"I thought it was best to arrest her away from her house," Hogan said. "I knew she had children and I didn't want to alert the whole neighborhood, just on the off chance that Sara Jane

119

Olson turned out not to be Kathleen Soliah. So we stopped her minivan and got her out of her vehicle and into ours very quickly. The first thing I said to her was, 'FBI, Kathleen. It's over.' "

But Olson wasn't about to admit to her true identity. Hogan told Olson that one of the most difficult things about investigating her case was trying to pronounce her real name, Soliah. It was a trick question, but Hogan's prisoner wasn't going to be found out that easily. Hogan, who was wearing an *America's Most Wanted* T-shirt, then asked Olson if she knew that she had been profiled on *AMW* recently. Hogan reports that Olson "sort of giggled."

Real funny.

Hogan and the other officers took Olson to the nearby Ramsey County jail — where a fingerprint check confirmed her identity.

Sara Jane Olson, suburban housewife and popular soccer mom, was — absolutely and without question — also one of the 1970s most wanted fugitives. Her real name was Kathleen Soliah.

The question immediately arose: how did this seemingly ordinary and unassuming woman achieve such a radical transformation?

Little by little, the answer would emerge.

It turns out that in 1976, after the arrests of the other SLA members, Kathleen Soliah fled back to Minnesota, the state where she had been born and raised until the age of eight. There, she told people her name was Sara Jane Olson — a clever identity to assume in a state largely populated by the descendants of Swedish immigrants and where one of the most common family names is Olson. Still in her twenties, Olson fit right into the local campus scene, and she went to work as a live-in cook at a fraternity house connected with the University of Minnesota.

She also did volunteer work at a counter-culture bookstore called the May Day Collective. Sara Jane Olson, apparently, was an unusual kind of fugitive: she was spending less energy on hiding out than on getting right back into a busy and fulfilling public life.

Sometime later she met a man named Gerald "Fred" Peterson, a doctor who had studied at Harvard and was now serving his internship in a Minneapolis hospital. He and the woman he thought was named Sara Jane Olson were married on March 12, 1980. They soon had a daughter and later moved to Africa, to the country of Zimbabwe, where Dr. Peterson, a socially conscious physician, thought his medical training could be put to good use. In Africa, his wife taught English as well as drama. Her interest in acting later led her to star in a number of local theater productions when the family moved back to Minnesota.

(I'll give Olson credit for this: she must be some actress. After all, for twenty-five years she's been acting like she never heard of the Symbionese Liberation Army and doesn't know how to build a pipe bomb.)

By the late 1980s, the Peterson/Olson household contained three daughters and was ensconced in Highland Park, one of St. Paul's fancier neighborhoods. Olson and her husband, now a highly regarded emergency room physician, became avid joggers and were often seen trotting through the neighborhood's tree-lined streets. They also entertained frequently, throwing fund-raisers for a daughter's soccer team and for local political candidates who were attuned to Olson's liberal values. Again, Olson's cooking skills were on display. Cheesecake and other desserts were a specialty. Friends remember that Sara's entertainments were always elaborate, and the home-cooked food she served at these events was invariably delicious.

During all these years, no one in law enforcement knew this tranquil outcome of fugitive Kathleen Soliah's run from justice.

But back in Los Angeles, retired police captain Mervin King couldn't forget the day he'd been in charge of the terrible shoot-out with the SLA in Compton, California. About Kathleen Soliah, he told *People*, "You don't like to have a loose end like that." So he kept reminding his detective son, Tom King, about the case until Tom was finally in a position to put the LAPD back on Kathy Soliah's trail.

The day after Sara Jane Olson was arrested, the LAPD and FBI announced that *America's Most Wanted* was responsible for the capture. So the entire world was looking for comment. And not everyone was being very positive about it.

Least of all the friends and neighbors in Olson's well-groomed, upper-middle-class suburb, who were trying to come to terms with the fact that their effervescent, sociable PTA mom was also a wanted terrorist.

Of course, no one wants to think they're friends with a terrorist, so the reaction is understandable. "Everyone who's heard about this is shocked," neighbor Mary Kate Kennedy told our correspondent on the scene. Another neighbor, Pat Kramer, talked about how Olson often attended local block parties. "She'd bring a casserole like the rest of us did," Kramer said. "There was nothing unusual about her at all."

But, of course, there was. Most moms who bring a hot dish to a neighborhood party aren't one of *America's Most Wanted.*

It was also the day after the capture, June 17, 1999, that I appeared on NBC's *Today* show, hosted by Katie Couric and Matt Lauer. Couric asked me what had made *AMW* reach so far into the past to bring this case back into the public spotlight. I explained that it was because the FBI had asked us to. They challenged us. And once we had made up our minds that airing the story was the right thing to do, we knew we were going with it all the way. But Couric also asked the question that my staff and I knew was going to come up once law enforcement had Soliah in custody as a result of our help: why did we reach so far back in time to look for this particular fugitive? Referring to the woman who now called herself Sara Jane Olson, Couric asked me, "John, do you have any mixed feelings at all about her arrest?"

I gave her a truthful answer. "I always do," I said. "You know, you wonder if people change. You wonder if people can be rehabilitated. This lady was wanted for some very serious things. Police cars were bombed. Three police cars were blown up in San Francisco alone. They attempted to kill police officers in Los Angeles. Bombs were found under police cars, and those bombs could have gone off in crowded streets and hurt or killed many people. And this was a dangerous group. I think people have to remember that they shot it out with police and six of them were killed. Their intent was to create chaos, murder and mayhem."

And, I might add, people have to remember that mother, lying dead on the floor of a bank.

But others were already sure that the American public, as well as Kathleen Soliah's intended victims, should just forget about her crimes, and were castigating *America's Most Wanted* for bringing her in.

No more than three days after the arrest of Sara Jane Olson, Minnesota state representative Andy Dawkins and state senator Sandy Pappas both made public statements of support and sympathy for Olson. That, however, did not sit well with the governor of the state of Minnesota,

Jesse Ventura. On his weekly radio show, the governor criticized Sandy Pappas's suggestion that the allegations against Soliah didn't constitute "real crimes." "I think pipe bombs underneath squad cars is a real crime," Ventura said emphatically. "What would [Pappas] suggest is a real crime?" He added that he thought the sympathy declarations by both Sandy Pappas and Andy Dawkins were "beyond belief."

When Ventura made those statements, Soliah was being held in the Ramsey County Adult Detention Center not far from her suburban home. She remained there for three weeks. In early July, she waived her right to fight extradition to California. Governor Ventura had made it clear that he stood ready to sign whatever papers were needed to send her back to the state where she was wanted. "She's California's problem," he said.

Soliah was flown to California, where she spent a month in jail before friends and family back in Minnesota raised a million dollars to pay her bail. Shortly thereafter, her defense lawyer, Susan Jordan, successfully petitioned the court to officially list Soliah's name as Sara Jane Olson, the name under which she will eventually be tried.

The media quickly jumped on the Olson bandwagon, painting saintly pictures of the wonderful liberal soccer mom who baked cookies and read to the blind.

God bless her, but you know what? All

through these legal maneuverings, the newly minted Sara Jane Olson never once apologized for the events she was such an integral part of back in the 1970s. She was full of praise for her supporters and those who were designing a Web site for her and raising money for her bail and legal defense, but not a word about those whose lives she'd come close to destroying.

Through her lawyer, Olson expressed her feelings about her current situation: Olson is "anxious to get the matter behind her . . . and go back to her regular, exemplary life. She's innocent," her attorney Susan Jordan told the press.

Well, that's for the courts to decide. Prosecutors tell us they have a wealth of evidence linking Sara Jane Olson to the crimes of the SLA; for example, they found Olson's fingerprint in one of the locations where the SLA made bombs.

And if Patty Hearst is subpoenaed to testify, we'll probably hear a firsthand account of how Olson helped to carry out the agenda of terror created by the Symbionese Liberation Army.

Still, Olson is acting like *America's Most Wanted* helped to snatch an innocent housewife right out of her kitchen for no reason at all. In October of 1999 she told the Minneapolis *Star Tribune*, "My pending trial is a witch hunt in the guise of a conspiracy case . . . with the apparent goal to take me off the streets for the rest of my life. I am being tried not for what I'm accused of, but for the crimes of the SLA."

Well, that's a convenient dodge. If she

believed she was innocent, she's had twenty-five years to come forward and say so, to do the right thing and let a court and a jury make that decision. And unless she's going to pretend she's not Kathleen Soliah, then whether or not she's legally guilty, she still has the weight of moral guilt on her shoulders, the debt she owes to the victims of the SLA crimes.

Chip Burrus of the FBI doesn't exactly agree with Olson's position that she's been prosecuted for no reason at all. "I personally don't understand it," he told *America's Most Wanted*. "The audacity of someone to think they can stay out on the lam and live a normal life when they've disturbed the lives of so many others — it's just a mystery to me."

But you know what really surprises *me* about this case? It goes beyond Olson's lack of contrition. I'm used to the fact that criminals don't tend to take responsibility for their own actions. No, what gets to me is that for someone who tried to stay out of the spotlight for so long, she did a really quick about-face. I think her fifteen minutes of fame kind of went to her head.

In December 1999 she released a cookbook that she and her friends are selling to help raise money for her defense. And you know what they had the nerve to call it? *Serving Time: America's Most Wanted Recipes.*

The cookbook contains pictures of herself as Sara Jane Olson in supposedly humorous poses: for example, one picture shows her "framed" (by

127

a picture frame) in a mocking pose with her hands in the air, as if she's being arrested. In another, she's holding up a plate of cookies while also clutching a handful of twenty-dollar bills. She even tries to make light of the charges against her: in the introduction to her cookbook, she writes that in the 1970s she belonged to a food-buying club called The Food Conspiracy. And so, she concludes, "I guess I do admit to once being a member of a conspiracy."

When some people suggested that pushing the cookbook with its tongue-in-cheek illustrations might not be the best way to demonstrate that she's just an average wife and mother who's being persecuted by a vindictive government and its law enforcement officers, Olson offered this comment: "Well," she said, "we all gotta have some fun in this."

Oh, really?

I recently took a trip to Parker Center, the headquarters for the LAPD. In front of the building stands a monument — a granite and marble fountain engraved with the names of the police officers who lost their lives in the line of duty.

It's not fun.

In fact, you'll never see a more sobering sight. The fact that someone could be charged with trying to put more names on that monument, and then laugh about it, putting her carefree attitude on display, is a slap in the face to everyone who ever carried a badge. Even if she's innocent, taking such a cavalier stance to such a painful issue is reprehensible, and everyone who purchases one of these cookbooks — in the name of raising money for her legal defense — needs to know that they're helping her thumb her nose at the system one more time.

Meanwhile, as she awaits trial, the woman now known as Sara Jane Olson walks the streets free. The rest of us can only wait for justice to be done.

Actually, there is one more thing to be done.

Remember that Soliah's alleged partner in crime, James Kilgore, is still on the loose. We haven't forgotten about him, and neither have the FBI or the LAPD.

I know there is someone reading this right now who has information about James Kilgore.

And I hope that person has the guts to come forward and call 1-800-CRIME-TV.

I have faith that you will.

And I believe that James Kilgore has reason to be worried about his long run finally coming to an end.

Because justice delayed is not, after all, justice denied; and, as I think we've made perfectly clear with this case, *America's Most Wanted* has a *very* long memory.

3

Death Rides
the Rails

It all started because our Web site went down.

Just after Christmas in 1998, the *America's Most Wanted* Web site, www.amw.com, stopped working. It was a technical problem: the company that was running the Web site for us technically went out of business.

It would be months before we had amw.com up and running again, and executive producer Lance Heflin didn't want to lose the communication link we'd established with our viewers. So he decided to put his personal E-mail address out as the show's temporary E-mail site.

It was a move he regretted immediately.

The next Monday, when he walked into his office and logged on to AOL, he couldn't believe his eyes. There were hundreds of E-mails from viewers across the country: commenting on the show, praising us and complaining about us, begging us to do stories, deriding me for one comment or another I'd made on the air, or telling us about stupid things that judges had done all across the nation — a flood of information.

At first he thought this was just a big pain in the butt: his electronic mailbox was clogged every morning with all this stuff. But as he started reading through the E-mails, he got a little addicted. The pure sound of people talking directly to the producer of the show gave him the clearest sense he'd had in years of what the show was doing right, what it was doing wrong, and what he could change to make it better. He started coming in an hour early each day, just to read the E-mails and pass them on to the staff.

About a month later, on February 2, he read an E-mail about a doctor, Claudia Benton, who was murdered in her home in the small Houston suburban neighborhood of West University Place. It didn't seem like a case we would do: there was very little to go on. No one had been charged in the case. The husband was out of town at the time, and to a cynical, hard-bitten newsman like Heflin, that always raised suspicions.

The letter, though, was extremely heartfelt. The writer, a friend of the doctor's, had been a crime victim herself; in a plea directed to me, she wrote, "We personally know, as you do John, how murder can affect the lives of a whole family, and a whole community. It is my prayer that you will help West University solve this crime . . . so that all of us can rest in peace."

Lance printed out the E-mail and passed it on

to the show's managing editor, Steve Longo, the guy in charge of putting researchers and producers on cases. At any given time, he has about fifty more cases on his desk than he can handle. He put the letter aside.

And everyone forgot about it.

But not for long.

In the next couple of days, Lance got such a torrent of E-mails on the case — all from different people, all individually written, all extremely heartfelt — that he realized he was on to something unusual.

Eventually he would relent and decide to take on the case.

At the time, none of us could have imagined that it would launch us on one of the biggest manhunts in our history.

Or that it would expose the terrible, hurtful tendency this country has to glorify killers and trample on the rights and feelings of victims.

Or that, three months later, I'd be at war, screaming at media outlets all over the country — the *Today* show, *Larry King Live*, CNN, *USA Today* — begging them, without any success, to help us catch a serial killer.

When Claudia Subiria Franco was just twelve years old, she left her hometown of Lima, Peru, to live with a family outside Houston for a semester as an exchange student. Hers was a big family, eight girls and a boy, and it was a close one; to this day, all of them still live in Lima —

all except Claudia. "She fell in love with our country," her host, Linda Montemarano, told us later. "Her dream was to be an American."

Years later, her dream — and another dream, to help children less fortunate than herself — began to materialize.

She returned to Peru to pursue a medical education, with the goal of getting her doctorate in pediatric research; she worked hard but maintained a vibrant social life. At a party she met an American who spoke to her in Spanish; she was multilingual — she had gone to a German boarding school run by nuns, and so her second language was German, English being her third — but rarely got to practice her English. So they switched to English and talked the evening away. Soon they began dating; eight months later her American, George Benton, was transferred by his company to Scotland. They stayed in touch, and the distance made them realize how much they missed each other.

They soon married, and after she finished medical school, they moved to America. A few years later she gave birth to beautiful twin girls. She delayed her residency by a couple of years so that she could devote her time to her children. But then the job offers started coming, and she started accepting.

She was the center of the family's life, a woman at once strong and tender, playful but brilliant. "She packed everything she could into life," George told us. "She didn't do much light reading, though, I tell you that. She liked *Architectural Digest* and *Metropolitan Home*. She got those at home, as well as three or four medical journals. It seemed like she always had some fifteen-pound book cracked open, and I'd just be sitting there reading the newspaper."

George worked in oil refinery management, a job that took him to many Third World countries. It was the nature of their relationship that they both made sacrifices for each other: when Claudia got a research position at UCLA, George moved the family there; when he spent three months in Africa, she took over the role of single mom.

Wherever they went, there was a quality about Claudia that everyone noticed: an ethereal quality, a warmth and a sincerity and a cheerfulness that affected everyone she met. Soon the couple moved to a well-to-do suburb outside Houston, where Claudia became an internist and researcher at Baylor University Medical Center.

"She had an incredible relationship with her patients," said Norma Gutierrez, a colleague. "A great bond. She developed friendships with them all."

"There was something that burned in Claudia to make it better for people, and the patients she saw knew that," said Mike Frazier, an administrator at the hospital. "She had a kind of a contagious smile, a genuine warmth and love for the patients that she saw. She always wanted to do

134

more for them, to go the second mile, and they knew that."

But her kindness extended beyond the patients, to the people with whom she worked.

"She looked after the people in the lab," remembers Patricia Cox, a grad student at the time. "I remember once I got sick, and she was the one who noticed, she was the one who forced me to go to the ER to get it checked.

"She would do the little things that other people never thought about doing," Cox said. "She helped me pick out some baby clothes for my new baby niece. Another postdoc was getting married, so she went with him to help him pick out a suit for his wedding. She was there for everyone — whether it be advice on picking a new apartment or condo or whatever you needed."

"One of the things about her was her spontaneity," coworker Trena Cormier said. "Like, if you were working with her in the lab around six o'clock, she'd suddenly say, hey, do you want to come over for dinner, you know George is making steaks. And she'd always be showing up with one or two of us in tow, so George always had to be prepared to keep on his toes."

The colleague who knew Dr. Benton best was Huda Zoghbi, who worked in the lab with Claudia. As strong as she was with patients, Claudia could not resist the lure of pure scientific research — the chance to wander into the unknown and return armed with answers,

answers that could save lives. She had become fascinated with trying to cure a rare genetic disorder known as "Angelman's Syndrome," a crippling disease that often strikes young children.

"She was very inspired by the idea of using genetic research to try to understand neurologic diseases of children, so she approached me about spending some time in my laboratory doing the genetic research," said Zoghbi. Dr. Benton spent a year and a half in the lab, sometimes for sixty hours a week, so the two women grew close. Zoghbi was excited about working with Dr. Benton, as were the Angelman's Syndrome patients she treated. She was, to them, a beacon of hope.

But Doctor Claudia Benton was far from the image of the stoop-shouldered workaholic. To see her shopping with her twin daughters — now twelve years old — at the Gap, giggling over the fact that Mom was so petite that they could swap clothes, you'd never take her for a neurologist struggling hour after hour in a silent lab seeking the cure for a rare disease.

Doctor Benton had just started a rotation at work during which she would be on call as the genetics consultant at Texas Children's Hospital. That meant a lot of evening phone calls, a lot of late-night trips to the hospital — a cycle which meant she had less time to devote to the family.

A few weeks earlier, George had mentioned that he wanted to go visit his family in Arizona for a while; they'd been asking about the girls and really wanted him to bring them out. Claudia said, Why don't you wait a few weeks, until I'm on call — then I won't mind being alone so much.

George agreed to postpone the trip, and Claudia felt better. Still, as the day approached, she realized just how much she would miss them, in spite of all the tumult of the on-call cycle.

That Friday, she left work early to see George and the kids before they took the late plane to Arizona, giving them one last hug and kiss in front of their beautiful home, then watching as they piled into a friend's car and drove off to the airport.

She went to get a haircut, and then went to a nearby restaurant to attend a Christmas party for the Baylor Department of Human and Molecular Genetics. Trena and her other friends noticed right away when Claudia walked in — or not so much walked as half-danced, half-sashayed over to their table.

She seemed, they said, in such high spirits — excited about Christmas coming, excited about the puppy she was secretly planning to get for the girls. A little later, as Trena was leaving, loud laughter pulled her attention back to the dance floor, and she looked over to see Claudia leading a conga line, her head back, her arms in the air, waving good-bye, and laughing as though she hadn't a care in the world.

As she danced, a train rumbled off somewhere in the distance, slowing down as it crossed into a residential neighborhood — Claudia's neighborhood, in fact. The trains cross several times every day; and on one recent day, a mysterious figure dropped from one of those trains in the shadows, the crunching of his footsteps in the gravel roadbed masked by the rumble of the engine, by the squealing of the heavy metal wheels against the tracks, and by the mournful whistle of the train, a whistle of warning as it approached a crossroads.

As far as we can tell, this is what happened that night.

Claudia came home from the party, walking into the large, empty house, locking the front door behind her. Around 10:30 P.M., she talked to a colleague at the hospital, going over a patient's case. A little while later, she fell asleep in her bed, in front of the TV.

She did not hear as the intruder managed to open the garage door and sneak into the house.

He quietly walked into the living room, where he picked up an African statue from the mantelpiece, a metal figurine about eighteen inches tall.

But as far as we can tell, he was not there to rob the house.

As far as we can tell, he was there for one purpose.

And the purpose was murder.

Any one of the wounds inflicted by this demon presence in her bedroom would have been mercilessly painful: where he swung the heavy African statuette and brought it crashing down on her face, where the knife went through her back and punctured both her lungs, where the force of the attack fractured her right arm at the elbow. As I looked at the autopsy report later, I would see two things: the fury, the overkill, the maniacal power of the attacker, and the strength, the courage, the bravery of Dr. Claudia Benton, who clearly struggled and struggled to stay alive, to stave off the attacker, to remain in this world for her daughters who needed her, for her patients whose very lives hung in the balance, for her husband, who loved her more than life itself; but it was life itself that drained from her as she rolled, it appeared to me, onto her right side, trying in vain to offer herself some protection as he brought the statue down, again and again, then left her there in unbearable agony as he went to the kitchen to retrieve a knife — she must have still been alive, or why would he go get the knife? — plunging the blade into the body of the petite woman, a body now drenched in blood, blood everywhere, blood from the nineteen blunt force injuries to her head and face, blood from the three stab wounds on her back, the pain of the multiple skull fractures so unbearable that she finally, mercifully, slipped out of consciousness, her soul leaving her small, crushed frame to suffer the final indignity as the madman ripped off her silk pajama bottoms, tossed them aside, placed a plastic bag over her head, and defiled her lifeless form. The only sound in the room, then, was that of one man's heavy postcoital breathing, a sound as solitary as the whistle of a train in the distance, emanating from the throat of a predator as evil and uncaring and unforgiving as the devil himself.

It was clear from the start that robbery was not the motive for this attack; the extreme violence of the attack was not consistent with someone trying to get in, get stuff, and get out. And the intruder took only a few small items, leaving many valuable items behind, items left in plain sight where he could not have missed them.

A jewelry box had been spilled open, but the most expensive pieces were left behind. (One of Claudia's sisters told us later that there is an old superstition, *"Los ladrónes nunca roban perlas porque se llevan mala suerte"* — thieves do not steal pearls because it will bring them bad luck.)

A string of pearls was left behind on the floor.

So, if robbery was not the motive, what was? The next logical conclusion was that this was some sort of perverted sexual predator.

Well, I have dealt with hundreds of sexual predators in my years as a manhunter. There is a pattern that emerges from their attacks. We have learned something of their motives, and their methods and we can predict, to some degree, what their behaviors will be.

This one was different.

For most sexual predators, the uncontrollable urge to violent sex builds, over time, until they believe themselves incapable of controlling it. Like a smoker who must, must, must have a cigarette to quench the aching emptiness in his chest after three days of forced abstinence, like an alcoholic whose body is battered by violent tremors for want of a single shot of Jim Beam, like a heroin addict who feels sick in a hundred ways that only one medicine will cure, these men experience sensations often expressed as a perception of physical pain, or other hallucinatory ailment, which they believe only violent sex will cure. I remember one killer we caught, an otherwise seemingly normal truck driver who occasionally picked up teenage girls in truck stops, raped them in the back of his truck, and killed them. The tipster who turned him in said he'd given only one enigmatic sentence of explanation for his actions: "Sometimes," he had said, "I just need to do that."

In almost all of these cases, the sex must be accompanied by fear on the part of the woman: it is this sense of absolute power and control, of sex mingled with terror, that satisfies the predator. They are insecure, weak men, men for whom sex is not enough to satisfy the desire — they must see their victims cower and plead and beg for mercy, or the need is not satisfied.

And just as predictably, once that need for violent sex — and, in the more violent cases, sex and murder — is fulfilled, there is a quietude, a silence, that settles over these predators. They are almost remorseful, shamed by their need, and at the same time satisfied by their action. The violent deed has the desired effect of quieting the demons, and they can rest. It is usually some time before the need for this sick, cruel, horrible act rises again.

Again, as I read the autopsy report later, I did not just see one of those predators here.

I saw something much worse.

First off, the enormity of this attack, the incredible overkill — a term cops use when a killer produces many, many more injuries than would have been necessary to murder someone — told me that this was not a situation of a demented predator seeking to frighten his victim, or even to kill his victim, either for pleasure or to leave no witness; this was a man who had gone beyond that controlled rage into an uncontrolled, psychotic state. More importantly, the fact that the rape occurred postmortem further told me that he was outside the realm of the rapists we usually dealt with — it was not the terror in his victim that he sought during the sexual attack; to him, this was more a reward for a job well done. That told me he was sicker, more inhuman, more remorseless, and much more dangerous than the men we usually hunted down.

And finally, there was no period of remorse, of shame, after the act. He did not run away immediately, filled with guilt and self-loathing.

Instead, he went into the kitchen.

He fixed himself a snack.

And he sat there, slowly filling his stomach, unconcerned that on a floor above him a woman lay, face down on her bed, dressed only in a gray sleeveless top, drenched in her own drying blood.

And when he was done, he grabbed Claudia Benton's keys and walked through a back door, climbing into her red Jeep and driving it, slowly and carefully, off into the night.

When Doctor Claudia Benton missed her call time at the hospital the next morning, her friends were immediately a little concerned. "There's no way she would miss a call," Patricia Cox said. "She is not that kind of person. She is always on time, always there."

The word spread: gee, could her car have broken down? Hey, did you hear she hasn't answered her pager? Does anyone know if she has a cell phone? Should we call George at his parents' in Arizona, or would that worry him unnecessarily?

About two in the afternoon, someone called Trena, Claudia's friend, asking if she knew how to get in touch with her. Trena had done some house-sitting at the Bentons'. She remembered how Claudia always told her how safe it would be to house-sit, that there hadn't been a murder in the neighborhood since 1985. Trena loved house-sitting for Claudia, actually, sleeping in that huge bed, having the nanny make you coffee in the morning.

Now Claudia's words were coming back to haunt Trena. That afternoon in the lab, they were holding their annual Secret Santa party. As they were exchanging gifts, Trena wondered aloud, "Should we continue with this party? I mean, Claudia's missing."

Her coworkers tried to reassure her: "You know Claudia. She's so spontaneous," someone said. "Maybe she forgot she was supposed to be on call and left to go to Arizona with her husband and the kids."

But at the end of the party, one gift remained unclaimed.

It was Claudia's.

Finally, Trena and a few others decided that enough was enough. They called the police and asked them to check out Claudia's house.

About an hour later, Trena was standing outside the office of the department secretary when she heard a woman scream.

"She's dead," the woman said. "She's been murdered."

I'm going to be honest with you: we've seen some crappy police work in our twelve years at *America's Most Wanted*. A crime scene is like a delicate, intricate castle made of wafer-thin

144

crystal: the slightest wrong move can shatter it beyond repair, make the case forever insoluble. We've also seen some bureaucratic nightmares: fingerprints that sat at the FBI lab in Washington, D.C., for months and months, leaving a case to stagnate and a killer to walk the streets.

But this time, it all went right: the cops on the scene disturbed nothing but went about their business cleanly and professionally. The autopsy was so thorough that we were later able to develop a clear understanding of the killer's modus operandi. And, more importantly, the cops found the needle in the haystack, the clue that would identify the culprit and put a face to the evil: a fingerprint.

The fingerprint traced back to a mysterious drifter, a man who'd been arrested once before — seemingly insignificant, but actually most important — for trespassing on railroad property and carrying a gun.

For we would soon learn that this was how he traveled, the old hobo way, by jumping freight trains. He went by many, many aliases, but we decided to go with the one that seemed most likely to be his real name.

Rafael Resendez-Ramirez.

The man we would come to call the Railroad Killer.

It would be another month before the E-mails started flooding Lance's mailbox. It's not unusual for us to get hundreds of letters or

E-mails on a case, but they're usually a form letter or a copied electronic file, sent to us again and again. What made this so unusual was that, of the hundreds of letters, no two were the same: each person told a personal story of being touched by Dr. Claudia Benton, of how she cared for them, of how they loved her, of what a role model she was for all the children she came in contact with. It was an outpouring of love and devotion the likes of which we'd never seen.

But the letters that finally turned the tide for Lance came not from all these friends and relations and well-intentioned acquaintances.

They came from her husband.

The first call to George Benton in Arizona, on the day he lost his wife, had come from the lab, asking if he knew where Claudia was. He immediately started forming scenarios in his head: she's sick and upstairs in bed, she left her beeper down in the kitchen, and she turned the phone off so she could sleep.

His mind would not even entertain the worst possibilities.

But the second call to George Benton in Arizona came from the police. They told him a woman had been found murdered in his home. She had not yet been identified.

In this moment, George Benton could hide the truth from himself no longer.

George Benton is not an emotional man. He is almost stoic, stolid in his manner and controlled in his speech; but his honesty and self-awareness are disarming.

"I have to maintain what composure I have," he told us later. "It's my responsibility to my children. Once you have to tell your children that their mother's been murdered, after that, you'll never do anything that difficult in your life."

Lance read the letters from George, about the bond everyone felt with his lovely wife, about the work she had done, about the pain this murder had caused, about how baffling a crime this was.

"It's a complete mystery," George said. "An unbelievable mystery.

"It's like, something evil just dropped in from nowhere."

We assigned our Texas correspondent, Ashleigh Banfield, to see what she could dig up on the case. As soon as she got to West University Place, she was made aware of the connection.

"West University, Texas, is an affluent neighborhood, with tree-lined streets and gorgeous homes," Ashleigh reported that night. "So how did evil manage to drop into town?

"The answer may lie just fifty yards away from the crime scene — on the other side of the tracks."

It all fit together. A drifter riding the rails comes into town. Just fifty yards from the railroad tracks, he spies an affluent home, an attractive woman. He must have found a vantage point from which to track the family's movements — it could not just be coincidence that the attack came just hours after Claudia's husband and children left town.

And on the other side of the tracks, Ashleigh, accompanied by the lead detective, Ken Macha, found a transient encampment — what we used to call a hobo jungle — the denizens of which come and go with the trains.

Together, Ken and Ashleigh picked through the rubble of the camp. They found mattresses, grocery carts, whiskey bottles, a cleaver; interestingly, they found several Bibles.

The detective told Ashleigh that he believed Resendez was living at that camp.

Ashleigh stayed at the camp after the detective left, questioning the transients she encountered, trying to get a clue as to where Resendez might have gone.

Nothing.

With the exception of the photo taken during his 1995 arrest for tresspassing on railroad property and carrying a gun, we didn't have a clue.

Most likely, not even his real name.

"We don't even have a true, correct Social Security number," Macha admitted. "He keeps using fake numbers and fake names wherever he goes."

Two days after the murder, Claudia Benton's red Jeep was found in a parking lot in San Antonio, Texas.

It was found right by the railroad tracks. Most

likely he ditched the car, hopped a freight train, and was gone.

He left behind no clue as to his destination. Nothing at all, except — to ward off the *mala suerte*, the bad luck — a pair of Claudia Benton's pearl earrings.

Rafael Resendez-Ramirez would have no bad luck.

It was going to take much more than luck to find him.

Nothing came of our airing of the case — we didn't get a single decent lead — and, as sometimes happens at *America's Most Wanted*, the case languished for a little while, put on the back burner as we went on to other cases. I know that sounds cruel, but it's a fact of life at *America's Most Wanted*: there are always a hundred more murders to look at, a hundred more families begging to have their case on the air, and with a small staff, sometimes we don't stay as focused on a single case as we'd like to.

But in late May, Lance asked a few of the producers to make a routine "update swing" — to check up with their cops on their recent cases, to see if there were any cases to be revived. One of the reporters assigned to this task was Anne Garofalo, a fresh-faced young producer who'd just returned from working in Los Angeles to be with her family here in Washington, D.C. The Benton case was the first one she had worked on for us, so the first call she made was to Ken

Macha, the lead detective. They hadn't had a bad relationship while working on the story, but it wasn't a great one, either, and Anne wasn't expecting him to tell her much.

She certainly wasn't expecting what she was about to hear.

"It's funny that you should call this morning," Macha said. "We just got confirmation that at the beginning of May, there was a double homicide — a pastor and his wife."

The couple, it seems, hadn't shown up for church one Sunday. When police went to check out why, they found they were in their bed, bludgeoned to death with a twelve-pound sledgehammer that was taken from the toolshed.

There were some parallels to the Claudia Benton case: in both cases, the women were sexually assaulted. In both cases, the motive clearly wasn't robbery. In both cases, the assailant took off in the victim's truck.

In both cases, the victims lived right next to the railroad tracks.

And there was one more thing.

"We just got the results of the DNA from the crime scene," Detective Macha told Anne.

"It matches the DNA from the Benton crime scene."

I got the call from Lance a few hours later. As always, Lance was all business: he wanted to talk about the million details that we had to work out. Ashleigh Banfield and Anne Garofalo would cover Weimar, Texas, where the pastor and his wife were killed. We'd send Ed Miller, our Los Angeles correspondent, to follow up leads on Resendez. I'd anchor the coverage from the Crime Center in Washington. Lance went on for twenty minutes about the details of the crimes, on which cops were playing with us and which weren't, and which victims' families were talking and which weren't, and which stories we were killing to get this all into the show, and what time we were feeding footage to Los Angeles for the promo department to put out promos on the case — the million details we need to get straight before we can get a show on the air.

I was listening, and I wasn't. Because over and over in my mind, I kept hearing a voice saying the same thing:

We've got another serial killer on our hands.

The cops were not calling him a serial killer yet — for the police, that is a very specific term, used only within a series of distinct definitions — definitions involving the number of murders, the frequency, the intervals between murders, the motives — and technically, this case didn't yet fit the criteria. But I knew in my gut what was coming. Because I knew how unusual this murderer was. This evil, demented lunatic was riding the rails, dropping off the trains in random places, and murdering the most innocent people in their homes. He'd already killed a doctor, a pastor, a pastor's wife. This guy, because his motives are so inscrutable, his movements so random, was going to be almost impossible to track. I knew the police agencies down there were in way over their heads. They were, as far as we could tell, making all the right moves, but their chances of finding this guy were slim.

And there was one other thing worrying me: as far as we could tell, the FBI still hadn't chimed in on the case. They were, in fact, unusually silent.

"Lance," I said, "we have got to find this guy. This is like everybody's worst nightmare. Who is gonna get this guy if we don't? What chance do those police departments have? And when the hell is the FBI gonna get off its ass and get something going on this case? What are they waiting for? And what is everybody else waiting for? Why isn't anyone else in the media covering this? I have CNN on right now. Why isn't CNN putting this guy's picture up? Didn't they learn anything from Andrew Cunanan?"

The minute I said his name, I realized — that's exactly what was going on. We had another Andrew Cunanan on our hands. Cunanan had killed, and killed, and killed again, and no one took much notice. *America's Most Wanted* kept airing that case and offering everybody our footage to try to garner some other nationwide coverage, and nobody cared one whit. I screamed as loud as I could wherever I could be heard, and no one paid attention to him until he killed Gianni Versace. Then, of course, his picture was everywhere — but it was way too late.

Well, I'd be damned if I was gonna let that happen again.

Anne Garofalo was stunned by the news of the second murder scene. She spent the day in frantic phone calls, setting up her shoot in Weimar, Texas, the next day. That night at the gym she ran the fastest mile she'd ever run in her life, the adrenaline of the hunt forcing her legs to pump faster, to push harder. After a fitful couple of hours of sleep, she flew into Austin, then drove into the town of Weimar, Texas.

Anne's heart was in her throat as she drove into the sleepy little town of two thousand, one of those towns where everybody seems to know everybody else — and certainly, everybody seemed to know Pastor Skip and his wife, Karen.

There are only two places to eat in Weimar: the Texaco station, where they have great barbecue, and the Dairy Queen, where Anne filled herself with corn dogs as she listened to the stunned townspeople trying to cope with this murder, all of them wanting to tell her about the decent pastor and his wife, and their quiet, loving ways.

"It's hard to describe," said Glen Schoeneberg, a member of the pastor's congregation. "When they walked into a room or they were in your presence, they did just make you feel like things were okay and you were a little better than you ever thought you could be."

Anne met up with police chief Bill Livingston, and they headed up to the church, and to the Sirnics' modest home behind it. "It's just sheer shock," the chief was saying as he drove, his voice unusually emotional for a cop. "All the people I have talked to, even the old-timers, no one can remember a murder in Weimar, Texas. Ever. There was some talk about a fight in a saloon years ago, that they think somebody got killed, but no one remembers for sure. But we've had nothing like this."

The gravel crunched beneath the car's wheels as Anne and the chief pulled around the church to the Sirnics' home.

She did not fail to notice the railroad tracks that ran right next to the home.

It was a chilling scene for Anne: the cat was still hanging around the house, waiting for the owners who would never come home again, owners whose shoes were still sitting on the welcome mat. Karen Sirnic was an avid gardener, and near the front door dozens of plants, ready to be put in her garden, still sat in boxes.

The day was boiling hot, and the house had been sealed by the forensic team after they had examined the house for evidence, so as Anne approached the house the stillness was even more palpable, the air not moving at all, as though the house itself were holding its breath, waiting for the Sirnics to return. There was a strange dissonance to the scene: the house was impeccably neat, and yet there was a layer of black dust everywhere — the fingerprint dust left behind by the forensic team, dust undisturbed in this burning afternoon.

The cat, unafraid of these unknown visitors, sat on the roof and meowed. Its food bowl was empty.

Anne and the chief walked around to the back of the house, to the toolshed. The Sirnics kept an orderly shed, with little labels marking where every tool should go: RAKE read the label next to the rake, HOE beside that.

Farther down the row, there was a label marked SLEDGEHAMMER.

That slot sat empty.

Police believe that Resendez, after ditching Doctor Benton's car in San Antonio and riding the rails for a while, hopped off a train in Weimar, Texas, and randomly picked the Sirnics' home.

They believe that as the Sirnics slept, he crept into the toolshed, emerging with the sledge-hammer. Early reports were that he used a glass cutter to slice through a window pane on a back door off the carport, reaching his hand through to open the latch; but Anne had found no broken glass. More likely, the door was unlocked, because no one locked their doors in this town.

After getting in, he walked through the house, the sledgehammer over his shoulder, soon finding the room where this pastor of a small congregation, this man of few possessions who did not preach to his flock but rather engaged them in conversations about God, lay sleeping next to his wife, the church secretary who also sang in the choir and ran the youth program. He heard their slow, rhythmic breathing in the dark, walked up next to the bed, and swung the sledgehammer in a high arc, and then down, two fierce, powerful blows, crushing the skull of Pastor Skip Sirnic and his wife, Karen, their blood spattering the wall and sheets, their lives gone in an instant.

Then, once again, the intruder committed the most unearthly of acts, placing a blouse over the crushed skull of Karen Sirnic, sexually assaulting her, and then, when he was through, walking out of the room, leaving the bloody sledgehammer leaning casually against the wall, then going down to the kitchen, and fixing himself a snack; a smug, crazed figure, sitting in the dark, knowing full well that once again he would get away with murder.

No one had thought anything of it on that Saturday morning when Pastor Skip's 1998 Mazda pickup was missing from their driveway. Even though no one saw Skip and Karen in town, people figured they were probably headed down to New Bielau. In addition to being pastor of the 375-member Weimar United Church, Skip Sirnic was pastor at the small Trinity Evangelical Lutheran Church in New Bielau, a small community eight miles south of Weimar.

Those two. Always on the go. So busy.

But everyone was concerned when they had to start services without the couple on Sunday. It certainly wasn't like them to be late.

They were disappointed, too. Everyone was especially looking forward to seeing Skip this day, to wish him well and shake his hand.

It's not every day the pastor has a birthday.

So they walked out behind the church to the parsonage and knocked on the door of the Sirnics' humble abode.

But there was no answer.

Anne knew the odds were against us again. Resendez had a thirty-six-hour head start on the authorities — the murder had taken place on a Friday night and was not discovered until Sunday morning. Resendez had stolen the Sirnics' Mazda pickup; then, in a curious turn of events, police discovered it in San Antonio, right near the place where he had left Claudia Benton's red Jeep.

That meant he almost certainly jumped a freight train again in San Antonio.

And that meant, once again, that he could be anywhere.

Late that Thursday afternoon, Anne was screening her piece for Phil Lerman, the co-executive producer. The next day was taping day for us, and there was the usual mad scramble to get all the pieces done for the show. Cindy Smith, another producer, sat in the room as well, watching the Sirnic murder piece with Anne and Phil, waiting her turn to screen her own piece

157

after Anne was done. After watching Anne's story, Phil and Anne were going over a couple of minor changes they felt would make the piece stronger when Cindy heard herself paged over the office intercom. She leaned over Phil's desk and called the receptionist, telling her to forward the call into Phil's office.

Phil and Anne were huddled around the screening cart, going over their notes, so they didn't notice at first when Cindy started repeating into the phone:

"Oh, my God. Oh, my God."

But they froze at attention when they heard her say:

"Resendez-Ramirez? Kentucky? Oh, my God."

Suddenly they were all talking at once: What about Resendez? Was he caught in Kentucky? What happened?

Cindy, ignoring her colleagues' pleas, said into the phone, "Thanks. I'll call you back."

Cindy's big blue eyes showed white all around them, and for second she could not speak.

"Phil," she finally said, "do you remember a rape case from Kentucky that they kept trying to get us to do? A guy and his girlfriend were walking on the railroad tracks, and he was killed, and she was raped, and you guys kept turning it down because there was no suspect?

"Well, now there's a suspect.

"They've definitely tied it to Resendez-Ramirez.

"Only this victim survived. She's the only one who's ever seen Resendez and lived to tell about it."

For a moment, no one breathed, everyone staring at one another in amazement, an unspoken question floating over the room, a question that would soon be answered:

Yes, the victim would talk to us.

Yes, she would help us catch the Railroad Killer.

There's not a whole lot to do on a Friday night in Lexington, Kentucky, but sitting by the tracks and listening to the trains was a popular pastime.

That's where Chris Meier and his girlfriend, whom we called Sarah in our stories, found themselves one evening in the early fall of 1997. It was just after classes started at the University of Kentucky, and they'd left the year's first party to walk down to the tracks.

"He used to go and listen to the trains all the time," Sarah told us later, "and we waited, but a train never came, so we got up to go back to the party.

"That's when this guy approached us."

He was a smallish man, with a small mustache. Sarah felt no fear until she noticed that in his hand he carried a screwdriver — the point stuck out, like a weapon — and when she heard him speak a menacing order to Chris, an electric chill of fear ran through her.

159

"Get down," the man was saying to Chris. "Get down."

Chris got on the ground, and Sarah did, too, trying to appease the man, trying desperately to figure out what he wanted.

"I just did whatever Chris did so I wouldn't upset the guy," Sarah said. "I was always told, 'Do whatever they say, and they won't hurt you.'"

The man started rifling through Chris's backpack looking for money; Sarah, knowing that they didn't have a dollar between them, again tried to appease the man. "We'll give you our MoneyMover card," she pleaded. "We'll give you as much money as you want. You can take our car, here's the keys, take 'em."

At that, the man's face froze into a fearful grimace. "I don't want 'em," he growled.

Chris was now pleading with the man. Just don't hurt Sarah, he said. Just leave her alone.

"His only thoughts," the cops told us later, "were to save his friend."

But the man got angry and told Chris to shut up, and then went at him.

Sarah couldn't see what the man was using to tie Chris's hands behind his back, and then hers, and then their feet; they lay bound, and now gagged, on the railroad tracks. They sat that way, in a freakish tableau, like the victims in an old silent movie, until the man began to drag Chris away. Sarah could see the pain in her boyfriend's face as the man dragged him across the gravel, so she wormed her way along next to him, to avoid the same bloody, painful passage.

But the blood, and the pain, were just beginning.

Now in the ditch beside the railroad tracks, the man tried to figure out what to do next.

"He seemed flustered," Sarah said, "like he seemed to be moving really fast, and like he didn't know what he was doing."

The two were lying on their stomachs, but Sarah managed to work her gag off and rolled over onto her side, and tried to talk to the man, soothingly, calmly.

"I kept saying, 'Just let us go, we'll get you anything you want,' but he kept getting really angry that I could get my gag off. Then I got my hands untied, and I tried to untie Chris, but I couldn't, so I just kept talking to him.

"He just kept walking away, and coming back, and walking away, and coming back . . ."

Sarah's voice trailed off as she remembered what happened next.

It was like a dream, the vision of the figure in the shadows walking away one more time, coming back, this time carrying — a board? A stone? Sarah couldn't quite make it out, but she could see that the man held it in two hands, bringing it crashing down on Chris's head in a single blow; like a dream, as the man walked over to her, lay himself on top of her, and stuck the screwdriver into her neck, saying to her as her blood oozed from the wound, "Do you see? Look how easily I could kill you"; like a dream, as she looked over at Chris, his mouth filled with blood, asking the man to turn Chris's head to the side so that he would not choke on his own blood, surprised as the man complied, walking over to Chris, bending over his body for a moment, and then returning to her and saying, "Don't worry about it. He's gone."

I always counsel women when they are in this situation to keep talking. Try to engage the attacker in conversation. If he sees you as a person, there is less chance that he will be able to objectify you, to use you for his sick ends. At this moment, the man was behaving like a typical sexual predator, placing Sarah in a position of fear first, then moving on to his attack. Sometimes, sometimes, sexual predators can be dissuaded from their actions in this moment if you can get them talking.

Instinctively, Sarah knew this, and even though her boyfriend lay, bloody and near death, just yards away, she held her composure and asked him his name, and told him hers.

"I was just trying to have him put a face to me and know me, that I was actually a person. I was just doing anything I could to become like his friend," Sarah remembered.

But in a moment, his anger returned.

Again, he lay himself on top of Sarah.

And as she pleaded, "Please, whatever you do, just don't kill me," he violently raped and beat her, breaking her eye socket, breaking her jaw, leaving her beaten and bloody.

An odd peace settled over Sarah; she didn't cry through the ordeal, and while the thought momentarily occurred to her that she might die in this place, in this moment, a voice in her head told her no, this is not your time. When the brutal attacker had finished with her, she asked him, calmly, to put her pants back on, and lay calmly as he took her ring and earring, and watched as she saw the man hurry away. She did not know that her boyfriend had just become, according to the police, the first murder victim of the Railroad Killer, nor that she would be, to the best of our knowledge, the only person to ever survive his attacks.

Chad Goetz, a University of Kentucky student, was watching TV when a young woman ran screaming across his front porch and through his open front door.

"She was frantic, scared, and her face and head were covered with blood," Goetz later told a reporter for the Louisville *Courier-Journal*.

Now the calm had deserted Sarah, and she was crazed with fear, almost in shock. "I didn't realize that I had been hurt," she said. "And when I got to the hospital I had a broken eye socket and a broken jaw and I had to get sixteen staples in my head and of course, where he stuck me in my neck, I had the stab wound there, but I didn't know I was hurt. My mom was there, and

I called her over to me, and I didn't even ask her if Chris was still alive. Everybody was hush-hush, nobody would talk to me, so I called my mom over, and I just said, 'Chris is gone, right?'

"Because I knew."

Now, two years after the attack — and just hours after the police called us that Thursday afternoon, tying all the murders together — Anne caught the next flight out to go meet Sarah, who was still in shock over the naming of a suspect in Chris's murder.

"When I got the call at my apartment, I didn't believe it," Sarah told Anne, "because there haven't been any leads before; I was in the mode of not getting too excited because it might not be true. I was in disbelief until a few days later."

The interview had taken place in Anne's hotel room, because Sarah said she'd feel safer there; her sister and the detective accompanied her. After it was over, Anne excused herself, went into the bathroom, and sat and cried for a very long time.

When she pulled herself back together, she went out and hugged Sarah, then got ready to go back to the editing center we'd set up in Texas. Thanks to that woman's courage, we now had a much better picture of how the suspect operated; if, in fact, it was Resendez, then we had a clear understanding of how he had progressed, starting from a normal sexual-predator modus operandi in Kentucky in 1997, to the much more dangerous, violent, unpredictable monster we began trailing two years later. She was able to give us lots of clues — what he looked like, what he sounded like — that would aid in the chase.

She also gave us one other thing.

People always ask me, John, why do you put these women on TV? If you are such a victim's advocate, and if you want to make sure no one is re-victimized by the media the way you were after your son was murdered, why do you do these interviews? You know how painful they are. You know how traumatic they are. Why don't you just put the fugitive's picture up on the screen and be done with it?

It's a fair question.

But there's a good reason.

First of all, we never force anyone to go on camera. The bonds that develop between the victims we profile and the producers of our show are bonds that last for years, and they last for one reason: we treat victims of crime — all victims — with grace and dignity. We don't hound them with phone calls, we don't camp out on their lawns, we don't run after their children with cameras, we don't do the hundreds of things I see every week on the nightly news.

But within the very strict framework of how we treat crime victims, there is a sober reality. And as cold and hard as it is to say, it's sometimes difficult to get the public to pay attention, even to the most horrendous crimes.

At this moment, as word was spreading that

the Railroad Killer was now believed responsible for four murders and a brutal rape, the story was still getting zero attention outside of the local press and *America's Most Wanted*. We knew we had to have a way to cut through the apathy, to break through the noise of everyday distractions and a thousand other news stories. We knew we had to have a way to make people stop and listen, a way to say, hey! This is real! This really is happening! This man is out there! He will kill again! Help us stop him!

And Sarah, brave soul, gave us the means to do that.

We did not show her face, we did not say her real name, but the power of her voice hit home. She focused attention on this case the way a thousand cops could not. I could plead with the audience until I was blue in the face — and I did — but my words could not raise the clarion call that her words could.

With her words, perhaps we could catch a killer.

Before Anne went back to Texas, she had one more stop to make. Thomas Meier, Chris's dad, had called her, to tell her that she could accompany the family on a journey they were making, a very, very special pilgrimage.

Until then, they had never been to the place where Chris was killed.

Now that his killer had a name, they felt they had to go there, to put a kind of closure on the

166

act, to say a special good-bye.

They stood silently for a long time in the hot sun, his father, his mother, and his sister Elizabeth, all staring at the spot where their beloved Chris had had his life taken far, far too soon.

Softly, Elizabeth spoke. "You wonder what was going through his head," she said.

"The fear, the rage," said Dad.

"He'd be twenty-three now," Elizabeth said.

"That's right," said his mom. "As of yesterday."

As usual, we taped the show on Friday, for airing on Saturday. By Friday night, cops from all over the country were showing up. Bill Livingston was coming in from Texas, the cops from the Meier case in Kentucky were headed in, and we were about to meet up with our newest ally in the case: a Texas Ranger by the name of Drew Carter.

Carter was the very model of a modern Texas Ranger: lean and lanky with the ever present white Stetson of the Rangers, he was sort of like a Marlboro cigarette in a cowboy hat. Slow talking and Texas-polite, he would become a regular fixture down on the Crime Center set over the next few weeks.

But for Carter, this wasn't just work.

This was personal.

When he was five years old, Drew Carter told his parents he wanted to be a Texas Ranger. The Rangers have a big place in the folklore that surrounds a boy growing up in Texas. It wasn't an

167

easy goal: you have to be a trooper for eight years, then take a statewide test, and only a small percentage of the top scorers even get to become candidates. Those who survive the many tests are the cream of the crop — and even of those, very few get in, because there is very little turnover: one leaves the Rangers only by retiring or getting killed.

He was a Ranger for just five months when he was assigned to the Claudia Benton case — but he quickly showed his mettle. It was he, along with another Ranger, who started finding the pattern in the Resendez attacks. After the Sirnic murders, he was chatting with a buddy of his, the way Rangers tend to do: Carter would call into the barracks, just to see what was going on, and he and his pal Brian Taylor would chat about everything from football to murder.

In one of those conversations, they started noticing similarities between the Benton and Sirnic cases — the proximity of the railroad, the randomness of the attack — so they decided to compare DNA samples, calling the lab and asking to be bumped to the head of the line — "and lo and behold," remembers Carter, "it matched."

Carter was now on the case full-time, and though his slow dispassionate Texas drawl belied his true feelings, we knew he was deeply committed to the case.

"I grew up along a set of railroad tracks, and my parents still live there," Carter said. "The tracks are up a grassy hill in our backyard. A mile and a half north, those same tracks pass in front of Claudia Benton's house.

"What's to say," Carter said in that slow drawl, "that he might have just as easily jumped off the tracks at my parents' house, instead of Claudia Benton's?

"Everybody is a potential victim of this guy.

"He has to be caught."

Before we even got to air with that week's *America's Most Wanted*, he would be proven right.

Twice.

Just as we were finishing taping, seventy-three-year-old Josephine Konvicka was finishing up a phone call with her daughter. Josephine lived just outside Weimar, Texas, the town where the Sirnics were killed, just about a mile from the railroad tracks; she had lived there alone since 1986, when her husband, George, died, and after that — unlike most people in this rural area — she always locked her doors. Josephine probably turned in around midnight.

The next day, when her daughter came to check on her and feed her cows, she found a broken window in the house. Inside, her mother was dead, her head beaten in savagely with a heavy tool from the shed.

Fingerprints at her home, police said, matched those of the Railroad Killer, Rafael Resendez-Ramirez.

And the next day, the body of twenty-six-year-old Noemi Dominguez, a former elementary school teacher, was found in her Houston home. She had also died from a blow to the head. Her 1993 Honda Civic was stolen — and once again, Resendez was considered the prime suspect.

The numbers were mounting: Claudia Benton. Skip Sirnic. Karen Sirnic. Chris Meier. Josephine Konvicka. Noemi Dominguez.

The pace was increasing. His madness seemed to be intensifying.

We needed a good tip, and we needed it badly.

On the next broadcast — Saturday, June 12 — we would get one tip that seemed extremely promising.

The FBI would go crazy for this tip.

Except for one thing.

For the first time in our history, we were not going to give the hot tip to the FBI.

Not right away, anyway.

The real story of what happened to Resendez-Ramirez has never been told, because it involves a little secret. The secret is this: the FBI, in addition to its unsurpassed ability to catch fugitives, its unparalleled efforts to nail bank robbers, and its unfailing professional ethic, has a unique ability to piss off other law enforcement agencies. The cops and sheriff's deputies who show up on Friday night aren't always happy to see their FBI counterparts, with their smart suits, their big budgets, and what some perceive as a better-than-thou attitude. "Feebs," some of them smirk, a derogatory nomenclature intended to indicate that their investigative skills were much more feeble than the agents themselves believed them to be.

We have, in fact, seen many cases where a local cop did all the footwork to solve a case, but the FBI came in at the last minute, caught the fugitive, and took all the glory. Privately, my friends in the FBI acknowledge this: positive publicity, they say, is essential for the bureau to keep doing its job — it keeps the public behind them, it diffuses criticism from media disasters such as Waco, and it helps a lot when budget time rolls around and the government is trying to decide how much to allocate to the FBI each year.

Well, this was one case where the FBI was pissing everybody off. Especially the people who were working hardest on the case — the Kentucky homicide cops, the Texas Rangers, and the U.S. Marshals.

They had been working this case, 24-7, from the very start. Privately, there were grumblings about the FBI: the bureau had come into the case late, its agents seemed to be more interested in hogging the spotlight than solving the crime, and, most importantly, while all the other agencies involved were working well together, the FBI was playing everything close to the vest, refusing to share some information, leaking information that shouldn't be leaked.

And I'll tell you one other little secret: our producers were starting to get pissed off at them, too.

It started on that Friday night, the night before the broadcast. The FBI had finally gone into high gear on this case, putting Resendez on their Top Ten list, and between them and the Texas Rangers and the U.S. Marshals there were hundreds and hundreds of law enforcement officers on the case. The FBI set up the main task force office in Houston, and Anne was headed down to Houston to see what they could give us. But from the beginning, the patronizing attitude of the FBI agents put her on edge.

Agent Lloyd Diaz had already called to make sure that we were going to have a crew at the command center that Saturday night, to make sure that the FBI was getting publicity as they took our tips.

Anne had explained, politely, that our tips came in to our hot-line, not theirs.

Diaz sounded perturbed. Can't you forward your calls to our hotline? he demanded.

The answer, again, was no.

Let me explain one thing: the reason *AMW* is so successful is that people trust us. They trust us to tell them the truth, and they trust us to keep their anonymity when they ask for it. A lot of people who would never call the FBI do call us, because of the bond of trust that we have developed with our audience. And I'd be damned if I was going to betray that trust for anyone, even the FBI, even on a case as big as this one. And the FBI knows it. The whole business of "Well, we thought you were forwarding the phones to us" was a bluff. We hadn't done it in 546 shows, and we weren't going to start now, and they knew it.

We did agree to shoot some b-roll at the task force but refused to forward the phones, and we figured that was that. But when Anne and her crew got down to Houston that evening, they were met with more of the patronizing attitude she'd encountered over the phone.

"So, did you transfer the phones?" said agent Brian Loder.

Anne told him that no, we didn't, and no, we couldn't.

Loder put a condescending hand on her shoulder. "Well, I think you guys need to get someone in there to get those phones working right," he said, his voice dripping with sarcasm. ("He did everything but call me 'missy,' " Anne remembered later.)

The situation went from bad to worse. Anne was accompanied by Mark Barnard, the sergeant on the Kentucky case, and the two of them walked into a side room to talk.

"Excuse me, miss, but you're not allowed in this room," PR man Rolando Moss told her. "This is the war room. There's classified information in this room."

Anne and the sergeant looked around.

The room contained a map, a Pepsi can, and a table.

Anne then walked into the larger room, along with Sergeant Barnard. The two FBI agents, Loder and Diaz, came walking up.

From the looks on their faces, Anne could tell something was up.

She knew, of course, what it was: the team back in our Crime Center in Washington had called to tell her that Noemi Dominguez's car had been found, in a small town near the Mexican border. This was bad news, because it meant that Resendez had probably slipped into Mexico, which would make him even tougher to find.

Agent Loder said to Barnard, "There's some information that's come in." He stared at Anne, stared back at Barnard, stared at Anne.

After twelve years of working with the FBI, most agents understand that there is a partnership with *America's Most Wanted* that they can count on: we never release information that they ask us not to release.

But Loder didn't see it that way.

"All you have to do is tell me to leave," Anne said, "and I'd be happy to."

"Well now, you wouldn't mind, would you?" chuckled Loder.

Anne excused herself, saying she was going to the ladies' room. She motioned to her crew, and motioned to the door.

They all left.

A few minutes later, she was beeped again by the law enforcement team back at the Crime Center in Washington.

"I have some information for you," one of the officers said. "And we want to get the Marshals and the Rangers on it right away. Can you live with that?"

Anne understood this coded conversation: we want to give these guys a chance to work the lead before the FBI comes in and bigfoots everyone. In other words, he was saying that they wanted to hold off from informing the FBI about the tip for a few hours.

Anne looked back at the task force building. She thought about Loder and Diaz.

Totally against *AMW* policy — although I can understand why she reacted this way — she replied, "I can live with that."

The tip was, indeed, a hot one. It came from someone claiming to be a Resendez family member. The caller had enough information about the family — information we knew but which had not been released — that we were certain it was the truth.

Drew Carter had decided it would be easier to deal with the family if he could move quietly. And moving quietly meant keeping the FBI suits at bay for a while.

The caller gave Carter the address of Resendez's sister, Manuela, in Albuquerque, New Mexico.

That Monday, Carter left our studios and

jumped on a plane, eager to see if the sister would talk to him.

We had managed to develop a pretty strong profile of Resendez, partly from information we got from the bureau and the Rangers, and partly from a lot of legwork by our reporters here and in Mexico. We knew that he was born about seventy-five miles outside of Mexico City, in Puebla; that he was abandoned as a baby and raised by his grandmother; that he started stealing at the age of twelve, was already in this country at sixteen, and at nineteen was already convicted of burglary, car theft, and assault of an elderly man in Miami. The cop on that case says it was a harbinger of things to come: in all his years on the force, he had never seen such a brutal, senseless assault.

Resendez was sentenced to twenty years for that assault.

He served only six of them.

Now, I want you to think about that for a minute. Because every time I hear something like that, it makes me furious. Do you realize that if we had one simple rule in this country — that people who commit violent crimes serve the time that they are sentenced to — Doctor Claudia Benton would still be alive today? That Pastor Skip Sirnic and his lovely wife, Karen, would still be alive today? And Chris Meier, and Josephine Konvicka, and Noemi Dominguez? Because the heartless bastard accused of their murders would not have been free to jump onto freight trains, to move through the night, to enter the homes of decent people who are sleeping in their beds, who are where they are supposed to be, and where they are supposed to be safe, people who have never harmed anyone in the world, to enter their homes and beat them until they are dead, and continue beating them long afterward, and to have sex with their dead bodies. He would not have been free to do any of this, because he would still be serving time for the brutal assault on an elderly man in Florida, a crime for which a judge felt he should serve twenty years in prison; he would still be serving his time, and that would have been the end of that.

Instead, we had a serial killer on our hands.

And damn few tips about where he could be.

There was only one advantage we did have in this situation. Unlike most serial-killer cases, where you have a modus operandi but no named suspect — think of anything from Jack the Ripper to the Son of Sam — this time there was a picture for the media to circulate, there was a face for the media to find.

There was only one question now:

Why didn't anyone in the media give a damn?

In my last book, when I criticized other media outlets, the reviewers beat me up: they said I was just trying to make the competition look bad. Well, what they don't understand is this: when we get to the point where we have a serial killer on the loose — like we did with Cunanan, like we apparently did again here — it's not a matter of competition anymore. We want the other media to get involved. We want to see his face plastered everywhere. Yes, there is a certain part of any TV producer that wants the story you're involved in to be recognized as a big story, and at the same time you want to retain some exclusivity on that story — but when lives are at stake, you have to put the ratings aside and do what's right. We were trying to do that. But for some reason, we were barking alone in the wilderness. Our producers were pleading with their contacts in the other media to get this guy's picture on the front pages, on the nightly news — but even with six murders under his belt, they kept getting the same answer: sorry, it's a local story.

Our coexecutive producer, Phil Lerman, is the former national editor of *USA Today*. I asked him to call his buddies back at the paper, and see if they could get the ball rolling. I've seen it a thousand times: the media operate in a pack mentality. They don't mind missing a story as long as everybody else is missing it, too — but if *USA Today* has it, then *The New York Times* has to have it. And if the *Times* has it, *The Washington Post* has to have it, and the *Chicago Tribune* and the *Los Angeles Times* will pick it up, and the producers of the national nightly news programs will yell at their assistant producers about why they're missing this story, which must be big because it's on the front pages of every paper.

I remember Lerman telling me about working on deadline at *USA Today*, and they would have someone fax them the front pages of *The New York Times* and *The Washington Post* the moment they came off the press, just to make sure that *USA Today* hadn't buried something inside the paper that everyone else thought was front-page material. Never mind using your own judgment — it was more important to make sure your judgment didn't look foolish when compared to everyone else's judgment.

I was hoping that this time it would be *USA Today* that would get the ball rolling. Phil did, indeed, call some editors at the paper and told them where to look for the story on the Texas wires.

And the next morning, we picked up the paper and looked through every page, and not a word about Resendez.

And the next morning, it was the same thing.

And the next.

And the next.

And it was the same all over the country. Outside of Texas, there was scarcely a word.

I truly believed that Resendez could be caught, and I usually am cocky enough to believe that *America's Most Wanted* can catch just about anyone. It was pretty clear this time, however, that we were going to need some help. But how could we get the other media on board?

Fortunately, I was able to catch a break.

A break that let me hold the rest of the media hostage.

It had been more than a week since the Railroad Killer had last struck, and we knew in our hearts he was about to strike again. We were getting ready for our next show — we had three more stories on Resendez-Ramirez ready to go and had named him our Public Enemy Number One — when the news came in that Katherine Soliah had been caught, after twenty-five years on the run. As I said earlier in this book, there was a lot of controversy about this capture — a lot of people saw her as a poor defenseless soccer mom being picked on by big bad *America's Most Wanted* — and the media were lining up to hammer me. They couldn't wait to get me on live TV and try to rake me over the coals on this one.

Now, I know how TV works. I know the people calling up for these interviews — from CNN, from Larry King, from MSNBC, from the *Today* show — are low-level "bookers." They don't have the authority to make deals; they're just under enormous deadline pressure to get a face in front of the cameras, and they live and die over being able to do that very quickly.

So I stalled them.

I told them I would come talk about Soliah — if, and only if, they would also let me talk about the serial-killing Railroad Murderer, and show his picture.

I knew this would screw up their plans: they'd have to go get the okay from their supervisor, who would have to get the okay from his or her producer. I knew they'd have to give in, because they had already committed to giving air time to the story, and like it or not, I was in the center of the controversy.

Besides, how could it hurt them? Here I was, handing them the biggest news story of the year, a known serial killer on the prowl, riding the rails, slipping into small towns, slipping away again. It was two for one: beat up John Walsh on the Soliah case, and get a big scoop on another case as well.

And then the answers started coming back.

No, thanks.

Not interested.

We've never heard of this other case, so it's not a big story.

I couldn't believe it: it was so incredible, and so infuriating. No one else has done this story, so we don't want to do it either. I started calling the producers directly, begging, pleading for time. We bargained with Larry King: we'll give you twenty-five minutes on Soliah if you give us five minutes on Resendez.

They offered two minutes on Resendez.

We settled for three.

By the end of the day, though, we had gotten the word out: it was just a minute here, a minute there, but at least the other media outside of Texas had finally run a picture of the suspected

Railroad Killer.

And soon, the snowball would grow.

Finally *USA Today* ran a little mention of the murders in its Nation Briefs column. The very next day — surprise! A few papers around the country ran the AP wire story on the case. The next day *USA Today* carried a longer story; the day after that *The New York Times* ran a long story — and by the end of the week, literally hundreds of stories were running all over the country; there were reports every night on the nightly news, and we had to assign one person full-time to deal with the calls from other media requesting interviews and footage.

Now, you'll notice that, for more than a week, nothing else had happened on the case — no new bodies found, no new leads that anyone was talking about. So why did hundreds of editors and producers suddenly decide this was a big story?

Simple.

Because everyone else did.

It was now the middle of June, a full month and a half after the Sirnics were killed, a full month and a half after the Benton and Sirnic and Meier murders were linked, a full month and a half since it became apparent to everyone involved that we had a serial killer on our hands, a full month and a half since the FBI started pleading with the media everywhere to run the face of this suspect.

My favorite question came at a news conference a few days later, when a reporter asked the FBI, Why have you taken so long to publicize this case? Couldn't you have protected the public better by getting the word out sooner?

So to those who say I criticize the other media for self-serving reasons, I raise that same question. To them, I say: had the newspapers and the networks started running this guy's picture along with us back when this all started, if they hadn't waited for the rest of the pack to help them decide this was a national story, then we might have caught this guy before he bashed in the skull of a seventy-three-year-old woman, before he murdered an elementary school teacher, before he slipped into Mexico, before the rest of his heinous acts still to come. Those who failed to run this story have to live with that knowledge, and I believe they need to be reminded of it, or the next time it will be more of the same. We have proven one thing in our nearly thirteen years at *America's Most Wanted*: the media can be a powerful, powerful tool. I just think those who have been entrusted with that power should learn how to use it better.

Our problems with the FBI continued. Suddenly they were not returning our calls, not granting us interviews, not faxing us their press releases. At first I was worried that it was retaliation for giving the Texas Rangers the head start on the lead with the sister — agents, as tough as they are, can be damned petty — but it wasn't that.

It was a syndrome we'd seen many, many times before.

Now that the "big boys" were finally getting into the game — Brokaw and Rather and Jennings and Koppel and the *Today* show and *Good Morning America* and CNN and all the rest — the FBI felt they didn't need us anymore. Why go on dinky little *America's Most Wanted* when we can be on all three nightly newscasts?

I couldn't believe it.

The media monster we had helped to create had now backfired.

It had eaten us alive.

I felt like we were the poor stepchild. The FBI came to us when no one else would help them. But as soon as the big guns came into town, they tossed us aside.

It was as though they were saying that the nation's top media manhunters were no longer needed on the manhunt.

Well, we still had a lot of allies in the FBI — guys whose cases we helped solve and who owed us a favor — and one morning, one of those guys decided to return that favor. He called us, off the record, with an astounding bit of news: Rafael Resendez-Ramirez had been arrested by agents of the Immigration and Naturalization Service on June 1 in New Mexico as an undocumented alien. But there had been a communications screwup — the INS didn't have a record in its computers that Resendez was, at the time, the main suspect in the Benton and Sirnic murders — and the next day, Resendez was kicked out of the country and sent back to Mexico!

Two days later, he would be back in the United States and would begin his killing spree again.

We called our main contacts with the FBI to confirm the story.

And a funny thing happened.

Now, the FBI needed us.

They needed us to keep this information quiet.

It would only harm the investigation, they told us, to let Resendez know that we were aware he had crossed the border. Please, they said, keep this information quiet; when we're ready to release the information, we'll give it to you exclusively.

We asked only one thing: that the FBI stop freezing us out. That they let us do our jobs. That they bring us back into the fold.

A flurry of phone calls, apologies, and promises later, the agreement was made. We would withhold the information.

Two days later, our FBI contacts came by for our next taping. As promised, we were leaving out the information about the screwup in New Mexico.

Neal Freundlich, the show's senior producer,

was chatting with them when his cell phone rang. He didn't speak; he just listened. Finally, he said, "Oh, really? How interesting. I'll call you back."

He turned to the FBI contact. "You promise that when you're ready to release the information, you'll tell us first?"

"Of course," he replied. "That's what we agreed to."

"Well," said Neal, in his usual friendly, matter-of-fact tone, "you're a big fat liar. You're holding a press conference in Houston as we speak, releasing the information. And you didn't even bother to invite us.

"Excuse me, I have a show to produce."

The media were now in full throat on this case, screaming about the government screwups, digging up every piece of information they could about Resendez. His face was everywhere — even landing on the cover of *People* magazine.

I was glad that, finally, the media had picked up on this story; I knew now that the world had gotten a lot smaller for Resendez-Ramirez. As a crime fighter, I was ecstatic.

But I will also admit that, as a victims' advocate, it was also a bittersweet moment for me.

Of course I knew that the main goal here was a law enforcement goal, and that having his picture everywhere was the best way to achieve that goal. As I said, we worked hard to get there.

And yet, once the media frenzy begins, I'm

always a little sad, because they get so caught up in what they see as the myth and the romance and the excitement of the killer that they quickly forget about the victims.

For example: to this day, with the exception of what you've read in this book, there has been no article ever written about the life of Claudia Benton. No article discussing her life's work and ambitions, her background, nothing. Her picture ran, with the other victims, in the stories about Resendez; there was a single quote about each of them, which is par for the course, but that's it.

I can't help but wonder what the families of the victims felt when *People* magazine decided to track down Resendez's wife, Julieta Dominguez, in Mexico, and quoted her as saying, "My Angel" — the name she knew him under — "never showed any sign of violence with me. He was a perfect gentleman. When I was pregnant he would massage my legs and help me put shoes on my swollen feet before work."

Gee, isn't that wonderful. A half-dozen people have been murdered and I'm supposed to feel sympathy for the killer because he was nice to his wife when she was pregnant. Where the hell do these magazine people get their values?

Of course, the greater good was being served, so I really shouldn't complain at all. But I couldn't help feeling sad when, for example, I read a letter to the editor that Dr. Benton's brother-in-law, John Benton, wrote to *People* magazine after their profile of Resendez:

> I would like to thank you for showing [Resendez's] face . . . but I would like to ask that *People* also consider a story on Claudia. I do not think I can fully tell all the good that was in this person's heart. Born in Peru, she was a wife to a husband who has worked years in Third World countries, mother to twelve-year-old twin daughters and a friend to all. She was a person who took time to sit and talk with a seven-year-old who was feeling forgotten. She took in a young woman who had had a problem in her life, giving her a home and a shoulder to lean on. She was a pediatric neurologist who dedicated her life to helping people in any way she could, who left behind many children and parents who had a great belief in her. She poured her heart into people, only to have her life wasted by a person who should not be considered a human being. Why is it that all the articles I have seen list the victims only as names but tell all about the suspected killer's life and story?

Good question, John.
Good question.

But when a killer's on the loose, you've got to suck it up and move on, because there's work to do. I knew that we had to develop better information on the killer, and I knew we had the right man for the job.

Ed Miller, our L.A. correspondent, was our newest team member. He'd just come over from the TV show *Hard Copy*, which had been canceled. I'll admit that I was a little worried at first: those *Hard Copy* stories could be pretty tabloid, and I was concerned that we not let the tabloid mentality creep into *America's Most Wanted*. Critics who don't know our show think of us as tabloid TV, but our viewers know what we're really about, and they know how careful we try to be about not crossing that line.

Well, the minute Ed got on the job, he allayed my fears. He clearly "got it": he was tender and gentle in dealing with victims, and ruthless in his pursuit of Resendez. "This was new for me — actually getting to be on the side of the victims and the cops. It was new for me, but I liked it very much," said Ed, a big, burly blond guy with a kind of intense gaze whenever he was working.

And at this point, it appeared that he was working nonstop. Every time I looked up, there was Ed — in Texas, in Indiana, down in Mexico — actually going door to door in Mexico with a picture of Resendez to see if he could pick up fresh leads. I know people accuse us of forgetting, sometimes, whether we're television producers or cops; sometimes, I must say, we are guilty as charged.

And now, Ed was headed to Gorham, Illinois.

Because now there were two more bodies.

"They were good, decent, gentle people," Bill Morber, the brother of one of the victims, told us. "They didn't deserve to have happen to them what happened to them."

As a former prison guard, George Morber was not the kind of guy who spooked easily. He was used to being around thugs, and he knew how to handle himself.

At eighty, George's wife had taken ill; after taking her to the hospital, he began living in a trailer next door to his daughter, Carolyn, and her husband.

Their trailers were just a hundred yards from the railroad tracks.

When Carolyn's husband came home at 1 P.M. on June 15, he found his in-laws both brutally murdered.

These deaths were soon linked to Resendez-Ramirez.

And now, another town went through the cycle of shock, disbelief, unbearable sadness, and then anger — anger that the killer still had not been caught.

Drew Carter, the Texas Ranger at the heart of this case, was picking up new leads, too. He had developed a friendship with our staffers, especially Anne Garofalo — "I didn't eat out anymore in Texas," Anne said afterward. "I was always at the Rangers' office for pie and Dr Pepper, or at their houses for dinner." So while playing his cards close to the vest, Drew was still giving her enough hints about what was going on with Resendez's family that Anne — with a little of the dogged telephone work she became famous for around our office — was able to piece together exactly what was going on.

And it was pretty exciting.

On June 14, when Drew Carter left our studios and jumped on that plane to New Mexico, he wasn't sure whether Resendez's sister, Manuela, would talk to him. But he tried a different tack with her: he said that he wasn't there to ask her questions but to answer any questions she had, because he was sure she had some.

Drew has a disarming straightforwardness and fairness about him; he strikes you, immediately, as a man of his word. Somehow, this came through to the sister, because she decided to trust him.

Manuela agreed to the meeting.

She kept repeating that she didn't know where Resendez was. Drew, quite honestly, told her he believed her. That wasn't why he was here, he said.

Then he took a chance.

He asked her if she would help find him.

And, a bit to his surprise, she said yes.

"Initially, there was some denial there, but she is a woman of great faith," Drew told Anne later, "and I believe she thought she was doing what was right, even though it was painful."

He told Manuela that he thought it would be helpful for him to talk to other family members.

She said they lived in Juarez but added that she had to think about whether to tell him how to find them. She had to pray first.

Drew left, but that night, he got a call from Manuela.

Here are the names of his relatives in Juarez, she said.

Here is how to find them.

Vaya con Dios.

Four days later, Drew Carter traveled south, to Juarez, Mexico, where he gained more information about Resendez than he had in all the months of the investigation. He learned, among other things, that the fugitive's real name was Angel Maturino Resendiz; that he had been spotted just ten days earlier in Rodeo, where his wife and child lived — just ten days!

The next week Drew made contact with the wife and retrieved some items that were taken from the crime scenes. First the U.S. Marshal assigned to Mexico talked to her, then Drew brought her up to Houston to meet with her himself.

Things were moving quickly now. Family members were giving him more and more information. They were trusting him, believing him, opening up to him.

Through it all, they painted a portrait of "Angel Maturino" that was terribly at odds with all we already knew about him. He was a kind man, a gentle man, a religious man, they kept saying. He could not do these terrible things.

And yet, as Drew continued to talk to them, they came around to believe that Drew was an honest man, and that his only interest was in getting Angel into custody without anyone getting hurt.

On Sunday, July 11, Drew Carter was off on a fishing trip when his cell phone rang. It was another call from Manuela.

She wanted him to come see her in Albuquerque.

She needed to talk to him.

And what she had to say was incredible.

Angel had made contact with her — through a third person, she was quick to point out — and he said that he was tired of running.

He was ready to give himself up.

And the family agreed that the person he should give himself up to would be Texas Ranger Drew Carter.

The Zaragosa Bridge in southeast El Paso is a quiet and relatively lonely place; pedestrians mostly use the other three bridges that link Mexico to the cotton fields and garment factories of El Paso.

Drew Carter stood alone on the bridge and waited. Behind him were other officers and some of the fugitive's family members, including Manuela. It has been a frenzied couple of days since that cell phone call on the fishing trip: a hasty run to Albuquerque, faxes back and forth with the district attorney to work out agreements

193

on matters Resendez was insisting on before surrendering — promises of his safety in jail, regular visitation rights, a psychological evaluation — all brokered through the sister.

But now, at 9 A.M., it was almost peaceful to just be standing and waiting, waiting for the moment the entire nation had been waiting for but not a soul was aware of, except for Drew Carter and his team, the family of Angel Maturino Resendiz, and — if the family was telling the truth, and there was no reason to believe they were not — the fugitive himself.

It was a moment of high drama; Drew would later say he felt like he was in a spy novel, making the exchange on a bridge.

Finally, through the glare, Drew could see a pickup truck pull up from the Mexican side and stop. Two men got out, one of them small, almost frail; they walked toward Carter and then stopped, just shy of the U.S. inspection booths. Carter walked toward them and approached the smaller of the two men. Instinctively, the manners long bred into him overwhelming the feelings he felt toward this man, he reached out his hand. "Hi," he said. "I'm Drew."

The other man took his hand, but said nothing.

He didn't have to; Drew knew who he was.

Finally, the long hunt was over.

As Drew Carter, Texas Ranger, escorted his prisoner to the American side of the border, slipping handcuffs on the hand he had just shaken, his mind stayed focused, the way a cop's mind does, on the little details: what is the next step. How will we get him to the plane to Houston. What time will the hearing be.

But he also allowed himself a moment to think about Claudia Benton, and the Sirnics, and the others who Maturino was accused of killing; he looked down at this man, wondered how he could have been capable of such violence, and thought: Well, at least there won't be any more crime scenes.

There is that.

And for a hardworking Texas Ranger, what better way to celebrate your thirty-second birthday?

The trial was mercifully short: although he was technically being tried only on the murder of Claudia Benton, his lawyers said that Maturino admitted to all the killings but was insane.

At the end of the trial, the woman we called Sarah, the only woman to survive the attacks, took the stand. Her brave testimony brought everyone in the courtroom to tears, even the lawyers: "I've been doing this more than thirty years," said Harris County District Attorney John B. Holmes, "and I've never had an occasion to tear up in a courtroom, until today."

"I told her," said prosecutor Devon Anderson, "that she was my hero."

It took less than two hours for the jury to find

Maturino guilty, after which the judge imposed the sentence.

Death.

Allowed to speak, Maturino complained that he thought the conditions of his surrender — Drew Carter had told the family he would be treated "humanely" — precluded the death penalty. "That police officer lied under oath, and I don't think it's right," he said.

But thank God the judge saw through the killer's empty, foolish attempt to save his worthless hide. And God bless Drew Carter, who gave the argument just as much credence as it deserved: "I think that as far as fairness goes," he said after the trial, "he got a lot fairer shake here during this entire proceeding than any of his victims or his victims' families received, and that's all I'm going to say about that," Carter said. "I'm in no way compelled to enter into a credibility war with a convicted serial killer."

And so, for the families of Claudia Benton, of Skip and Karen Sirnic, of Chris Meier, of Josephine Konvicka and Noemi Dominguez, of George Morber and his daughter Carolyn, there is some measure of justice, some measure of closure. There was another victim, four months after all the others: Leafie Mason, an eighty-seven-year-old woman in the small town of Hughes Springs, Texas. When she was seven years old, she lost her father to a freak of chance, when he fell below a slow-rolling boxcar. Eighty years later, another slow-rolling boxcar brought Resendez-Ramirez to her town, where he selected her home at random and beat Leafie Mason to death. For months, the cop on the case insisted that this case matched the Resendez-Ramirez murders; but there were so many such claims that they couldn't all be checked out.

After Ramirez (now known as Maturino) was caught, it was found that his palm print matched a palm print in Leafie's house.

She was the ninth victim. In the months that followed, Maturino would confess to several more murders — although his final grizzly tally may never be known.

There are lessons to be learned, and there are people who will never learn them — like the woman who runs a Web site dedicated to telling the world about the man she calls the "Angel of the Railways," running the letters and so-called poetry he spews forth from his prison cell. Under the guise of social science — that we as society need to understand the message of these miscreants — she decided it's her calling in life to give "a communications medium for this special class of the disenfranchised." I can't begin to tell you how furious I get at this sort of horse manure, and I won't dignify it by repeating any of Maturino's writings here. This man has taken nine lives — I don't even want him walking on the same planet with good and decent people anymore, let alone imagine wanting to hear his self-serving, self-centered "point of view." The only feeling I would like to hear him express is regret, or remorse, or in some way indicate that he at least understands what he has done to all those families — but instead he puts forth semiliterate claptrap that some people seem to find fascinating. I can only say to the woman who runs that Web site, I pray that your family never suffers what Maturino made so many families suffer, that you never have to learn how searingly painful it is to find your mother's killer, your brother's killer, your sister's killer made into a martyr; that you never have to learn what it is to be re-victimized by the media, the way the fascination with Maturino continues to re-victimize all those families.

These are not the images to leave this story with: I prefer the image that our producer Neal Freundlich found while working on a field production in Seattle right after the capture. He and Anne had been talking about sending some souvenir to Drew Carter, something to remember them by, and to thank him for all his help. During a break, Neal wandered into a magic store and stopped dead in his tracks: there on the wall of the store was a poster — a poster that now hangs, matted and framed, in Drew Carter's home.

It was a poster from the 1930s, advertising a magician who went by the name Carter the Great. In the poster, he is playing poker with a small, red, horned creature. The magician is holding four aces, and the caption reads:

"Carter Beats the Devil."

4

The Mother and the Mission

The place looked like something you only see on the evening news. At first glance, you could mistake it for a refugee camp in the Third World. It was a courtyard, surrounded by mud-brown brick buildings — most of them falling apart. The buildings stretched eight stories into the sky. On the ground level, there were little concrete porches, separated from one another by low-slung dividing walls, reminiscent of a dingy stable. Filthy water flowed down the faces of the buildings — a constant stream supplied by faulty plumbing. Moss and mildew covered the brick in patches.

The courtyard itself was strewn with little bits of broken glass, the kind that stay around so long they blend in with the dirt. At one end of the courtyard there stood a dilapidated swing set. The swings were mostly gone; those that remained were barely hanging from twisted, rusting chains. These former swings were surrounded by a few cracked concrete benches.

But still, children played, as children always will. Little boys and girls steered their bicycles and trikes around rain puddles that never seemed to dry, picking at pebbles hiding among the few patches of grass that were strong enough to live in this wasteland.

It could have been Beirut or Sarajevo or any war zone in the world. But this was not a foreign land. It was Stamford, Connecticut. This was the courtyard of the public housing project called Southfield Village. And in the past, it had been a war zone. The kids of Southfield Village had seen more than their share of violence in the courtyard.

But this day was going to be different. On this day a little girl was turning eight years old. On this day, the third of July, there would be a party.

On this beautiful day, nothing could go wrong.

In 1993, Stamford's South End neighborhood was the setting of a great struggle. Parents and community leaders were waging a battle to keep their kids in school, just long enough for them to apply to college or at least get a legitimate job. There was another option obvious to the kids, an option too many of them chose: drugs. There was an abundant supply to sell and use. Plenty for everyone.

John Ruffin was one community leader who was trying to win the battle. Ruffin was a successful businessman who was such a big name in the community, he was known simply as "Name." Name had a past: he once served twenty-two months in a Connecticut prison for drug dealing and assault charges. In fact, before the prison term, he was one of the biggest dealers on the South End. But now he was taking the righteous path.

Everyone in the community knew Name. He routinely threw block parties and picnics to promote goodwill among people in the neighborhood. He even started a youth organization called the Nation. As he told the newspaper reporters he invited to one of the early Nation meetings, he wanted to see the young people succeed. He told the teenagers that there was more to life than the ghetto. He claimed to ascribe to the teachings of the Reverend Louis Farrakhan, and he was every bit as charismatic.

Name Ruffin preached this gospel and appeared to practice what he preached: drug use will only lead to a dead end. He wouldn't dare use drugs. He had seen firsthand how drugs were killing Stamford junkies little by little, one day at a time.

But that was only half of Name's story — the public side. What was really going on was far more devious.

Name saw, firsthand, the devastation the drugs were causing — because he was also the man supplying the drugs.

What the general public didn't see, and what the citizens didn't talk about, was the fact that

Name was nothing more than a benevolent crime boss, moving massive amounts of cocaine and other drugs onto the streets. His income came from selling narcotics to the same people he claimed he was trying to save.

The Nation, operating under the guise of community leadership, was leading the community straight down a path of lawlessness. Name was the Godfather. Modeling his operation after that of his hero, John Gotti, Name became a philanthropist of sorts in Stamford. At Thanksgiving, Name, along with members of the Nation, would give out turkeys to the needy. At Christmas, they would hand out toys and bicycles. Name provided for the community with one hand so he could keep their mouths shut with the other.

Name knew that if he started sampling from his own drug supply, he'd lose his empire, like so many others before him. So Name felt justified preaching that drugs were the pitfall. That was in public; in private, he was digging the pit.

Many of the residents of the South End knew the Nation was nothing more than a drug-pushing street gang. But they weren't talking.

The cops knew it too. They just had a hard time proving it.

Name wasn't a hands-on dictator when it came to organized crime in the South End, but like a true Mafia godfather, he had to give his blessing to every crime that went down. He needed his taste of the profits, and more importantly, he needed to be in control.

So when a new drug gang moved into the South End in the early 1990s and set up shop, the Nation went on alert.

The competition came from New York; Brooklyn, to be precise. A small group of Jamaican drug dealers that became known to the cops and to the Nation simply as the Jamaicans. At first, the amount of "product" that the Jamaicans moved was so small that it wasn't worth Name's time or effort to stop them. Name had a mapped out section of the South End that he considered his "neighborhood." And as long as the Jamaicans weren't crossing into his territory, Name would let them slide.

Backed by their connections in New York, the Jamaicans slowly began to increase their business. Their big breakthrough came in the form of an abandoned building at 609 Atlantic Street. It was a rundown property that served as a flophouse — a shell of a place where addicts could go to smoke their crack pipes in peace and anonymity among their fellow crackheads. They would get their supply from their nearest Nation or Jamaican retailer and then head on over to 609 Atlantic to light up.

It turns out that one of the Jamaicans was a savvy businessman who came up with a bright idea: why force the customers to travel long distances for their fix? If they're going to be at the crackhouse anyway, why not just sell the crack there? And that's exactly what they did. This entrepreneur and his partners set up a twenty-four-hour Crackmart at 609 Atlantic. There was always someone on-site to provide the rock. The concept was an instant hit. Word spread quickly that the Jamaicans were open for business on Atlantic Street.

The Jamaicans had set up shop just a half block outside Name's "turf" — not technically a violation of the unwritten law of the streets, but close enough to cause trouble. Big trouble.

In order to get to the Nation dope dealers, customers had to travel right by the Jamaicans' crackhouse. Addicts were getting cut off at the pass. The Nation's profits were suffering, and that would not be tolerated.

One of the Nation members who had already set up shop in the South End decided to tell a group of Jamaicans to get lost. As a response, he received a bullet in the butt.

That set the tone. The Jamaicans weren't going to just go away.

Two days later, Nation members went into retaliation mode with a military-style attack. Armed with automatic weapons, they conducted a commando-like assault on the house at 609 Atlantic. Standing boldly on the front lawn, Nation members opened fire on the front of the building. More than a hundred rounds ripped through the crackhouse. Amazingly, no one was hit. But the message was sent: the Nation was telling the Jamaican crack-shop keepers that they'd better get off the block.

The street term for this is "broadcasting" — when you send a message so loud and clear that everyone in the community gets the news.

The news sent a chill through the neighborhood: the Nation and the Jamaicans were in a state of war.

Saturday, July 3, 1993, was a hot, sticky day in Stamford. The kind of day where the air gets wavy and looks like water where it meets the ground. It was the kind of day where you want to take it easy and relax. It wasn't the kind of day for a lot of aggravation.

It was the day before Independence Day, and Stamford would be holding its annual fireworks display at nightfall. Everyone was hoping it would cool down by the time the fireworks went off. Just a little.

Over on the east side of town, a seven-year-old girl named Jasmine Merced was getting ready to go to the birthday party at Southfield Village. Jasmine was a petite little girl with a pretty caramel complexion, the gift of her Italian mother and Colombian father. She always wore her hair in two braided pigtails that swung behind her when she walked. Jasmine was a happy kid, but a quiet and sensitive one: her high, squeaky voice belied her spirit, wise and sensitive beyond her years. Jasmine noticed other people's feelings the way few kids do, and she would be very concerned about the things she did and said, if she thought they would hurt someone.

That sensitivity came through on this day, because Jasmine knew the birthday girl was hoping for a specific toy; Jasmine couldn't remember exactly what it was, and rather than disappoint her friend, she got her mom to agree that they would pick up the birthday girl and take her to the toy store to buy the gift herself.

It was the type of thoughtfulness that people noticed about Jasmine; the kind of thing that parents pray for in their child. And together with her sister, Crystal, who was two years older, Jasmine had a way of melting her mom's heart. "Sometimes I would just say 'I need a hug,' " their mom, Rita Volante, told us, "and my girl would come running up to me and hug me. I remember a friend of mine saying, 'I wish my daughter would do that once in a while.' "

On most days, that was just how Rita and her kids got along.

On this particular day, however, the kids were driving her nuts.

They woke up a lot later than they were supposed to, and the house was a mess. Rita, in her typical mom way, told them that if they didn't get the place straightened up, they couldn't go to the party.

Rita was sometimes strict with the girls, but she had to be. Divorced from her husband, Rita had moved with her kids from the Bronx to Connecticut to give them a better environment. She worked as an instructor at a Head Start program that a lot of the kids from Southfield Village attended; and between working and raising the kids on her own, she developed the kind of let's-just-get-this-done attitude that gets a single mom through the day.

They had scheduled some serious cleaning. They went through their closets and separated the things that they really didn't have use for anymore. The girls protested: did they really have to get rid of this? Why that, Mom? I use that all the time! All throughout the day, the girls did a good job of getting on Rita's nerves. She was looking for a reason not to have to go through the hassle of taking them to the party, and the girls were one step away from giving her the excuse she needed.

Maybe, Rita thought, we just won't go to this party over at Southfield Village.

Maybe we just won't go.

But at about two-thirty that afternoon, Rita got a call from Agnes Adams, the aunt of the birthday girl. Agnes reminded Rita that she'd promised to give Agnes a ride to a nearby store — to buy a brand-new bicycle for the birthday girl.

Well, that settles that, Rita thought. She told Agnes she was running late, but she would be there.

Of Rita's two daughters, Crystal was probably more excited to be going to the party. She was very outgoing and loved playing with lots of other children. Jasmine was more introverted. She could deal with one or two other kids, but she became very shy around big groups. Today they would both get their fill. But they weren't planning on staying at the party too long: Jasmine didn't care much for Southfield Village, and Rita didn't want to be there after dark. They planned to come home early and get ready to watch the fireworks. Something they could do just as a family.

Rita hung up the phone and told the girls to hurry. Crystal and Jasmine had already picked out their outfits, and Rita started to fix their hair.

She told the girls how close they came to not getting to go to the party.

But we are going to go, she finally told them.

You kids are lucky.

Name Ruffin was taking it easy on the third day of July. He was hanging out at his town house with his brother Marcellus Ruffin, along with a group of Nation members, including a close friend named Marvin Wooten. The men were kicking back and relaxing, some were lifting weights in the back — it was too hot to do much else — when Name's girlfriend, Teneria, burst in with some shocking news.

Teneria, who was pregnant with Name's child, told the group that she had been attacked in Southfield Village by two women — the girlfriends of two of the Jamaicans, Christopher Carter and John Roper.

Teneria said she was sprayed with Mace, but she still tried to fight back against the women.

208

Carter and Roper broke up the fight by restraining her instead of their girlfriends. This, according to Teneria, left her vulnerable and allowed the women to get a few more cheap shots in at the end of the fight.

Name admitted much later that he wasn't normally the type of guy to get involved in other people's fights, even his girlfriend's fights, but he felt that his unborn child had been put in danger. What's more, Chris Carter was no stranger. Carter was known on the streets as Mad Max. He was one of the Jamaicans who had conducted business at 609 Atlantic.

The Jamaicans had encroached on Name's neighborhood, they'd threatened his livelihood, they had shot one of his associates in the butt, and now they had attacked his girlfriend and unborn child.

It was time to take care of business.

This is the brutality of street gangs, a brutality born of a selfish, self-centered ego: if I am wronged then I will strike back, no matter who gets hurt in the process. And so the violence echoes back and forth, escalating as it reverberates, until neighborhoods are ruined, lives are ruined, entire generations grow up in a culture of violence and fear — all to satisfy the wounded ego of some street thug.

Investigators think that Name didn't actually ask the other guys to help settle the score. He didn't have to. Like dutiful soldiers, they knew that if their benevolent leader had a problem, they were obligated to help. They volunteered their services.

Name made a phone call.

It was a call for weapons.

One or more of the Nation's members went to a safe house where the gang stored their arsenal of firearms. It wasn't long before a large duffel bag arrived. Inside, there were guns — lots of them. The men took their pick of the assorted Glocks, 9mm's, and .380s from the duffel bag. And among the sidearms was a special weapon in a cloth carrying case. This particular gun was not up for grabs. This was an AR-15 assault rifle — the kind of high-powered weapon the U.S. armed forces have been carrying into battles since the 1970s. This was Name's pride and joy.

The group split up into two cars. Marvin Wooten, whose nick-name was "Smash," drove a Mazda RX-7. Marcellus Ruffin and two of the other Nation members were crammed into the car. It's a two-seater, so two men had to ride in the hatchback. They had to keep the door open so they and their weapons would fit.

Name, Teneria, and the rest of the crowd rolled out in an Oldsmobile 98.

They were headed for Southfield Village.

Rita and the girls arrived at Southfield Village at about 3:45 P.M. The first thing they did was pick up Agnes and head to the store. The bike had already been purchased and assembled; it just needed to be picked up. From there, they went back to the party and surprised Agnes's niece with the bicycle.

It was the hottest time of the day.

Most of the parents just dropped their kids off at the party. The adults who stayed, as Rita did, remained inside, helped out with the party, and tried to stay out of the heat. Agnes's apartment was on the ground floor. The entrance opened out into the courtyard. The position of the apartment gave it more circulation than most, but it was still too hot for the kids to stay inside. They went out and played in the courtyard.

For some reason kids aren't bothered by the heat as much as grown-ups are. They were bundles of energy, running this way and that; it seemed like every kid on the block was at the party, playing together without a care in the world.

And they were in good company. After all, this was their yard, and it was the Saturday of the Fourth of July weekend. Entire families were out enjoying the hot day as best they could — tossing the ball around, grilling hot dogs, listening to music, setting off firecrackers while little kids squealed in delight — all the things that people do on a summer weekend. A lot of the people from Southfield Village were out in the courtyard.

Including Chris Carter and John Roper.

The group in the Oldsmobile and the group in the Mazda were disappointed. They thought

211

they would find their prey, the Jamaicans, in front of one of the buildings; that would have made for an easy drive-by attack. But when they weren't there, the gang realized they would have to take the offensive and go on the hunt. They split up, half entering the courtyard from one side, half from the other.

C.J., one of the older children, had just returned from a nearby store with candles for the cake. Just in time for the kids from the party to come inside from the courtyard and get something to eat.

They all sang "Happy Birthday to You," and the birthday girl blew out the candles. The kids were anxious to get a piece of cake and a scoop of ice cream, so the parents had to get control. They made the kids line up from smallest to tallest to see who would be first in line to get their plates. Some of the other kids from the complex who had crashed the party were eyeing the goodies, too. There was plenty of food, so Agnes and Rita invited them inside to get what was left over.

Now they had a small apartment filled with rambunctious little kids, all holding paper plates loaded with ice cream and cake. And it was hot. Far too hot for all of these kids to be underfoot. And just think of the mess.

All of the children were sent back outside.

Into the courtyard.

The Nation Group that went through the dark

breezeway was keeping a close eye on the court-yard ahead of them. They could tell that it would be a task to find their targets amid all the people in the courtyard. Their eyes were more attuned to the bright light they had just walked out of than to the dim light of the breezeway.

This could have been the reason that they had passed right by Carter and Roper.

But then, one of the Nation crew cried out.

There they are.

And Carter and Roper were off and running.

The two men ran faster than the hunters could draw their guns. The Jamaicans darted toward the other side of the courtyard. If they could make it there, they could duck for cover into another breezeway. The only thing that lay between them and sanctuary was the court-yard.

The courtyard full of people.

The courtyard full of kids eating cake and ice cream.

But Name and his crew didn't care about the kids, or the parents, or anything that was in their way.

They only cared about revenge.

They raised their weapons.

And suddenly, the brilliant sunshine, the blinding heat, the beautiful sounds of laughter and music that wafted above this perfect Independence Day weekend, all of it, all of it, was shattered, shattered in an instant, in the time it takes for a finger to move on a trigger.

Rita Volante told us what she remembered:

"We had just finished up and were putting the ice cream away. That's when everything really got crazy.

"I thought they were firecrackers, because it was the day before the Fourth of July — firecrackers had been going off all day all over — until C.J. came to me and said, 'They're shooting.' We really thought they were firecrackers. Loud and very consecutive, like firecrackers going off. It wasn't 'pow' and wait and then 'pow.' It was 'boom boom boom' one right after another. It was just a continual flow of bullets."

Now, those of you who have children already know this, and those of you who have never had children may never understand. There is a protective instinct that kicks in. You may have seen it on nature specials when a lioness or mother bear will fight to the death anything that comes near her cubs. Humans have this instinct, too. Once you become a parent you're willing to do anything to save not just your child, but any child near you who's in danger.

That's what overcame Rita and her friends.

"When we realized that they were shots instead of fireworks," said Rita, "we panicked. We ran toward the door to try to get the kids inside. The kids were running in on their own, and we were pulling in some of them, trying to get as many of them in the area as we could into the living room. They were, of course, scared; so they were panicking, they were screaming, some of them were crying. We were trying to move them in as quick as we could and then try to check to see if everyone was there. It seemed like all the kids were inside.

"It was crazy. It was chaos, total chaos. It was like living a nightmare. You see those things in movies, they're not supposed to really happen.

"The adults that were there were hollering to get down. Some of the kids knew enough to get down on their own. But it was difficult, because we wanted to make sure everybody was inside. Some of them were small, and we didn't want to take the chance that they were still out there. There was one little one who was still out on the porch, and Agnes reached out and grabbed him and pulled him inside, it was one of her nephews. He had just panicked and froze there.

"I know, when both of my daughters were inside, I took a deep breath and I thought everything was okay.

"I felt a little relieved."

Somehow, with all of the bullets whizzing by them, Carter and Roper had managed to make it to the breezeway right next to Agnes's apartment. They had taken cover, and investigators say they were returning fire with the weapons they had on them. Bullets were whizzing back and forth across the courtyard.

Little Jasmine had made it into the safety of

the apartment just seconds earlier. She appeared to be fine, except for a stain on her blouse.

At first Rita thought it was Kool-Aid.

It was not.

The ground outside Agnes's apartment was strewn with pieces of half-eaten cake and paper plates with globs of ice cream melting in the heat. One plate was different from the others.

It had a neat hole carved into it.

A bullet hole.

This was Jasmine's plate.

Just moments before her mother saw her enter the apartment, just moments before her mother mistook the stain on her blouse for Kool-Aid, Jasmine had been running, as fast as she could, still clutching her ice cream and cake. The bullet was traveling at such a high rate of speed, it was unclear whether she was shot in the back or in the chest. Either way, it entered Jasmine's upper body, passed through her lungs, and came out through the other side, passing neatly through her paper plate in the process.

And now Jasmine collapsed and was not moving.

"One of the kids said, 'She's bleeding!' " said Rita. "Jasmine had on a dark two-piece shorts outfit. It was navy blue with little tiny flower buds in it. So it was dark and you really couldn't see the blood. When the child said, 'She's bleeding,' I still didn't know that it was her. And then I saw Jasmine tug on Udine, one of the adults at the party. I couldn't hear all of what she said to her, but it sounded like she said, 'I've been shot.' And at that point Jasmine just collapsed into her arms. And Udine started screaming to me, 'Let's go. Let's get her to the hospital,' because I froze up at first, I couldn't believe this was happening.

"I ran into the kitchen for my purse, to get my keys. Udine had Jasmine, and she ran outside. I ran after her. I recall bullets going by me. We were running toward the car, and the shooting was still continuing. She was carrying Jasmine, and when she got to the car, she bent down on the ground and covered her with her body so she wouldn't get hit again.

"I was on the ground also. I was trying to get my keys out and get them up into the lock. And all I could think about was, if I get shot, I can't drive her to the hospital, and we need to get there as soon as possible. We got inside the car, Udine in back of the driver's seat with Jasmine in her arms. We started to pull out, and as we pulled out another of the adults from the party jumped in on the passenger side.

"I was driving as fast as I could. I was pretty much in a state of hysteria. I was screaming, I was trying to reach behind me and touch her. Udine said at some point she felt the tension on Jasmine's hand loosen up. It was a ride that probably lasted about three minutes, but seemed like a lifetime was going by. As I was driving, police cars were passing, and I was trying to get their attention by blowing my horn and flashing my lights. I guess they were responding to the same call and had no way of knowing that I had the child in the vehicle going the opposite direction."

Lieutenant Doug Baker of the Stamford P.D. was one of the first detectives to arrive on the scene. He heard a broadcast about a shooting in Southfield Village, "which is not an unusual occurrence," he told us.

When he arrived at the courtyard, there were large groups of people gathered around. The uniformed officers were already trying to seal off the area with yellow tape. Shell casings were scattered everywhere. One of the officers informed him that a little girl had been shot. Baker instructed two detectives to go to the hospital and check on the girl's condition.

The kids from the birthday party were doing their best to come outside and get a look at the commotion. The adults were trying to keep them in. In all, there were between fifty and sixty kids around when Baker arrived. Most of them had stopped crying. It was the adults now who were holding back tears.

Some of the bystanders were able to give Baker the play by play: six guys with guns coming from the building across the way. Two other guys running across the courtyard. The first guys shoot, the other guys shoot back. Several dozen people are caught in the crossfire. Two women carry a little girl through the barrage of bullets.

It was incredible that nobody else was hit.

As the detectives did their work, Rita was arriving at the emergency room with Jasmine.

"Udine and I took her inside," Rita told us. "The nurse was aware that we were coming in. They brought her into a room where they started working on her. The last thing I can remember is laying her on the table, and them cutting her shirt open so they could try to save her.

"During the time they were working on Jasmine I was not allowed in the room. I was fighting and had to be secured not to be in the room. They had to hold me back. I would have liked to be in there, but I understand they needed to do their jobs. They brought me into a private room in the back to wait. Udine stayed with me for awhile, then she left to go change — she had a lot of blood on her."

Detective Patrick Mooney was one of the men sent to Stamford Hospital. Rita couldn't see what was going on, but Detective Mooney saw it all.

"There were twenty-four doctors, nurses, technicians in the trauma room, all working on Jasmine Merced, all trying to save her life," he said. "She had lost a lot of blood at the time. There were people going crazy bringing in blood and fluids and setting up different things around the stretcher.

"The doctors were doing everything possible. Give me this, give me that, get this, hold this, do that, let me hook this in, this, that. They were getting in each other's way, some of them, at the time. And the reason I say twenty-four, I was just standing back watching, and I counted the people because I had nothing else to do.

"I did see one or two of the uniformed officers. They couldn't even stand to watch the little girl; they were walking away teary-eyed. After about forty-five minutes, the doctor in charge called it off and said it was useless to go any further. They pronounced her dead at that time."

Detective Mooney paused as he remembered the moment.

"Everybody was walking around, looking away," he said. "There was a chill that goes through your body — everybody."

In another part of the hospital, Rita sat and prayed. "I tried to maintain some hope and faith that she was going to be okay," she said. "But there was a feeling inside that I knew — from the ride there, it just felt like something had left my body. It was a darkness that came over me. Something was just missing. It's a strange terrible feeling. It's like a part of you is just gone. And they still hadn't told me that — they didn't need to. I could feel it."

It is in this crease in time when a parent's sixth sense comes through, the electrical connection between parent and child, the moment when you know what the doctor is going to tell you before he says it. I have heard this from so many parents who have found themselves in this horrible moment, illuminated by the sickly glow of overbright fluorescent hospital lights, their sense that the most important person in their lives has somehow left their universe, and they feel a chill in their bones, and before the doctor says a word, they know.

A moment later, the doctors broke the news to Rita.

"They told me she didn't make it. They explained to me what the bullet had hit and the damage it had done. Every time they would close her up, or sew her up, something else would open up. A main artery had been hit, and the bullet had punctured her lung, so she was bleeding internally too severely. They said normally they would have stopped fifteen, twenty minutes into a procedure like that, but they continued for about an hour in some type of hope or effort that they would be able to bring her back."

And a little while later, Rita headed home, for the first time, without one of her children.

How did we come to this? How is it possible that we have spawned a generation of criminals, a generation of thugs, with no regard for human life? What human being could see a child in front of his windshield and not slam on the brakes, could see a child walking into traffic and not pull her back, could see a child lost and crying and not say, there there, don't worry, we'll find your mommy? And yet, these inhuman monsters were even worse — it was not chance that threw the innocent children in their paths, it was intent. They planned on taking revenge for an insult, they saw that their path of revenge took them through a courtyard filled with innocent children — and they didn't give a damn. They raised their guns, they pulled the triggers, their bullets whizzing by the tender bodies of squealing, laughing innocent babes; they heard the children's terrified screams, heard the mothers' anguished cries, and then lifted their guns and pulled the triggers again, not stopping even when their bullets tore the flesh from one of those children, took her from this earth far, far too soon.

I will never understand how these monsters can so selfishly, so recklessly, so cruelly move through the world and leave such sorrow and loss behind them, and not give a damn; and I will never stop my crusade to find them, to hunt them down and put them behind bars like the animals they are — for there is no lower form of life than those who would harm a child and, I believe, no greater calling than protecting children, when we can, from the scum of the earth.

Back at the crime scene, word spread that little Jasmine Merced had died. Newspaper and television reporters were getting reactions from the residents. One little girl cried, "We can't even have a birthday party. I want to get out of the Village."

The birthday girl talked to another reporter.

"My mother told me to tell you I'm nine, and I hate the Village. I don't want to live here anymore."

The news of Jasmine's death ate at Douglas Baker and the other investigators. Nothing could go wrong with this investigation. Everything had to be perfect. This girl's murder must not go unpunished.

That night, Rita had to take care of her other daughter, Crystal, while she was still in a state of shock.

"I'm not really sure whether I slept that night, I don't remember sleeping," she said. "I was really very concerned with Crystal, and if she was going to be okay. I sat with Jas's picture in my arms and Crystal was asleep on the couch. The doctors had given her something to help her sleep. I just still couldn't believe it happened.

"I kept thinking, hoping, that it was a dream, that it wasn't true, even though I knew it was. I'd been there. I'd seen it. I had to hope for something and that was the only thing I could. A mother's biggest fear is to lose your child, and it had happened. And it wasn't something I could have prepared for. I didn't have time to tell her how much she meant to me, how much I loved her. I wanted some sort of reassurance that she knew that I loved her, that I would never do anything that would put her in jeopardy, or anything that would harm her. I would never let anything happen if I had control over it, or if I knew. But I didn't.

"I was outraged that this could happen — that a good time, a birthday party, something that's supposed to be normal for children to go through, would end in such a tragedy."

What is unbelievable to me is that, in addition to the loss of her daughter, Rita was hiding a second, secret wound. It was a wound that would take a lot longer to come to the surface. And just like the bullet ripping through Jasmine's flesh, this wound would prove to be just as fatal.

Normally, it's close to impossible to get any information from witnesses at Southfield Village. At the crime scene there were several people who could tell the officers what happened, but when it came to actually identifying the participants, everyone had excuses: I didn't really get a good look. They were all wearing ski masks. They had bandanas over their faces. It was understandable that people would be hesitant to talk. They knew Name was involved, and as much as they might hate the Village, they still had to live there.

No one knew that, in addition to having just lost a child, Rita was suffering another pain, a clandestine one. She did not let on to anyone. But stoically, forcefully, she made the rounds of the neighborhood. More than a hundred people had witnessed what happened out there. And no one has anything to say to the police?

Not this time, thought Rita.

Someone shot my daughter.

And every one of the men involved in this shoot-out is going to pay.

No one knew why Rita was so fearless; clearly, she was taking her own life in her hands, going up against Name Ruffin this way, boldly insisting, quite publicly, that her neighbors come forward to testify.

Thanks to her, one by one, a few witnesses did come forward.

It wasn't much.

But for now, it was enough.

John Roper and Chris Carter were arrested within two days of the incident. More information led to the arrests of two of the Nation associates reportedly involved in the melee, Charles McDougal and Dwayne Goethe. A third Nation associate, Torik Baldwin, was able to hide out for a week or two, but he was taken down as well. Even the big fish, John "Name" Ruffin, was picked up. (The investigators didn't regard his brother, Marcellus, as a suspect until much later.) That left just one participant out on the run — Marvin "Smash" Wooten.

No one's quite sure how Marvin Earl Wooten got the nickname Smash. It's just one of those names that followed him around like the trouble he got into.

Marvin Earl "Smash" Wooten grew up in a working-class neighborhood in Stamford. Smash's first tangle with the law came in March of 1988. He was just out of high school. The

Stamford P.D. received a tip that cocaine was being sold out of a house on Liberty Street — Smash's mother's house. The cops didn't have enough to get a search warrant, so they just decided to go over and check things out.

Lieutenant Doug Baker of the Stamford P.D., the same detective who would later be among the first at the housing project shoot-out, happened to be part of the team that went over to Smash's mother's house, and simply knocked on the door. Now, had Smash stayed quiet and pretended he wasn't home, the officers would have just walked away and come back later. But Smash panicked.

Just a few seconds after they knocked on the door, the officers heard glass breaking in the rear of the home. They darted around to the back of the house to find Smash jumping out the window. He led the officers on a foot chase. He lost. The officers, now with probable cause to search the apartment, went in — and found some six hundred vials of crack. Smash and his mother were both arrested. Smash admitted that the crack was his, so the possession charges against Mom were dropped.

Smash was sentenced to four years, but with the way the justice system works, he was back out on the streets by November of the same year. He joined forces with Name Ruffin in 1991. Smash had an in with Name because he and Marcellus Ruffin had been best buddies back in high school.

In the years that followed, Smash started to make a career as street-level drug supplier. They're the guys who get large "packages" of drugs from heavy movers, and break it down into quantities that can be sold to the guys who sell it on the street corners and in flophouses. Smash would never go out and sell to the consumer himself. He didn't like to get his hands dirty. He was a sharp dresser who drove nice cars, wore flashy jewelry, and kept a lot of cash in his pockets at all times.

And he became a cool customer. The cops knew what he was up to, but they could never catch him in the act. Once, while preparing to do a bust on an apartment, the narcotics squad saw Smash strolling down the hall, leaving another apartment on the same floor. The cops patted Smash down and found a thousand dollars cash on him. They confiscated the money as possible drug proceeds. Most of the dealers on the streets would have pitched a fit if they lost a grand but Smash didn't bat an eye. Smash couldn't explain how he got the cash, but the cops couldn't prove it was received from drugs sales so Smash just got away.

Later, he even got half of the money back.

So, Smash was no stranger to the Stamford P.D. when Detective Pete DiSpagna was assigned to be lead investigator in the hunt for him. He and his partner, Duncan Stewart, followed every lead that came their way. They were relentless in their pursuit of Wooten; the memory of what happened to Jasmine Merced would not let them rest.

In September, they got their chance to take him down. They received enough information to conduct a search and seizure on an apartment in Bridgeport, Connecticut. There was good reason to believe that Smash was there, selling drugs out of the residence.

On September 24, DiSpagna and his colleagues joined members of the Bridgeport P.D. in executing the warrant. They moved in at 6 A.M., so they could catch Smash while he was still asleep. When they entered the apartment, they found a pound and a half of crack cocaine, a machine gun, and $4,000 cash.

This was Smash's place all right.

But Smash wasn't home.

They decided to stake out the place. Some of the officers waited inside Smash's apartment. Others were posted in the hallway and laundry room. DiSpagna and Stewart set up in a shop across the street. And they waited.

For five hours, they waited.

Finally, at about eleven o'clock, Smash Wooten pulls up in a Mazda RX-7. This is the moment everyone was waiting for. Everyone's on foot, just waiting for Smash to come inside the building.

Before Smash could even cut off the engine to his car, a man comes running out of the building — he's a limousine driver, one of Smash's neighbors. This man runs up to the car, waving his arms and yelling, "Get out! The Five-O's are here!"

Smash doesn't hesitate. He takes off at high speed. The cops are caught completely off guard. They're not prepared for this scenario; no officer is in his car, no one can chase him.

Smash Wooten wins round one.

The next break would come just a couple of days later, on September 26. The task force that was tracking Wooten put out an NCIC alert on the description and plate numbers on the RX-7. Police dispatchers across the region sent out the broadcast. Meanwhile, Detective Stewart was following a lead that Wooten might be headed to the train station in Norwalk, Connecticut.

An ambulance driver who happened to hear the alert radioed in that he saw the car. The driver was in Norwalk, in the vicinity of the train station, and he had the RX-7 in sight. Stewart called for backup to meet him at the train station. They got there just before the RX-7 did. When the Mazda drove up they forced it to stop and moved in to arrest the driver.

But Smash wasn't driving. They searched the train station. He wasn't there either. Somehow Smash bailed out before the cops could move in.

Smash Wooten wins round two.

Smash had successfully skipped town, and although there were a few unconfirmed sightings in and around Stamford, it would be a while before he surfaced again.

In March of 1994, New York City was experiencing a rash of taxicab drivers being viciously and indiscriminately killed for their money. A special team of detectives was assigned throughout the city for the sole purpose of trying to identify cabbies who were about to be robbed.

On March 26, two detectives from the Thirty-second Precinct took note of two young black males riding as taxi passengers. The detectives felt they looked nervous — nervous enough that the cops pulled the cab over to question the men. After a little chat, they searched the guys. They found more than cab fare: they found methamphetamines, marijuana, and a ton of drug paraphernalia. They also found a loaded 9mm pistol.

The man with all the goodies was named Tyrone Davis. His friend was Curtis Edwards. The cops took their pictures and fingerprints, and then threw the guys in the slammer.

Two days later, a woman claiming to be from Harrisburg, Pennsylvania, showed up and put up two $5,000 bonds for Davis and Edwards.

When the fingerprint check for Tyrone Davis bounced back to the Thirty-second Precinct, it didn't match with anyone named Tyrone Davis. It did match with one Marvin Wooten. By the time the NYPD realized who they were dealing with, Wooten, his buddy, and the mysterious woman from Pennsylvania were all long gone.

Smash Wooten is knocked down but gets up and wins round three.

The Stamford detectives continued to work their leads. The New York story all fell into place, because they were getting information that Smash and Marcellus Ruffin might still be together and were probably running drugs between New York and Harrisburg. They gave this information to the FBI and the Harrisburg P.D. On June 22, agents moved in and took down Marcellus Ruffin. But once again, Smash was nowhere to be found.

Smash Wooten wins round four.

At the same time Marcellus was being taken down in Harrisburg, his big brother Name was on trial in Connecticut.

Thanks to Rita, there were several witnesses ready — reluctant, but ready — to take the stand.

Rita had put a lot of time and effort into being aware of every legal twist of the case from the beginning. She did her best to be at every hearing and session.

"When arrests started being made it was like, these people weren't even human," Rita said. "They don't deserve life. They had no respect or no regard for anyone that was out there. This was daylight. There were at least sixty people out there, and a great number of them children. And they continued shooting. They continued shooting even after they knew someone had been hit. No remorse, no nothing.

"One of the accused had decided to turn

231

state's evidence, and he agreed to testify for a very lenient sentence. And I wasn't part of that decision," Rita continued. "I just feel that victims, or families of victims should be aware of it. It's not something you'd like to read about in the paper. I realize that his testimony was necessary to get the men who were really responsible for what happened that day, but it doesn't make it any easier."

But it was about to get harder still.

In September of 1994, Name Ruffin and Charles McDougal went on trial on charges of manslaughter and conspiracy to commit murder, criminal attempted murder, and manslaughter.

Because of the presence of Name Ruffin, the threat of violence hung in the air, and no one could avoid it.

The sheriff's department knew Name's people still had a giant stash of weapons, knew that they were not above intimidating witnesses — or worse — and were taking no chances.

At the beginning of the trial, police sharpshooters were posted on the roof of the courthouse and on the police station next door, scanning the crowd for any signs of trouble. "More security precautions were taken than at any trial before or since," remembers Bruce Hudock, the man who prosecuted the case.

Inside the courtroom, the sheriff's department had taken the extraordinary precaution of stationing two deputies with loaded shotguns inside the door. Hudock realized that this was

232

going to be just too much for his witnesses; he told the judge that he could not prosecute the case in this atmosphere of almost unbearable tension and fear. Reluctantly, the judge decided to evict the deputies with the loaded guns.

Many people might have been afraid to come forward in the courtroom, with Name Ruffin sitting just a few feet from the witness stand, staring at you and daring you to testify.

Rita was not one of them.

She was one of the first to testify.

And she did not waver.

Without a shred of fear, she took the stand and started off the prosecutor's case, and by the time she was finished, the tone in the room had shifted. The other eyewitnesses came forward to testify, buoyed and emboldened by Rita's strength on the stand.

Next a parade of technical experts — investigators, ballistic experts — laid out the hard evidence.

And then the star witness took the stand.

The man who had turned state's evidence was Nation member Torik Baldwin. Baldwin was able to explain the infighting between the Jamaicans and Nation, and explain the sick, thoughtless, irresponsible assault in the courtyard.

Baldwin testified, in chilling detail, how he nearly assassinated an innocent bystander at point-blank range, just moments before the gun battle broke out. "We saw someone run across the courtyard and someone came out the door," Baldwin said. "I put the gun right in his face, but Marcellus said, 'Nah, that ain't him.' We kept running. Next we saw someone sitting on the bench, and then I ran through that hallway. As the guy was running, he pulled a gun. Dwayne opened up, then Marcellus. My gun jammed and I cocked it back after everybody started shooting."

Even more terrifying was his testimony about the moment Jasmine Merced was mortally wounded: "That's when I saw the girl running, and she just jumped but she kept on running."

Rita sat through the torturous hours and hours of testimony. And even though it looked like there was no way these guys could get off, the jury was still mainly dealing with one thug's word against another. There were a few other people who testified, but the strong witnesses who were so helpful in the initial investigation weren't as eager to testify in a court of law.

"We had been through about three weeks of a trial that was very frustrating, very difficult, and it became a battleground for the state's attorney and the defendants' attorney," Rita told us. "I was at the point where I wasn't sure what the outcome was going to be. The press had constantly said how difficult this was and put down the whole trial. They put a lot of doubt in my mind. After what I had been through, I knew that anything was possible. And I had to look at the reality of these men possibly walking out of there. And I wasn't sure I could live with that."

Rita sat in the courtroom with her mother, nervously awaiting the reading of the verdict. She sat directly behind Ruffin and McDougal.

"When the verdict was read and I heard that first, 'On the count of conspiracy to commit murder for John Ruffin . . .' When I heard 'guilty,' I was so relieved, happy, it was like 'Yes!' I closed my eyes and said, 'This is what I wanted.' "

Ruffin was also found guilty on the attempted murder charge, but he was found not guilty of manslaughter. Still, Rita was pleased with the two guilty verdicts.

She didn't have much time to bask in the glow. Just look at what this sick bastard did next.

"When they read off the verdict, John Ruffin turned around to me, and I could hear him say, 'Fuck you, bitch.' And it stunned me for a minute, because I couldn't believe it. Here was somebody who was so cocky and so bold through this whole thing — he's the victim, he was never there, he was being set up and all kinds of bullshit — and here he's got the nerve to turn to me who has done nothing, I didn't do anything to this man. Then he said, 'And your mother.' And I just lost it. I had kept my control through the whole trial, wanting to jump over there and get him. Thankfully the sheriffs and the state police saw and heard the same thing I did, and prevented me from going after him."

The reading of the guilty verdicts for Charles

McDougal calmed her down.

At some point or another in the investigation, every detective in Stamford's Homicide Unit did some work on Jasmine's slaying. A lot of the officers who had children of their own could see themselves in Rita's shoes. It tore them up to think that the same thing could happen to their own children. And at the same time, the long hours they spent working the case kept them away from home and away from their own kids.

In the summer of 1994, the tips on Marvin Wooten were still coming in to the Stamford cops, but as the weeks wore on, they received fewer and fewer leads. When wanted posters went up in Manhattan, an officer said Wooten may have asked him for directions to a nightclub. Other tips claimed Wooten was dressing up as a woman and hiding in Stamford.

Pete DiSpagna knew that Wooten had left the area. He wouldn't dare come back anytime soon. And there was little DiSpagna could do outside of Stamford — even less outside of Connecticut. He was concerned that Wooten would use his connections to disappear underground. He had to do something before he disappeared completely and the case went cold.

Pete's next break would come at a conference on law enforcement and the media. At the conference, DiSpagna met a sergeant who worked for the NYPD's Crimestoppers tip line. There was still a good chance that Smash could be in

New York, and he was hoping that Crimestoppers would take on the case. The NYPD had to decline. They already had a boatload of cases, and they had to stick with fugitives wanted for major crimes in New York. The only charge they had on Smash in Manhattan was a bench warrant for failure to appear on the charges from the time he was arrested in a cab under a fake name.

But the sergeant said he'd had some luck going to the shows *Unsolved Mysteries* and *America's Most Wanted*. The sergeant told DiSpagna that *Unsolved* was on a summer hiatus, but that he should give *AMW* a try.

He knew that we never take a break. Our office is running seven days a week, fifty-two weeks a year.

Detective DiSpagna contacted the show and got in touch with our reporter Tom Morris Jr. Tom, a father of three at the time (now four), was immediately drawn to the case. And after talking with the dedicated detectives and an impassioned Rita Volante, he knew we had to get the case on the air.

We knew that it was going to be difficult to get anyone to come forward in a case like this; we were sure there were people who knew where to find Smash Wooten, but we were also sure that those people were likely to be frightened about calling us. We knew that to break through that, we had to make people feel the outrage, the horror, the sheer inhumanity of the act of shooting up a courtyard while a child's birthday party is going on in full force. We had to find a way to make the heart-rending injustice of that moment break through the fear any tipsters might be feeling.

Those are the elements that go into deciding whether to present a story as a news report, or whether to reenact the crime. We knew in this case a reenactment would make the viewers feel what we were feeling: these are animals, inhuman animals, and not one of them deserves to be walking the streets.

As we previewed the reenactment in our offices, no one made a sound. The young actress who played Jasmine in the reenactment looked remarkably like the slain little girl. And when the gun battle broke out in our courtyard, you could feel the fear. For a moment you forgot you were watching a short film.

It all seemed so real — the girl running across the barren space, trying not to spill her ice cream, pressing the paper plate against her little chest, her little legs pumping as gunshots explode on all sides of her. She stutter-steps as her body lurches forward momentarily, but somehow she keeps running. Bullets appear to strike the brick walls, sending sparks flying above Agnes's head as she runs with Jasmine in her arms, her mother right behind her, dodging the same bullets. Then the little girl's body goes limp in the backseat during their mad dash to the hospital.

It was all very, very real.

Too real, in fact.

Once again, we had to walk the fine line: this had to be real enough to break through to the viewers, to make them outraged, to make them want to pick up the phone; but we didn't want to go too far, to make the piece exploitative, to make the piece so violent that people will turn away. I've talked about this many, many times: it's the hardest decision we make. If we "sanitize" the segment too much, the police get angry at us, saying we've not shown the criminals to be as awful and violent as they really are, that we've downplayed the crime. And I see their point. If we err in the other direction, we are accused of promulgating unnecessary violence on television, of taking advantage of the victims' pain, and that's something I will not tolerate on *America's Most Wanted*.

In the end, we decided to take out some of the most painful shots, to tone down the violence. I think we did the right thing; the final product was still a powerful, powerful document, one that I knew would stir an emotional response and, I hoped, a productive one.

The segment ended with Rita's personal appeal to our viewers to help catch Marvin Wooten: "He stole Jasmine's childhood from her. And also from the rest of her family. I think that's got to touch everybody somewhere. If anybody out there has any idea of his whereabouts, please help us."

Pete DiSpagna was in our studio on Saturday, November 5, 1994, the night the story aired. It was the leadoff piece in the show. He was optimistic that something good could come out of the airing, and before the segment was even finished, calls started coming in to the hotline.

Most of our viewers are well intentioned, but as with all of our cases, some of the tips were clearly off base. DiSpagna got calls from all over the country — from people who were sure they saw Wooten selling hot dogs in Shea Stadium, to people who were sure he was doing some off-road driving in rural Texas. All of the tips had to be taken with a grain of salt.

There were 180 tips in all, and a few more after we ran a short update on the case the next Saturday night. But in the end, none of them panned out.

Marvin Wooten had managed to slip underground. And he would stay there for a long time.

In the meantime, those who knew and loved Jasmine tried to deal with her death the best they could. K. T. Murphy School, where Jasmine went, constructed a small park. The teachers and students dedicated it to their friend Jasmine. There's a small bench in the park surrounded by shrubs and flowers that Jasmine's classmates helped plant.

It's a place where kids can go to read, or work with a teacher or tutor. It's a quiet place. It's a place Jasmine would have loved.

The kids needed a way to show how much they missed Jasmine. At the dedication ceremony, they sang and performed sign language to the song "Put Your Hand in My Hand." Rita told us that the kids reacted to Jasmine's death differently. "Some of them seemed able to go on with life as if nothing ever happened," she said. "Others, it really seemed to bother. They'd ask me where she was, and if it could happen to them. Some of them had trouble sleeping at night.

"I can remember one of the kids in her classroom said she was very brave. I thought they were saying that she was brave because she had been shot, and what a terrible thing it was. But the child explained it as, if something ever happened — like Jasmine did something wrong — rather than waiting until the teacher found out about it, or taking the chance the teacher would, she would be so upset about it that she would tell the teacher about it beforehand. She was very sensitive. She had a very strong conscience about what she did, and was really afraid of hurting other people's feelings.

"She thought, when she grew up, she wanted to be a doctor, because doctors make people better. And those people she had seen who were sick or had something wrong with them, she thought it would be the greatest thing if she could make them better."

Even at such a young age, when most kids feel

they are the center of the universe, Jasmine was always thinking of other people first. The fact that her life was taken by people who had the exact opposite view of the world was something that Rita just could not fathom.

"I don't ever see any one of them being a productive part of society, and my daughter — who I know would've been someone, would've done something to make a difference in this world — is gone."

Each week after the initial two broadcasts, Detective DiSpagna would receive a package of tips from us in the mail. Each week that package became thinner and thinner. Then there would be weeks where no tips would come in at all. Eventually, months would pass before a lead came into our hotline.

We knew that we had to get Wooten on the air again. It was one of those cases that had affected all of us greatly. In September of 1995, we decided to produce a "Top Ten Most Wanted Fugitives" special for Labor Day weekend. Some people made the understandable mistake of thinking that these were the FBI's Ten Most Wanted. They were not. We sometimes do feature the FBI's most wanted list, but this time, it was our own list — the guys we wanted to catch the most.

And Smash Wooten would lead off the show.

The first time Smash aired in 1994, Pete DiSpagna was full of hope that *AMW* would help take Wooten down. Now, as he and

Duncan Stewart made their second trip to Washington, their attitude was different. "The second time, we weren't as optimistic," DiSpagna admitted. "Leads were going nowhere. It got to be very tedious."

DiSpagna and Stewart had worked on this case, day in and day out, for two years. They had heard every tip, every rumor, every lie, and they probably knew more about the day-to-day goings-on of Smash's family and friends than Smash knew himself.

DiSpagna did get one glimmer of hope just before the broadcast. He met a cop from Washington state who was working on his fourth case with *America's Most Wanted*. This guy knew how powerful the show could be, because our viewers had racked up three captures for him. The detective told DiSpagna not to give up hope. "How do you know when you've got a solid tip?" Pete asked. "How do you know when it's the real thing?"

The detective answered, "When you hear the tip you need, the hair on the back of your neck will stand up."

The show hit the air at nine o'clock. The calls came in just minutes later.

When our operators take tips, they'll usually just write down the information the caller gives and pass it on to the officers on the case. There are a couple of exceptions: when the caller asks specifically to talk to an investigator, the operator will pass the call along; or if a tip sounds particularly solid, the operator — with the caller's permission — will flag down an agent or detective on the case to take over the call.

The program was still on the air when an operator held up her hand to get someone from Stamford. Stewart took the call as DiSpagna continued to read through the tip sheets. After a minute or two, Stewart called DiSpagna over to the phone. "You've got to hear this."

Pete took over on the phone call.

The call was from Akron, Ohio. The tipster was able to describe Wooten down to the last detail. The caller said Wooten had rented an apartment, but he wasn't planning on staying in Akron; he was just getting the place ready for his mother and sister to move in. This is what really got DiSpagna's attention: he had been keeping an eye on all of Wooten's family members, hoping that Smash would slip up and try to visit — and he knew Wooten's mother was getting ready to move!

The caller said that the mother and sister had even come into town to see the place. But Pete still needed more information to verify that this was a legitimate call.

"Can you tell me anything about the sister?"

The caller said, "When I saw her, she scared me."

It turns out that Marvin Wooten's sister was severely physically challenged, and the caller was accurate in the description of the sister's disabilities.

That's when the hair stood up on the back of Pete's neck.

This was the big break that DiSpagna and Stewart were looking for.

There was just one problem. The caller said now that he had taken care of the apartment, Wooten was ready to leave town.

DiSpagna got on the phone with an FBI agent who worked with the Ohio Fugitive Task Force. It was a Saturday night, so he had to reach him at home. "I could hear in the background the dog was barking, the baby was crying," DiSpagna told us, "but still he was very accommodating. He was a class act."

DiSpagna gave the task force all the information he had. Then he had to leave it in their hands and just hope that they could get the job done.

DiSpagna and Stewart were on pins and needles on the ride home from D.C. Would the task force get to Wooten in time? Had he already left town? Would anyone get hurt in the takedown? Would this just be another dead end?

Pete DiSpagna had plans to spend the rest of the holiday weekend with his family in New Jersey, so Duncan dropped Pete off and continued on to Stamford.

That afternoon, the Ohio Fugitive Task Force and the cops in Akron staked out a place that Smash was known to frequent. When a man matching Smash's description drove up, they moved in and cornered him. This time there was no limo driver to tip him off. No woman to bail him out.

And in a moment, the manhunt was over.

At about eleven-thirty that night, Pete was awakened by a phone call. Duncan Stewart was on the other end of the phone.

"They got Smash!" Duncan was telling him. "I got a phone call from the guys in Ohio. They got Smash!"

DiSpagna thought he was kidding. "I couldn't believe him," he told us. "I didn't have any reason not to believe him. After all, he's my partner and I trusted my life to the man. It just didn't sink in."

DiSpagna had to hear the news for himself. He made a call to Ohio. It was true. After twenty-six months of heartache, long days that dragged into long nights, Smash Wooten was in custody.

DiSpagna said, "All I could keep thinking was, this is really happening. This is *really* happening."

The Marvin Wooten in Akron, Ohio, was no longer the same man as "Smash" Wooten in Stamford. Wooten told the cops exactly who he was, and the fingerprints matched perfectly, but he was still Marvin Wooten in name only. This Marvin Wooten in Akron was disheveled. His once neatly cut hair was done up in kinky, sloppy cornrows. His clothes looked like they came from a thrift store instead of a boutique. When DiSpagna and Stewart came to the Mercer County Jail to pick him up, he wore stained blue jeans, white Nike sneakers, and a plain black T-shirt that was two sizes too big for him.

Even though he knew it was Smash Wooten, Pete DiSpagna had a hard time recognizing him. His face was skinny from all the weight he'd lost. He sported a beard and mustache. But those weren't the only reasons he didn't look quite like Smash anymore.

"Smash had had an air about him. It was the first thing you noticed," Pete told us. "But it was gone. You could tell he wasn't taking care of himself. Time had taken its toll. It wasn't any one thing that was drastically different. He just had a different look. He walked with a different attitude."

"Marvin Wooten?" Pete asked.

Wooten nodded his head in resignation.

"What's up, Smash?"

It was a long ride back to Stamford for the three men. Wooten wouldn't discuss what happened at Southfield Village. But he had plenty to say about his life on the run.

When Jasmine Merced was killed, Wooten left Stamford immediately. He never went back. On this point he was adamant. He knew Stamford was the last place he wanted to be when everything went down. The rumors of him dressing in drag so that he could stay in town were totally untrue.

From Stamford, he went to Bridgeport and rented an apartment. That was the scene of the near-capture where the limo driver tipped him off. He knew the heat was on, so he decided to go even farther away. He went to the train station in Norwalk. That's where the ambulance driver spotted him just before he got away.

He headed up to Manhattan. He didn't remember asking any cop for directions to a nightclub — in fact, he tried to keep a pretty low profile — but that didn't stop him from getting busted with the gun and drugs in the back of that cab. He wouldn't say who was arrested with him, or who bailed him out.

He had to stay on the move; he spent a little time in York, Pennsylvania, and then moved on to Harrisburg, as so many of our tipsters had told us he had.

At some point in Pennsylvania he hooked up with a running buddy — someone who could keep him employed in his trade and give him a place to stay. He also got together with Marcellus Ruffin. (Of course, they were probably together long before that, but Smash didn't want to give every detail.)

That's when the first airing of *America's Most Wanted* changed everything for Wooten — as we learned when he gave the detectives a rare explanation of what it feels like to be profiled on our show.

Wooten didn't see the broadcast himself. But it seemed like everyone else did. Marcellus was busted, and Smash's new friend took him to a place to stay in Baltimore, Maryland. And in

Baltimore, as in the remainder of his days as a free man, Smash was a minor celebrity, albeit an unwilling one. He tried to live a normal life, but people recognized him wherever he went. The man who used to drive fancy cars and wear flashy clothes was now trying to blend in as much as possible. He ditched his jewelry, lest it draw attention. He stopped going to clubs. He stopped going out to eat. He even stopped operating a vehicle, leaving the driving to his new buddy. Despite all of that, he would get strange looks from people who knew his face was familiar, but who just couldn't quite place it.

One day in Baltimore, Smash was walking down the sidewalk when he literally bumped into someone he knew from Stamford. This wouldn't have been a bad thing, except this woman was the grandmother of one of the co-defendants in the trial.

Time to leave Baltimore.

Smash's new friend could hook him up with people he knew in Akron, Ohio, so that's where they went. Smash's plan was to set up his mother and sister in the Akron apartment and then keep moving to another set of contacts in Cleveland. But Akron would end up being the last stop on their tour.

The reason he got caught, Wooten told the Stamford detectives, was because of the people he was hanging out with. He didn't accuse them of turning on him, but he said they had "worse judgment" than he himself did. Too many

people saw him, and too many people told their friends who he was. He said it was a living nightmare knowing that he would be recognized wherever he was. Smash knew it was just a matter of time, and it was a relief when the task force took him down. He was tired of looking over his shoulder.

At his extradition hearing in Akron, the judge asked Wooten if he had a lawyer.

"I don't want a lawyer," Wooten said. "I just want Connecticut to come and get me if that's what they want to do."

Wooten told DiSpagna and Stewart about his lowest moment. In the lockup in Akron, a group of detainees started to talk among themselves when Smash walked in. Smash could tell they were talking about him, and he had his guard up, ready to be harassed or attacked. One of the men finally was elected to approach Wooten. Wooten put on his toughest exterior and asked what they wanted from him.

The man said they wanted to know if they could have his autograph.

Wooten told the cops he found it very disturbing.

Poor baby.

September 7, 1995, was a hot day. Many men waiting for trains and buses sat shirtless, trying to cool off any way they could. Construction workers doused their heads with water and caught quick breaks under shady trees. Our

camera's wide-angle view of the Stamford sky-line shimmered in the heat.

Tom Morris and his camera crew went to Stamford to meet Smash when he arrived from Akron. Tom shouted out a couple of questions to Wooten, but Smash must have been all talked out from the ride home. The frail, tired-looking, defeated ex-gangster walked quietly into the jail for processing.

But Marvin Wooten wasn't the only person worn out by the chase.

Rita Volante met Tom and our crew not long after Smash was dropped off. And just as Marvin Wooten had changed, Rita had changed, too.

Rita had lost a lot of weight since we interviewed her the summer before. The skin on her face seemed to sag unnaturally, and in the bright hazy sunlight, her once golden olive complexion seemed pale. Her voice, when she spoke, was weak at best. Her eyes were tired and sunken, as if she hadn't slept in weeks. The audio tech had to put the microphone unusually high on her lapel and Tom had to ask her to speak as loudly as she could manage.

Rita explained to us that she'd recently been in the hospital. Problems with her heart. Too much stress. But she didn't want to talk about that, she wanted to talk about Smash finally being behind bars.

She'd found out about the capture on Monday morning when the Stamford cops came to her home. "I was surprised," she told us. "I was shocked. I was relieved. I was ecstatic . . . I don't know. I can't say enough."

Behind her tired eyes, a little spark started to grow as she talked about the end of a long journey.

"It's been a very difficult couple of years. I'm just extremely grateful that everybody involved was captured.

"This finishes it off for me, finalizes it. I know that I had done everything in my power to make things right. And it could never be right unless I can have her back; I can't do that. And this is the next best thing, is to have these people taken off the streets and see them get as much time as possible.

"And this way, other people wouldn't have to fear them, and hopefully some of these other guys that are out there might learn from this. Even if it affects just one person, changes one person's life. 'Hey, these guys I thought were great — now look at them. I wouldn't want to spend forty years behind bars or in jail.'

"People really showed great interest — they took it to heart. Everyone was a child at one time. If you don't have children, you were a child yourself. I enjoyed my childhood, but there are kids today who can't. They grow up too fast. There's too much violence out there."

Rita also wanted to praise the detectives.

"They were great. I wasn't just a number or a statistic or a case that got pushed aside. Everybody kept me going when I started to lose faith that we were actually going to catch him. I hope that after everybody's hard work, the justice system follows through and gives him the maximum amount of time."

We knew Rita had given a lot of herself to see the court trials through. And we knew that between her poor health and the court dates, she had quickly gone through two jobs and was in danger of losing her third. We wondered if she could put up with the stress and financial strain of yet another trial.

"I've gone through a couple of jobs because of my persistence and wanting to be there in court. But I will make every attempt in my power to be there."

When we aired the segment about Smash Wooten's capture, we ended the piece with a thought from Rita. Tom had asked her about Jasmine.

"Jasmine's spirit will always live on," Rita told Tom, her eyes looking calm, peaceful. "She lives on through me and through all the people she touched and all the people who knew her. For some reason she was taken. People believe a lot of things: that she was chosen, that her destiny was preset. I don't know; maybe, maybe not. But she's an angel up there. She's watching down."

Those were Rita's final words not only to our viewers, but they were also her final words to us.

A few weeks after that broadcast, Rita Volante died.

We learned later that she suffered from a

genetic liver condition. During this ordeal, she was so consumed with the fight for justice and with taking care of her surviving daughter that she didn't do the things she needed to do to keep the disease in check. In some ways it was a miracle that she survived as long as she did. Clearly, after Jasmine was shot, she was living for only two things — to make sure her surviving daughter, Crystal, was taken care of, and to see the day that Marvin Wooten was captured.

We did not know this at the time. When we heard the news about Rita at our office, we talked to her parents, to find out exactly what had happened.

"Rita died of a broken heart," her parents told us. "She died of a broken heart."

Prosecutors could never stick a murder charge on any of the men involved in the death of Rita's daughter — it was never clear just who killed Jasmine Merced — but in a very real way all of them were responsible — and in a very real way, all of them paid for it.

John "Name" Ruffin received a forty-year sentence for his conviction on attempted murder and conspiracy to commit murder. Later Marcellus Ruffin was rung up on conspiracy to commit murder, attempted murder, and first-degree manslaughter. He's doing forty years, just like his big brother.

Dwayne Goethe pleaded guilty to the same charges for which Marcellus was convicted. He was sentenced to three concurrent twenty-year hauls. Charles McDougal also got twenty years for conspiracy to commit murder, to be suspended after fourteen years.

The other players got lighter sentences.

John Roper, one of the members of the Jamaican posse, pleaded guilty to firearms possession charges. He served his time and was released before Wooten was even captured.

His cohort in the Jamaican posse, Christopher Carter, is also back out on the streets. Investigators believed it might have been a bullet from his gun that killed Jasmine Merced, but because the bullet was never found they could not prove it. In the end he was able to plead to risk of injury to a minor, and a firearms charge. He was sentenced to eight years, a sentence suspended after five.

Torik Baldwin got off easy because of the testimony he provided. He pleaded guilty to manslaughter, served three years, and was out on probation — but immediately violated his probation with an arrest on federal drug charges, so he's back in prison and will stay there for a while.

And as for Marvin "Smash" Wooten — he got what he deserved. He pleaded guilty and was sentenced to twenty years in prison.

And we can thank Rita for that.

In the year that passed between Jasmine's shooting and our first broadcast of "Smash" Wooten, two other people were gunned down in Southfield Village. Someone at the Department of Housing and Urban Development — someone who obviously needed a loose brick to fall on his head from eight stories up in order to get a clue — finally declared the high-rise complex unfit for living.

It's been torn down.

That is another testament to Rita; beyond pursuing justice for her lost child, she worked with her last traces of energy to make the neighborhood safer, not for herself, and not just for Jasmine's memory, but for Crystal — who now lives with her grandparents — and all of the other children out there who were in danger of losing their childhood.

The many police substations that now dot the area are testaments to Rita's strength and determination as well — for it is she who, before she died, realized that it just took the police too long to respond to crime scenes, and it is she who led the fight to have the substations created.

I'll never forget something Rita said in that final interview. This portion of the interview never made it on the air. But I remember that we looked again at the tape after she died, and one section stood out for me as her final testament. Her words were prophetic:

"I can rest. I was sick a little while ago, and one of the main things that was on my mind when I wound up in the hospital was: if something happens to me, it's not finished. I didn't do everything that I could do to make sure that this doesn't happen to someone else."

In the end, she did everything she could do. She made sure it was finished.

Finally, Rita can rest.

5

The Fugitive Who
Came to Dinner

I shouldn't be surprised by anything at *America's Most Wanted* anymore. After thirteen years, just about every bizarre thing that could happen, has.

Case in point: a few years back, a husband and wife from a small Florida town were on their way to visit Washington, D.C. They managed to get our publicity director, Avery Mann, on the phone and told him they were huge fans of the show, that they were seniors, and that their greatest wish would be to come tour *America's Most Wanted.* Something they said must have hit home with Avery, because he decided to give them the rare chance to visit the hotline in our Crime Center on a Saturday night while tips were coming in.

The couple were in their sixties, but they looked like a couple of kids at Disneyland as they came into the studio. The show was on, and the place was abuzz with activity, but the couple managed to corral one of the cops working a case — to ask him who he was chasing that night.

258

By sheer coincidence, the cop was from the same small town in Florida as the vacationing couple. Neither could believe it, and they spent a few minutes playing who-do-you-know-back-home.

Finally, the cop got around to telling them about the case he was working on — an urgent case we had just inserted in the show a few days earlier. A child had been abducted, and he had an artist's sketch of the kidnapper; there was good indication we could bring the child home safe and sound if we could find the abductor that evening.

The woman stared at the sketch. Something about it seemed familiar.

Very familiar.

And then it hit her.

It was her brother.

It turns out that the woman's brother, to whom she hadn't spoken in years, had a history of mental problems. Her identification of the sketch as being her brother turned out, indeed, to solve the case: her brother was, in fact, the kidnapper, and if it weren't for that one-in-ten-million encounter at our hotline between a vacationing couple from a small town and a cop on a missing child case, we might never have solved it.

That was, by far, the strangest coincidence I'd ever encountered in all my years at *America's Most Wanted*.

That is, until the case of Asgar Ali.

In February of 2000, Fox tried a little experiment: for publicity, they did a crossover between a reality show and a fiction show — *X-Files* and *COPS*. It was kind of cute, but it got us to thinking: why not team up the two shows that really could work together? Why not have *America's Most Wanted* and *COPS* team up to clean up one town? Someone pitched the idea to the network: first John Walsh rides with the cops on *COPS* as they take down whatever bad guys they can find, and then *America's Most Wanted* goes on remote from the same town to hunt down the fugitives they missed. It was a simple idea, and a fun one — but also one that could do some good — and the network said, go for it. The next stop of the *COPS* schedule turned out to be Jacksonville, Florida; so a few weeks later, I found myself headed down to Jacksonville and humming, "Bad boys, bad boys, whatcha gonna do."

I had already talked to our team about my trepidations about this crossover. I have always respected the program *COPS*, and had a great relationship with the show's creator, John Langley. I've always thought they treated law enforcement with great respect, and in that way performed a service, because they allow the general public to see just how dangerous every moment can be on the streets, how stressful a cop's job is, how any simple domestic call can erupt into violence, and how good most cops are at keeping things cool.

But I also have concerns, I will admit, about the children who appear on the show, even though their faces are invariably blurred (or, to be technically correct, "pixillated"). On *America's Most Wanted*, we have always been extremely careful about how we portray children and adolescents. And I've always had problems with *COPS* shows where they burst into a domestic abuse situation, where Daddy's been beating up Mommy or Mommy's stabbed Daddy, and you have three small children in the background screaming and traumatized while the cops are interviewing Mommy and Daddy and trying to decide whom to arrest. And even though their faces are blurred out, everyone in the neighborhood knows who they are — they've seen the house, they've seen the parents; how hard could it be to identify the kids? And these kids have to go to school, and get teased by their friends. And years later, when they've tried to put the incident behind them, and *COPS* shows up in syndication, and their friends or, later, coworkers, tease them — "Hey, I saw your dad beat up your mom on TV again last night" — I think it must be horribly traumatic for the children.

So the ground rules for the crossover were set: no domestics. We'd go out on the real crime calls. Into the danger zone, the mean streets after midnight.

I will admit this to you right now: I am an adrenaline junkie. I like hang gliding, fast motorcycles, hanging out of helicopters, that sort of thing. I think going to the edge tunes you into life, it heightens your senses. And so the idea of strapping on the bullet-proof vest and heading off into the night with the siren blazing gave me a kind of rush.

First I met up with Murray Jordan, the *COPS* producer, and I immediately knew we'd be okay: here was a seasoned, salty veteran, grizzled and no-nonsense. We had lunch, then made plans to meet at the substation and get the show on the road.

The first cop I was going to ride with was Russell Johnson, a big strapping blond buzz cut of a guy. As we were putting on our flack jackets, some of the other officers gathered around.

There is a tension at the beginning of any police shift, and most cops I know deal with it the same way — by joking, by razzing one another. It's almost a ritual, and so I wasn't surprised that they started razzing me, too. They were calling Russell "Pretty Boy" and hooting down the hall at us:

"Hey, Pretty Boy is riding with the big movie star!"

"Hey, it's Little Pretty Boy and Big Pretty Boy, together at last!"

"Hey, how many bad boys you gonna be able to catch between signing autographs, Pretty Boy?"

Russell just smiled and took it, and gave some back, and walked me out to the cruiser we'd be using for the night. It was an ultra-decked-out, state-of-the-art cop car, brand-spanking-new, with all the bells and whistles, including a dashboard computer.

"They'd never give me this if you weren't along," Russell told me. "I've T-boned" — crashed into the side of a drug dealer's car to stop him — "so they usually give me the junkers."

Russell was used to riding solo, but he was kind enough to accept me as a partner. I was thinking through how I'd react in a dangerous situation, and was kind of lost in my thoughts, so I never noticed how quickly we passed from the beautiful downtown waterfront area of Jacksonville to the toughest, meanest-looking inner-city ghetto area I've seen outside the Bronx — and believe me, we've shot on some of the toughest streets in this country.

Now my senses are heightened, I'm beginning to sweat in that heavy black flack jacket under my shirt, and we're ready for whatever comes.

It doesn't take long to get our first call.

We see a guy lying in the street, and he is not moving. He does not appear to be breathing.

I cannot believe that our first call is going to be a murder call.

We walk slowly up to the lifeless body in the street.

Russell reaches down and puts his hand on the victim's arm.

And the man rolls over, and looks up at me.

"Hey! John Walsh!" he says through a drunken slur. "Hey, man, my mother loves your show! She watches you all the time!"

I guess I was relieved, and a little embarrassed. The *COPS* crew that was taping us was a real A-team — two terrific guys, a cameraman and shooter — who handled themselves like pros; they'd run and gun with me and Russell, step for step, all night. I could see that they were trying to keep themselves from cracking up.

I suggested to our friend that a nearby bench was a better place to pass out, and we went back on our rounds.

Things got tougher later on. At one point — I was riding with one of Russell's cohorts — we came upon a crime scene with a man whose thumb had just about been cut off. It was a dispute between two men over a very attractive young woman, and we had to sort out who'd done what to whom. Then we got called on a burglary in progress, and when we got there, the other cop told me, you go around that side of the house, and I'll go around this side; and there I am, sneaking through an alley in a rough, rough neighborhood, and suddenly I realize, the other cop is carrying guns, clubs, handcuffs, Mace, and a radio, and I have . . . a flashlight.

I'm happy when we meet up on the other side of the house.

I got a sense of Russell's street smarts pretty early on, when we responded to a disturbance at a bar called J.W.'s.

"This your bar?" Russell asks me as we drive up.

Two officers are already at the bar, interviewing the complainant — a guy who's yelling about getting thrown out of the bar. He's saying that someone in the bar took his car keys, and that they're waiting for him to leave, and they're going to steal his car. Off to the side there's a little guy, a Jimmy Cagney type, agitating, yelling things at the guy who's trying to get his keys.

The two officers already on the scene are ignoring Jimmy Cagney.

"Rookies," Russell whispers to me. "Just out of the police academy. They got the wrong guy. Here, follow me."

I don't know how he knows he should do this, but he heads over to the little agitator. "Don't stand in front of him," Russell whispers to me. "Stand to his side."

I stand to Jimmy Cagney's right, and Russell is to his left; we are all facing the same direction. Russell turns to him and starts asking him questions about his involvement in the situation.

At that moment I notice that the guy has his hand in his back pocket.

"Do you mind if I look in your pocket?" Russell asks him.

The guy bolts.

Or, I should say, he tries to. Within two seconds, Russell has tackled the guy, has him on the ground, in a headlock; he is shouting to me, and I pounce on the guy, my foot on his back, my hands on his shoulders. Between the two of us, we have the guy immobilized. His eyelid is split by the fall.

His hand is still at his back pocket.

And under his hand is a gun.

I don't know how Russell had the street smarts to know this guy was trouble. These are, as they say in sports, the things that don't show up in the box score: another few seconds of this drunken rumble, and he could have pulled that gun. I could have been shot, Russell could have been shot, certainly the guy who lost his car keys had a target on his back — but it just goes down in the books as possession of a stolen gun, and we were on our way to the next call.

"Police work 101," Russell tells me when we're back in the cruiser. "Those two officers come on a scene, you got two guys yelling, the first thing you do is pat both of them down. This guy is a convicted felon, he's going away for a long time if we find that gun, so he has nothing to lose. He could have been very dangerous."

This is one thing I wish people understood better about cops — about street cops like Russell. They're in life-or-death situations every day, and most of what they learn they learn on the streets. Those rookie cops will be fine, once they've earned their street smarts — but there's just never enough time or money to train them properly before they get out on the street. In a lot of cities, cops get six or eight weeks of training, and then they're right out there, making decisions that will save lives or lose them. And when some brainiac politician decides he's going to save money by cutting the police budget, I think he should have to ride a shift like this before he makes up his mind.

That's what I'm thinking about as we roll up on a single-story tenement, where a riot is about to break out.

There are people everywhere, screaming, yelling: a bunch of kids have been beating up the seventy-five-year-old landlord. He let them stay in the house; now all they're doing is smoking crack, and refusing to pay rent, and refusing to leave, and when the landlord tried to kick them out, they pounded him, and we got the call.

We found the landlord, looking pretty badly tuned up, and a couple of other cops are on the scene, trying to calm things down and sort things out, and up on the porch is this punky-looking gang-banger kid who starts screaming at Russell. "Fuck you! Fuck you! Get the fuck out of here, you fucking pig!"

"Come down here!" Russell yells up at him.

"Come and get me you fucking pig!"

"You come down here, now, or I *will* come up and get you!"

The kid backs down, enough to walk up to Russell.

"Do you know who I am?" Russell says.

"Yeah, you're a fuckin' cop," the kid responds.

"Oh, yeah?" Russell answers. "Well, two weeks ago, you were passed out in a burning crackhouse, and I'm the guy who dragged you out. I'm the guy who saved your life. Remember me? You thanked me fifty times when you came out of your stupor with your clothes half on fire. And now I gotta take this from you?"

The kid was high as a kite, but he suddenly recognized Russell. His eyes got wide as he muttered his apologies, but the situation was defused. Everybody was calmed down — it was like the entire crowd exhaled at once — and the gang-banger kid went off quietly with one of the other officers.

And so it went: before my time with the Jacksonville cops was over, we'd be at a murder, a mugging, a few more fights, a lot of potentially explosive situations — and one by one, the cops would roll up, let the steam out, sort out the injured from the injurers, try to take the right one downtown, and move on.

All in a night's work.

At one point, I figured Russell and the *COPS* crew deserved a break, so before our shift I offered to take them to a nice restaurant for dinner; they wanted to stay close to the action, so we chose an American Cafe at the Jacksonville Landing. It is a beautiful, brightly lit but not garishly done waterfront, filled with the chatter of happy folks out for a party, situated on the St. Johns River, dotted with yachts, all framed by a beautiful neon bridge. As we sat outside at the American Cafe, there was no way you could imagine that you are less than a mile from those rough, tough neighborhoods these guys work, the neighborhoods that we'd head out to when our shift started.

Russell's boss, Sergeant Michelle Cook, was going to ride with us this night, and so we all crowded around a table at the American Cafe — me, Michelle, Russell, the *COPS* gang, and a few members of the *America's Most Wanted* team.

The waiter came and took our orders, and one steak dinner later, we headed out to the mean streets.

I know that the waiter recognized me — she was a fan of the show — but I can now tell you with certainty that while the waiter passed our orders along to the cook in the kitchen, she did not mention to the cook who the steaks were for.

I do know this story would have turned out very, very differently if she had.

Michelle Cook was a fireball of a Sergeant: a young, bright, bubbly, attractive young woman. I think because she's a woman she didn't get the kind of ribbing that Russell did. It's too bad, because I know she could have taken it: she had a great sense of humor, and an infectious laugh that helped ease us through some tense situations.

And there were plenty of tense situations to deal with.

At one point a call came over the radio. I didn't hear it, but one of the cops we were riding with was married to another officer, and he called out, "My wife has just responded to a homicide in zone two" — and we were off, at 110 miles per hour, sirens blazing. We arrived to find a young man lying in a pool of blood, a twenty-year-old kid, victim of a drug deal gone bad.

It was not a pretty sight.

It was one that these guys have to deal with every day.

Within a few hours, we caught up to the killer: he was spotted by some neighbors, who gave us a location; we radioed that to a helicopter, which managed to spotlight him; then the canines were called in and took him down. And now he's in the back of a patrol car, a seventeen-year-old kid who just committed murder, and he doesn't give a damn. I look in the window at him, and he turns to me, dead-eyed, void of any emotion.

A moment later, he turns away, puts his chin on his chest, and falls asleep, without a care in the world.

Later we came upon another burglary in progress: a great big guy was trying to climb a ten-foot spiked fence at a retirement home, and we caught up to him as he was halfway over the fence.

The guy's a scary-looking number: his head is

shaved, and he's all decked out in camouflage. We approach him cautiously because we can't see if he has a weapon. Russell's got his gun out; I'm wielding my trusty flashlight.

Suddenly, Russell grabs him.

"Hey, what do you think you're doing up there, pal?"

He turns to Russell and in the saddest voice says, "I've been stuck up here for forty-five minutes. Can you please help me get down, and then you can yell at me?"

I walk around him to get a better look and can see that one of the spikes of the fence has snared the man's pants, and another appears to have stabbed him in the chest.

The sound man produces a Swiss Army knife, which Russell uses to cut the man's pants free, and we all help push up on the guy's arms and legs to free him.

And then, in one sudden moment, this huge hulk of a guy comes crashing down, full force, right on my chest.

My elbow was killing me after that; I didn't find out until a few days later that he had fractured my elbow.

And as he's lying on top of me, and I'm lying there with my broken elbow, the guy kind of rolls over so he can see me, and his face lights up when he recognizes me, and he keeps smiling at me as they cart him off to jail.

I gotta say, I got fans in low places.

As we're walking back to the car, Russell turns

to me and says, "You know, it's really strange riding with you."

In early May, we started preparing our half of the double crossover — the episode of *America's Most Wanted* that would focus on Jacksonville's top cases. Among them: the stories of Tina McQuaid, a missing mother, and of Ricardo Tillman, the star receiver of the Jacksonville University football team. Tillman had been found murdered.

We also decided to air a brief blurb on one case that wasn't from Jacksonville — but cops in two other cities were very, very anxious to get it on the air.

The case started on February 19, 2000 when Detective Roger Spurgeon of the Indianapolis Police Department was called to a small one-level home. It was a typical February day, cold and overcast, and when Roger arrived at the home, cops already on the scene walked him toward a back bedroom.

Where he found the body of one Ama Butler, lifeless, bound, stabbed, and stuffed unceremoniously in a closet.

In a case like this, sometimes you make it simple. You look for the most suspicious guy involved and start your investigation with him.

That character popped up quickly, after just a few days of investigation.

Butler's cousin had broken up with her boyfriend, guy by the name of Asgar Ali. Ali was a bad egg — he'd already been arrested for stealing the cousin's car after the breakup — and though he was supposedly long gone from Indianapolis, guess whose fingerprint showed up at the murder scene?

That wasn't enough to charge a guy with murder, but it's sure enough reason to want to have a serious talk with him.

To do that, Spurgeon had to find him first.

Unfortunately, a store owner in Orlando found Ali before the detective did.

Ali — going by the alias Kishore Rattan — had been in the man's store several times, inquiring about a car the man was trying to sell. One afternoon, Ali said he was ready to buy the car but didn't want to carry that much cash around. Ali asked the store owner if he wouldn't mind accompanying him back to Ali's apartment.

The store owner, a trusting soul, agreed.

Bad mistake.

Once in the apartment, they signed over the paperwork on the car, and then, police say, Ali pulled out a knife and announced, "I am going to kill you."

The two men struggled, and the store owner managed to get the knife away from Ali — but it wasn't over. Police say Ali grabbed the man's necktie and tried to strangle him with it. Gasping for air, fighting for life, the store owner somehow freed himself and ran out the door.

So now there's a murder in Indianapolis that

Ali may or may not have something to do with, and an attempted murder in Orlando that he's charged with. Plus, it turns out that Ali, a native of Trinidad, is in the country illegally, and had been for ten years. He'd been in the custody of the INS, in fact, but they released him.

In fact, they released him on February 17, 2000.

Two days before the body was found in Indianapolis.

This was all too circumstantial for us to do a big case on — but we did have charges in the Orlando case, and since we were doing a remote from Florida anyway, we agreed to squeeze Ali's picture into the show.

In the fourth commercial break of every show — generally a very long break — Fox gives us back ten seconds to do what they call a "cluster buster" — a little tease letting the viewers know that the show is coming back after this wave of commercials. We used to use it as a coming-up-next promo; but a few years ago, we decided to use it as a chance to air one more fugitive. It's amazing to me, but we've caught more than a dozen fugitives off that "Break Four Tease."

So that's where we decided to air Ali.

Here's the sum total of all the copy that ran:

"Cops in Florida have charged Asgar Ali with attempted murder. He's also suspected in a brutal murder in Indiana. He uses the alias

Kishore Rattan. Call if you can help."

It's not much.

But it was enough.

We would actually catch Asgar Ali off that Break Four Tease.

How we would catch him, no one would believe.

Who would catch him was even more astounding.

And when we found out where he'd been hiding out — well, I still don't believe it.

Sergeant Michelle Cook and some of the other cops decided to watch the *COPS/America's Most Wanted* crossover shows at the Jacksonville Landing at a bar called Jocks and Jills. They were with a cameraman and sound man from *COPS*, still in town filming more episodes.

They had fun, and kidded one another, about their appearances on the *COPS* show, then settled in to see their fugitive and missing persons cases on our show.

Just before the show went off the air, their radios went off — a tip had come into the *America's Most Wanted* hotline. They were to check it out.

Michelle radioed back: which of the Jacksonville cases is the tip on? The football player? The missing mom?

No, the response came back.

It was from the case out of Orlando.

Michelle barely knew what case the dispatcher

was talking about. And as she drove over to the homeless shelter where the call came from, she was more than dubious.

"We figured we had to go. We just had to. Or we would never live it down. But we get calls all the time from people who think they saw someone on *America's Most Wanted*. We were so sure it was going to be nothing that the *COPS* guys walked in without their cameras."

But in the next moment, two other officers who had arrived on the scene first were walking out of the homeless shelter.

And the *COPS* crew was flying back to their car to get their cameras.

Because shuffling slowly between the two officers was a gaunt, dark-haired man, his chin on his chest. They brought him up to Sergeant Cook.

"Where are you from?" she asked him.

The man mumbled, "Trinidad."

"What's your name?"

"Kishore Rattan."

It took Sergeant Cook a moment. Why did she know that name? Why did it sound so familiar?

And then it hit her.

The Break Four Tease: ". . . he goes by the alias Kishore Rattan."

Now they're all headed back to the station house, chattering a mile a minute: could this possibly be the guy? We air three cases on *Amer-*

ica's Most Wanted, and the guy from the case that *isn't* ours is at a shelter five blocks from where we're watching the show?

Sergeant Michelle Cook bounded up the steps and ran to her computer, to call up the amw.com Web site and check out his picture.

The other officers stood behind her as she plugged into the Web site and called up the photo of Asgar Ali. It was identical to the man they had just arrested.

"That is so close," Sergeant Cook said.

"That is *him,* sergeant," one of the other officers responded.

"Without a doubt."

Another officer had brought "Kishore Rattan" upstairs and was guarding him in another section of the large room. "Hey, Pat," Sergeant Cook called to the officer. "Bring Junior over here so he can see his picture on the *America's Most Wanted* Web site."

Pat walked him over to where he could see over the sergeant's shoulder, with his face glowing bright on the computer monitor. "This is justice, buddy," the officer said, patting his shoulder. "This is justice."

Sergeant Cook looked once more at the picture of Asgar Ali, then turned to the suspect. "Who is that?" she asked. "Is that you?"

He did not respond.

She asked again.

"Partner, is this you?"

In a voice filled half with defiance and half

with weary resignation, he admitted, "Yeah, that's me."

Evan Marshall, one of the show's segment producers, was on "beeper duty" that night — the rotating task of being the person to call when we get a capture on Saturday nights. He was stunned by the news of the Ali capture. He knew this would be a big one.

He needed to get authorization to start rolling crews to report on the story; fortunately, he knew exactly where to find all the executive staff together.

They were sitting around a table at the wedding of our coexecutive producer, Phil Lerman.

Just as the band went on break, Neal Freundlich, the supervising producer, heard his cell phone ring. It was Evan.

"Capture," Evan announced. "Direct result. Asgar Ali, in Jacksonville."

Neal, at first, didn't understand him. Wasn't Asgar Ali from Orlando? Wasn't it the only case that's *not* in Jacksonville?

"No," Evan explained. "He's *captured* in Jacksonville. And get this — the same cops who were on *COPS* are the ones who went and arrested him."

"Get out!"

Neal told Lance Heflin, our executive producer, the news. He called me from the wedding.

I was dumbfounded.

Ali, wanted out of Orlando, was caught in Jacksonville just five blocks from where I had taken the cops to dinner.

And that's not even the half of it.

That same night, Sergeant Cook got a call with some background information on Ali — where he'd been working, how he'd been getting by.

It turns out that he was drawn to fairly upscale restaurants, where he'd get whatever work he could — cook, busboy, whatever they needed.

He'd been doing just that, in fact, in Jacksonville.

At the trendiest place in town.

The Jacksonville Landing.

"Let me tell you where it gets more interesting, though," Michelle said — as though this wasn't yet coincidence enough.

"I get a call a couple of hours later. And they say, 'Did you and Officer Johnson and Mister Walsh eat dinner at the American Cafe last Saturday night?'

"And I said, 'Yes, we did.'

"And he goes, 'Did Mister Walsh order steak?' I said, 'Yeah, I believe he did.'

"And the person on the phone says, 'Do you realize that Mister Ali works at American Cafe — and that night when you guys were in there eating, he was the one who prepared your food?'"

Well, I've chased fugitives, I've helped arrest

fugitives, I've conducted jailhouse interviews with fugitives — but this is the first time I've ever had one cook me dinner.

"It's a good thing he didn't know you were there," one of the cops said to me later. "Can you imagine what he would have done to that steak?"

There is, believe it or not, one more postscript to this story.

Remember the bar Jocks and Jills, where officer Cook went to watch the *COPS/AMW* crossover?

Well, guess where Asgar Ali was moonlighting while working at the American Cafe?

You got it.

He was a busboy at Jocks and Jills.

In fact, when he was arrested, he was still wearing a Jocks and Jills sweatshirt.

"Out of all the restaurants in the whole city that we could eat at," Sergeant Michelle Cook told me when I saw her later, "a murder suspect works at both of the ones we go to.

"This is better than fiction, John," she said. "You couldn't write a better script. This is something that I will tell my children and my grandchildren and anybody else who will listen, for the rest of my life."

6

Showdown
with the Unicorn

By the time we got to Woodstock, we were six, maybe seven strong.

I couldn't understand it. We had heard that there was going to be this gigantic concert — the Grateful Dead, Janis Joplin, the Who, and a dozen other musical icons of the times were on the bill — and I was excited to go. I figured thousands of other college kids from around New York State would be showing up, too; but when we pulled into town in my beige 1964 Volkswagen Beetle with the STOP THE WAR bumper sticker on the back — me and the beautiful blonde girl who would later become my wife — and walked into the first bar we saw, we were almost all alone. One other table of hippies was having lunch.

I told Revé I'd ask them what happened to the concert, and walked over to their table. It was an interesting group: a tall black man with the wildest hair I'd ever seen, wearing a multicolored shirt and waves and waves of beads; a tall, thin blonde woman next to him, apparently his girlfriend; and a few guys who looked like your run-of-the-mill stoned-out hippies of the time.

Yeah, this is Woodstock, the tall guy told me — Woodstock the town. The Woodstock concert, he said, is at a farm about twenty miles away, in a town called Bethel.

Through this whole conversation, I'm aware that Revé has come up behind me and is tugging at my sleeve. Finally, I turn to ask her what the problem is.

"Do you know who you're talking to?" she whispers.

"No. Who?"

"It's Jimi Hendrix."

So that was my brush with greatness at the time, me and the guitar legend, sharing a beer in a bar.

We got to Woodstock all right; and I remember the magical feeling of all these people hanging out together peacefully. And on the final evening, as I sat in the mud and listened to Jimi Hendrix blaring out his version of the national anthem, I thought just how much potential for good there was in this, the Woodstock generation.

Who knew that deep in its hidden recesses, there were those with such a deep potential for evil?

Ira Einhorn always claimed to be the cofounder of Earth Day. In fact, he wasn't even a member of the committee of thirty-three men and women who did create the event; according to the real founders, all Ira Einhorn did was hog the stage for a while.

But then, hogging the stage was what Ira Einhorn did best.

He was born Ira Samuel Einhorn in May of 1940 to a middle-class Jewish family in Philadelphia. Like mine, his high school pictures show a pretty normal, average kid. From an early age, he demonstrated precocious speech, and an accelerated reading ability. He also proved difficult: in the classroom, he was part prodigy, part anarchist.

When he embarked on his college career at the University of Pennsylvania in the fall of 1957, his intellectual range seemed limitless: he had a working grasp of physics, math, literature, philosophy, and linguistics. Unfortunately, his arrogance kept pace with his intelligence.

Ira didn't show up for class much, but was a voracious reader. "If you had a reading list for a course, and there were ten books you had to read, along with a hundred suggested supplemental readings, Ira would read the hundred suggested readings before he'd read the required ten books," friend Mel Richter told Steven Levy, author of *The Unicorn's Secret*, the first book to detail this unusual man and this unusual case.

But at the time, Richter and others could only be amazed at Einhorn and his split personality, so disciplined as a scholar and so slovenly as a human being.

Although Ira preferred smoking pot to attending lectures, his image of himself, and his reputation on campus, continued to grow. "Ira came all over you like the weather in Cuernavaca, rain and sunlight at the same time," said author William Irwin Thompson in his book *At the Edge of History*.

If Ira was an oddity on the Pennsylvania campus in the late 1950s — a sort of prehippie icon waiting around for the turbulent 1960s to happen — his life bloomed after graduation. "I'm trying to resolve my future," he wrote, as quoted by Levy, "but at present all I see is chaos — boy, do I love it."

In the mid-1960s, Einhorn traveled to Berkeley, ground zero of the psychedelic revolution that was taking place in America. For Ira, the era itself was a powerful drug, the atmosphere of irreverent freedom totally captivating the young rebel. He returned to Philadelphia, ready to proselytize for a tripped-out awakening.

Ira's "teachings" took the form of free-form lectures. He called them "Analogues to the LSD Experience," but they might be better termed "Welcome to the Ira Einhorn Experience." To groups of young hippies, Ira became the self-professed "Unicorn" — which is what *Einhorn* literally means in German — but also embodying his image of himself as a unique and gentle creature. As they sat, enthralled, Ira would expound on everything from Freud, Nietzche, Kant, Hegel, and Tolstoy, to McLuhan, Leary, and Lennon-and-McCartney. And his instinct for publicity — he once helped a local reporter for *Philadelphia* magazine hold a pot party, and staged his own be-ins, replete with body painting and daffodil exchanges — solidified his position as Philadelphia's king of the hippies. The fact that he rarely changed his clothes, the fact that he believed he could have any woman he wanted, the fact that he would often greet visitors to his house stark naked — all these contributed to the growing myth of the Unicorn.

In fact, he never became as well known as the other hippie leaders of his day, like Abbie Hoffman and Jerry Rubin; even among his devout followers — and their numbers were growing every day — there was sort of a suspicion about Ira, a distance people had to keep from him (and not just because of his legendary, growing body odor problem). There was something fascinating about Ira for the people around him, but also something vaguely annoying. For whatever the reason, he never grabbed the nation's attention the way the other hippie leaders did. But he did consider himself their peer, becoming more than passing acquaintances with Hoffman, Rubin, Allen Ginsburg, and the other stars in the emerging hippie firmament. (Ira claimed to have given Jerry Rubin his first hit of acid, though Rubin later claimed otherwise.) And when the hippie celebrities visited Philadelphia, it was Ira who would introduce them to the city, giving speeches and performing as their unofficial press advance man.

His rise to strange celebrity — or, depending on whom you ask, his ultimate hogging of the spotlight — came on Philadelphia's Earth Day on April 22, 1970. Senator Ed Muskie, popular for his fervent antiwar stance and expected to make a powerful speech in favor of the day's environmental themes, was scheduled to speak at 3:30 P.M., during a live TV broadcast. But when the moment came, guess who refused to leave the stage? Ira Einhorn, who had just finished one of his rambling speeches touching on Huey Newton, Chicago, and cosmic consciousness. He decided, without consulting anyone, to change the order of the program, so that the live broadcast carried not Muskie, but rather a rock-and-roll band playing backup to an oddly gyrating Ira.

According to Levy, Ed Muskie asked the organizers, "What the hell is going on?" But when they confronted Einhorn, Einhorn jeered, "I am not going to leave this stage. If you want to physically remove me from this stage, you can do it. These kids are *mine* now."

There was clearly going to be a showdown. The organizers led Muskie to the stage. Ira, finally, yielded the microphone.

But not before planting a big kiss square on Edmund S. Muskie's lips.

"Ira was the star of his own soap opera," remembers his good friend Stuart Samuels. "Everybody else was an extra. His ego just filled the room." This ego was especially apparent around women. "He just looked at women as if they were just objects, and he used them and treated them that way.

"Ira fancied himself a great womanizer," Samuels said. "You know, he said to himself that basically if he wanted any woman he could have them, and what he would do if he saw somebody at a party and he wanted them he would sit there and spend all the time with that person, in such an intense way, and he would look at them with such intensity, with his blue eyes, that he would just think that he could seduce anyone."

But despite all his braggadocio, his roomful of ego, his self-conscious self-boosterism, Ira Einhorn successfully seduced Philadelphia's business and political leaders. Perhaps they believed, like Einhorn, in his role as a self-proclaimed "planetary enzyme." It was his image of himself, the image of a man who could bring his knowledge of physics, astronomy, psychology, sociology, and a dozen other topics to bear on the great problems facing the world, helping business leaders find creative new solutions in the dynamic, changing environment of the turbulent Woodstock era.

If they only knew that his talk of nonviolence was a bunch of bull.

Levy uncovered two incidents, from earlier in Ira's life, that I believe show his true nature. To friends, these moments were aberrations, unexplainable glitches in the great aura of a man dedicated to peace.

To me, they show the true nature of a coward who uses the spotlight to blind people to the fact that he hasn't got the courage to admit how weak and pathetic he really is.

The first, according to Levy, comes in 1962. Einhorn was dating a coed at Bennington College in Vermont named Rita; she was an attractive young dancer but low on self-esteem. (Finding women like that was a pattern in Ira's life, as we'd find out later.) Einhorn was wildly infatuated with the woman — or, more accurately, infatuated with the idea of himself being in love. "The quote 'great romance of the century' was what was in his head, and he was fantasizing, but that wasn't what was happening at all," Rita told Levy.

When she finally got smart and dumped him, Einhorn couldn't handle it.

He showed up at her door.

She told him she was serious about ending the relationship.

He put his hands around her throat.

"It wasn't a rational buildup of temper at all," Rita later told Levy. "It was almost like, you watch one of those supernatural movies on television, and eyes change. Like a werewolf. It was like that truly. And so I knew when that happened, I was in the room with a madman."

Einhorn choked her until she passed out; fortunately, she survived the attack, and while she never pressed charges, she did succeed in having Einhorn banned from the campus.

On July 31, 1962, Einhorn wrote in a diary uncovered by Levy: "To kill what you love when you can't have it seems so natural, that strangling Rita last night seemed so right."

And that was not all. A few years later, the same pattern emerged: Einhorn's latest girlfriend, Judy, decided to end the relationship, and Einhorn wrote: "The violence that flowed through my being tonight . . . still awaits that further dark confirmation of its existence which could result in the murder of that which I seem to love so deeply. The repressed is returning to a form that is almost impossible to control. . . . There is a good chance that I will attempt to kill Judy tomorrow . . . the rational awareness of this fact brings stark terror into my heart, but it must be faced if I wish to go on — I must not allow myself to deviate from the self-knowledge which is in the process of being uncovered!"

A few months later, he insisted on meeting her for coffee at her apartment. She relented.

And while she had her back turned, she later told police, Ira beat her over the head with a Coke bottle.

"I was bleeding quite bad and attempted to ward off the blows from the bottle," she said later. "Ira then grabbed me around the neck and began to strangle me. I was trying to kick him and yell for help. While we were struggling I was knocked to the floor, I could feel myself going limp. At this point Ira let go of me and ran out."

So this is the fabled "Unicorn," as he dubbed himself, the proponent of nonviolence, the great synergistic thinker.

Just a coward.

Guys like Einhorn, to me, are the really dangerous ones. They feel superior to those around them and rationalize their actions as having some larger cosmic significance. Really, they are just like any neighborhood bully: picking on someone weaker in order to shore up their piddling sense of self-worth. That's why Ira needed all the media attention, all the accolades, all the sycophants sitting at his feet as he soaked in a bathtub, smoked a joint, and expounded on Marcel Proust. Underneath it all, he was just a scared little brat who got furious when he wasn't the center of attention.

But the businessmen who flocked to him didn't seem to notice, or mind.

For example, Ira forged a relationship with Bell Atlantic, convincing them that he was the perfect goodwill adviser to help them through some troubles in the community — such as neighbors objecting to a new switching station on South Street. In exchange, Bell Atlantic helped Ira reproduce and circulate a kind of pre-New Age newsletter, filled with the kind of "information" that Ira was gathering — for example, how to leave one's body, travel anywhere in the world, and return. Ira sincerely believed in this kind of stuff, and there were those in the business community who, while not buying the whole concept hook, line, and sinker, found it useful. Who knew? Perhaps one of these crazy ideas — like the idea of linking up lots of computers so people could pass information freely — might catch on one day.

Before long, those at Ira's lunches, and in his "information circle," were as varied as First Pennsylvania Bank's John Bunting, futurist Alvin Toffler, paranormalist Uri Geller, millionaire Charles Bronfman, and anthropologist Margaret Mead.

And because of Ira Einhorn's unique ability to make the nonsensical seem to make perfect sense — along with his excellent head for business, science, and technology — all listened to him with rapt attention.

No one had any idea of how truly, truly dangerous Ira had been, or how dangerous he was going to become.

No one.

Certainly not the beautiful blonde in the corner, sipping a cup of herbal tea.

It's not that Holly Maddux was destined to wind up in a big city like Philadelphia, but from a very young age it was clear that she would not live out her life in Tyler, Texas. As the attractive young girl was growing into a startlingly pretty teenager, everyone around her sensed that there was something different about her, something special, something unique.

"Holly was blessed with a tremendous intellect and curiosity about things, and that's what kept her going when she kept meeting up with certain mediocre aspects of life in a small town," remembers her sister Meg. Holly was the oldest of five children, four girls and a boy, and she and her brother, John, were older by a good bit — eight years older than Meg, their nearest sibling. So by the time Holly was a teenager, there was a houseful of small children to help take care of. And this suited Holly's sweet, giving personality.

"She was like a mother figure to me," says sister Buffy, who was five as Holly turned sixteen. "She was almost my parent, but also my playmate," says Meg. "She taught me a lot and was always fun to be around. She's the big sister I think anyone would want to have. She was extremely giving, very loving, always had a place in her heart for you. If she didn't know where that place was she would search herself and find that place where you fit in, and where she could embrace you and make you feel better."

It was Holly who turned the kids on to granola, who introduced them to the feminist ideas of the budding 1960s, who taught Douglas, the family parrot, to say "I love you, I love you," who sent them their first copy of *Our Bodies, Ourselves*; and although there is little memory of outright conflict, she must have been, to her little sisters, quite a contrast to their stern, conservative father.

Fred Maddux allowed, even encouraged, Holly to have and express her own opinions; possibly just out of a fatherly love of watching his young flower grow and blossom; possibly because, as the school valedictorian with perfect grades, she gave him so little to complain about; and possibly because he understood that his daughter was as strong-willed as he was, and that to try to control her would be to lose her.

But as she got older, the charm and grace of the young teenager took on a darker, sadder quality. There was something ephemeral about Holly, a solemn, serene quiet that settled about her, so that her perfect manners, once so endearing, now made her seem somehow aloof; her beauty, which had made her the kind of young teen others could not keep their eyes off of, now became a barrier that few teenage boys had the courage to cross.

"She didn't fit in, because she had this wonderful nature about her," remembers Meg. "She wasn't excluded — she just wasn't included in a lot of things.

"She definitely seemed as though she was of another time and place," says Meg. "She had friends, everybody said how much they liked her — but I can see that she could be very intimidating."

Part of it was her eyes: when you talked to

Holly Maddux, you felt transfixed by them, as though there was no one else in the world, as though what you were saying was the only thing that mattered. It caused people to open up to her, and she would listen, silent and attentive — and then later, they would feel exposed, vulnerable. "They would feel," says Meg, " 'Why am I telling this stuff to someone who has so much going for them, so much beauty and intelligence?' "

And so the girl who was Miss Everything — the school valedictorian, the girl literally voted "Most Likely to Succeed" — became more and more withdrawn. A girl who could have understood herself to be very, very special instead developed a low self-esteem, along with the kind of eating disorder that often accompanies it. She looked lovely; she treated her family with great love, her friends with the utmost kindness, her acquaintances with perfect respect — but inside, her fear and insecurity were growing.

Her dad wanted her to go to college in Texas, but, just as Holly was already living worlds away from Tyler, so was her choice of school: the elite Bryn Mawr, in the heart of a town that was being utterly transformed by the 1960s. College was difficult for her; still shy and withdrawn, she wasn't quite sure what to make of the turbulent free-love, civil-rights-marching, Vietnam-war-protesting community surrounding Bryn Mawr. After graduation she toured Europe, then returned to Philadelphia; after all these years, she was still not quite at home there. Philadelphia, after all, was nothing like anything Holly had ever experienced before.

Neither, of course, was Ira Einhorn.

"We met in either late September or early October 1972," Einhorn told a reporter for *Philadelphia* magazine. "I was having breakfast at La Terrasse and I saw her. There was an obvious attraction between us and I went over and I gave her my phone number. She wasn't feeling well psychically, and so she was going to Arizona, and when she got back ten days later I called her and she came over and saw me and I think it was an hour later that we were making love. That was a Thursday and by Monday she had moved into my apartment."

I suppose there's reason to believe Ira Einhorn's egotistical account of the beginning of the relationship. Holly's low self-esteem made her particularly vulnerable to a strong-willed, confident, controlling man like Ira. And as for Einhorn, sexual conquest was a big part of his self-image; at the time, it probably seemed like he was embodying the free-love values of the time, although in retrospect it's easy to see what he was really about.

The media has made so much of the image of Ira Einhorn that it's hard for people to understand that he's really not all that different from a lot of our fugitives. Men who feel the need to control women, to dominate them, in order to prove their own self-worth, are the men whose profiles fill our caseload. They find insecure women, and little by little, they come to isolate them from their friends and family. That's the first step: isolation. Make the woman feel as though she's lucky to have this guy, as though no one else would have her, and keep her so isolated and lonely that she can see him from no other perspective than the one he forces on her.

After the isolation comes the degradation: tearing down what little self-image she has left until she begins living her life trying only to please this unpleasable man, until he becomes the sole focus of her attention.

It's a type of emotional enslavement, this isolation-and-degradation pattern. We've seen it a thousand times at *America's Most Wanted*. Einhorn's friends wanted to think of him as a genius, a visionary, a leader — but he was just an insecure, controlling punk.

Nothing more, nothing less.

"Ira was such a dominant personality that when Ira and Holly were together, there were times when you didn't even think she was there," said Samuels. "She was like, in the background. She hardly spoke. She was almost like a paper figure; she never contradicted Ira in any way."

This, remember, is a woman who starred, intellectually, through high school and college, who certainly had more to contribute to a conversation than most of the sycophants Ira surrounded himself with — but who was being increasingly manipulated into a more and more subservient role. It's like these guys have some kind of radar they use to find the insecure women they can mold, and then they turn on that perverse system to begin molding them.

This became the pattern: "Ira's relationship with Holly was a very private relationship," Samuels said. "They would rarely go out together. They would rarely go to parties together."

And sometimes, at a party, Ira would decide to go home with someone else, and he would say quite matter-of-factly to a friend, "I'm going to go sleep with her. Would you make sure Holly gets home?"

As I said earlier, I lived through the heart of the sixties, and there's a big difference between free love and degradation. Don't tell me that was the culture of the times. Don't tell me a beautiful, tender, frail young woman like Holly isn't going to be devastated by that — and don't tell me Ira didn't know it full well. This was not some hippie guru experiencing the freedom of the time — this was a big jerk starting the process of degradation, just as he was finishing the process of isolation.

He took a big step in that direction in the fall of 1973, when Holly, for the first time, brought Ira home to meet the family.

"Ira's visit to Tyler," remembers Holly's sister

Meg, "brought with it a chaos of the spirits."

It was the fall of 1973. Ira and Holly had been living together for about a year. The idea of an unmarried couple living together was still new enough to raise eyebrows; and certainly, in conservative Tyler, Texas, it was a matter of great concern for Holly's parents. But they decided, in the best southern tradition, that they would be as polite as they could be to Ira Einhorn; and because this was the man their precious daughter seemed to love, they tried to accept him into their fold as best they could.

But Ira would have none of it.

"It was like guerrilla warfare," said sister Buffy, who was fifteen at the time of the visit. "He was doing anything he could to provoke Daddy. He was pushing buttons because he knew what things would really make my father grind his teeth."

It started from the moment he walked in the door. Ira insisted on throwing a big bear hug around the young girls; they were clearly uncomfortable — and so Ira would do it more and more, pushing and prodding them, turning their discomfort back on them.

At dinner that evening, Holly's dad was filling his children's plates, when he looked up and saw Ira grabbing food off the serving tray, gobbling at it like a starved animal.

"Dad," said Buffy, "aren't we going to say the blessing tonight?"

"Yes," replied her father, staring at Ira. He

began to say grace.

Ira just kept on eating and scratching at his poison ivy; watching the flakes of his calamine lotion fall onto his plate, then flicking them across the table with his fingers.

Ira ordered Holly around — "Go get me a fork!" "Go get me something to drink!" — and Holly, in some strange, numbed state, kept her head down and followed the orders barked at her by this overweight, unkempt man who was doing everything he could to be rude to her family.

"It was, 'go get me this,' and she would just take off and heed everything that he said," remembers Meg. "That showed me that she no longer had a reserve to resist, the ability to say 'It's right by the refrigerator. There's the drawer.' Her spirit had been squelched by him."

After this horrible dinner, Holly was still trying to salvage something of a warm family visit. She loved the book her mother had put together showing all her baby pictures, and invited Ira into the living room to look through it.

"No," he responded. "I want you to come brush my hair."

Her family looked away, trying to pretend they hadn't heard this. Her cheeks burned with embarrassment.

And she quietly picked up the hairbrush and did what she was told.

"I'm sure, internally, my parents were pretty outraged," says Meg. "But they didn't say, 'Hey, don't do that to my daughter,' or 'I can't believe you're eating like a pig.' They would just kind of smile and ignore the inappropriate behavior and say, 'Do you need more towels? I there anything else we can do for you?' They tried to put on as accepting a relationship as they could, for Holly's sake, because they knew this was someone special for Holly."

"I think he was trying to promote a big explosion," Buffy thought in retrospect, "so he could sever the ties and really get Holly alone."

Indeed, this would be the way Ira wanted Holly to view the dynamic: see, your father hates me because he's uptight. Your father hates me because I'm Jewish. You have to choose: it's him or me.

Later that night, Ira called Buffy into the back room where he was staying (he, of course, took the guest room, leaving Holly to sleep on the floor). "He said, 'Buffy, I've written a poem for you,'" she said. "It was some pretentious Jim Morrison-type stuff, free-form and way-out. The 'I am profound' stuff. I don't remember the poem; I do remember it didn't make any sense. Afterward, he gave me a big hug. And I know that right afterward I went to go wash, because I felt so dirty. It was like a used-car-salesman hug. It made me feel dirty then and it makes me feel dirty now."

Astoundingly, Holly's family made it through the weekend without ever blowing up at Ira. But Ira's actions had served their purpose.

Holly and Ira would never visit Tyler, Texas, again.

And now, Holly felt more alone than ever.

The relationship proceeded on its rocky way. Holly knowing she should leave Ira but never having the strength; Ira writing that he needed to be more gentle with Holly but never being man enough to change.

They would sometimes take separate vacations — and it was Ira, the professor of free love, the one who argued that their relationship should be open, who became insanely jealous when Holly once vacationed with another man. This, of course, is also part of that pattern of the insecure, controlling men who populate the *America's Most Wanted* docket — their insecurity translates into raging jealousy at the slightest provocation.

Finally, the arguments, the denigration, began to weigh too heavily on Holly; from somewhere, she summoned the courage to talk about actually leaving him. In May of 1977, she told her mother that she had a plan to move into her own apartment that fall.

In a desperate attempt to hold on to Holly, Ira took her on a tour of Europe that summer (although "took her" is probably a misnomer — Holly had inherited some money after a relative passed away, and that's probably what funded the trip. Ira was always very resourceful with other people's money). Things soured between them after just a week, and Holly returned to the States.

She was, for the first time in memory, ebullient. "Ira and I have agreed to split," she wrote to her sister Meg. "I'll be at Fire Island until September 5 or thereabouts — sewing, sunning, spending much time alone and unattached — Lovely!"

Adding to her buoyant nature: She realized that she had been misdiagnosed with diabetes. Discontinuing the treatments she was taking for the disease seemed to give her much more energy. "As I become more and more credulous of this new, healthy creature I seem to be rapidly becoming, so too do a number of my life-assumptions pull a shift. It's been great realizing I'm capable and ready to live alone."

Now, if we were dealing with any of a hundred different *America's Most Wanted* cases, our reporters would recognize this moment. The moment when the woman decides to break free is the moment when the insecure, overbearing monster who has been controlling her life says: if I can't have you, no one will.

In the years that have passed, many, many people have come forth to defend Ira Einhorn, saying that this brilliant creature could not have had such a reaction.

Not Ira, they say.

He's different.

At a dinner party one night on Fire Island, Holly met Saul Lapidus, a man who had summered on the island for several years, and they struck up an immediate friendship, taking long walks together and sailing on his boat. After just a few weeks, Saul proposed that the two take a long sail together. She told him that she'd think about it, and that she was in the process of breaking up with a guy named Ira Einhorn.

Saul knew the name. Knew it well.

His ex-wife had had an affair with Einhorn.

Ira, for his part, was now back in Philadelphia and frantic, trying to convince Holly to return to him. But she was holding firm on actually making a real, lasting break.

On September 9, 1977, at 9:30 P.M., Ira called Holly at Saul's New York apartment. He threatened her: if she did not return, he would rip up all of her clothes, and throw all her belongings into the street. Holly wasn't particularly concerned about most of her material things, but she was particularly fond of a lot of antique black lace that she'd brought back from Europe.

The next day, Saul Lapidus dropped Holly off at Penn Station. She'd been unsuccessful in finding anyone who could calm Ira down, so she decided to return to extricate herself once and for all.

Holly's presence indeed seemed to calm Ira down; they even went to see the new movie *Star Wars* with a couple of friends. After that, they returned to the apartment they had shared together on Race Street.

It is unclear exactly what happened after that. We later interviewed a student named Paul

Herre, who lived in the apartment directly below Ira's. He said that, since Ira was a large man, he was quite used to hearing him clunking around upstairs.

But this night was different.

This night, Paul heard something else.

"I heard a real sharp pounding on the floor," he told us later. "Then I heard a scream. The kind that sends shivers all over you. It didn't last very long.

"I still couldn't tell you why I didn't call the police," Paul said. In later years, he attributes it to his own naïveté, a country boy too embarrassed to say that he's not sure of a lot of what goes on in the big city, not wanting to appear to be too much of a rube, too much the country boy who jumps at every shadow.

And part of it, he admits, was also that the sounds emanating from the apartment upstairs scared him to death.

"It all stayed pretty vivid," Paul said. "The goose bumps I got really stuck in my mind."

On Sunday, Einhorn simply reported in his diary: Work on messy place. Toward that end, he purchased a steamer trunk. Late that afternoon, he contacted two young women who had met Ira a few months earlier; he was to be their "guide to the paranormal." Certainly, what he was about to ask them was out of the "normal" arena.

He met them along the Schuylkill River and

told them, "I've got a steamer trunk that has some very, very valuable documents in it. They're documents that belong to the Russians, and I need to get rid of it." His plan: to load the trunk into one of the women's 1976 Plymouth Volare and take it down to the river.

The women thought this was weird — even for Ira Einhorn — and were relieved when, after going back to his apartment, they realized the trunk would not fit in their car.

Later that month, Paul Herre, the student who lived downstairs from Ira, returned from his sister's wedding to find that his apartment was vacant. His roommate had gone to stay at the fraternity house on campus, driven out of the apartment by a mysterious smell, a smell that appeared to be coming from an apartment upstairs.

Paul located the spot on his ceiling from which the odor seemed to be emanating and found a dark stain there. He tried Spic and Span, then Clorox, then painting over the spot, then putting in an air freshener. His efforts worked, for a time.

But a month later a heavy rain brought back the spot in his closet, and the terrible odor.

October 2 is Liz Maddux's birthday, but the day passed without word from her daughter Holly. She was a bit hurt, and a bit worried: it was the first time that Holly had ever missed her birthday. A few days later, she did the one thing she hated doing and had rarely been forced to before: she called Ira Einhorn, to see if he knew where Holly was.

The response, in calm, measured tones, sent a chill up her spine.

"I was going to call you and see if you knew where she was," said Ira.

She asked him for details: had Holly been back in Philadelphia since her return from Europe? Had she moved into her new apartment?

He said that she had been back, but that her new apartment wasn't available, and she was very upset about it.

Days went by, and there were no developments. When your child is missing — I don't care how old she is, if she is six or sixteen or twenty-six — each morning brings a new emptiness, a new echo in your heart, a new level of dread. Two more birthdays went by that month — two of Holly's sisters — and there was no word, no sweet call, no pretty handmade card, no clever, thoughtful little gift, none of the things they had come to expect from Holly.

Liz Maddux called Ira again.

This time, Ira told her he had seen Holly the month before; while he was in the bathroom she went to the store and never came back.

He said he had checked with the hospitals, the police, and their friends, and no one knew Holly's whereabouts.

Later, investigators checked with those friends.

They said no, Ira had never called them.

R. J. Stevens ran the FBI office in Tyler, Texas. In late October the Madduxes called Stevens, asking for help in finding their daughter. A lot has changed since my son disappeared, in the way that law enforcement responds to missing children cases; but one thing hasn't changed — when it's an adult child who disappears, unless there's some hard evidence of foul play, it's hard to get the authorities involved. The Philadelphia police had been notified, but things were moving slowly; and the parents were desperate for help.

Stevens felt for the woman on the phone; but he knew that, without some evidence of foul play, there was nothing he could do. The FBI had no jurisdiction. He helped them file a missing person report but had to leave it at that.

Even though he had turned them down, there was a kindness about Stevens, a caring that was evident even over the phone. The family did not forget that.

In January of 1978, an article appeared in the local newspaper about an R. J. Stevens retiring from the FBI after twenty-eight years.

That same day, his telephone rang.

The Madduxes wanted to know if he could help them out now, on a private basis.

The curmudgeonly Stevens wasn't happy about the call. After twenty-eight years with the

FBI, his plan was to relax and catch up on his reading. Then he was going to dig into a novel set in the Philippines, written by an old FBI agent he knew.

But he did agree to go meet with them, just to give them a few suggestions on how to proceed.

But when he started hearing about Holly — reading her letters home, hearing about what a special girl she was — he started thinking, this is not the kind of girl who voluntarily cuts off all ties.

There's something wrong here.

And his instincts took over.

"I was just eaten up with curiosity," said Stevens. "Solving a crime is a great boost for me. I really enjoy a successful investigation. That's what I prided myself on in the bureau. So I thought, well, I am already up here, and it's not going to take too much of my time. I thought it would take a week or two.

"I didn't know it would take a year and a half."

On March 15, Stevens called Einhorn, asking for his help in locating Holly.

Einhorn said he was too busy.

The police had already interviewed him, and insinuated he had somehow harmed Holly to get to the money she inherited, he said; he was upset by the insinuation and no longer felt like talking.

Besides, he was busy getting ready for Sun Day, his latest project, and had thirteen people tying to raise $50,000, and this would keep him busy seven days a week.

At this point, Stevens played the investigator's game: just keep him talking.

So he asked Ira, don't you want to help Holly's parents?

No, Ira responded: he didn't like her parents and wouldn't help them find her. Holly is fine, Ira said. In fact, she'd called him to say she was okay. She'd just decided to make a break with her parents and didn't want to talk to them anymore.

Stevens argued that it was her friends, as well, that she had failed to contact.

Ira argued that she had just decided to make a complete break with the past.

Stevens argued that the family was just concerned for her well-being, that they had no intention of interfering with her lifestyle.

Ira said he didn't believe it.

"Tell me what happened the last time you saw her," Stevens said. He already knew the previous statements Ira had made: that he was in the bathroom when she left, saying she was going to the store.

"So that was the last time you saw her?"

"That was the last time."

"And you haven't heard from her?"

"Yeah, I got a call from her a day or two later, saying she was okay, but that she was going away for a while."

Bingo.

Stevens thought, well, Ira talked to Holly's

mother in the weeks after her disappearance. He would have mentioned that call to her. But in all his previous conversations, he'd never said anything about it. To an investigator, that's a big tip-off: Ira is starting to embellish his story, Stevens thought.

"It would be a lot easier if we just sat down and talked for a bit," said Stevens.

Replied Ira: "Just no time."

"After the conversation with Ira I thought we had a problem," Stevens said later. "He didn't seem concerned. He showed no desire to sit down. He was not at all forthcoming. You would expect a person in that position to be tickled that you were helping to try and find their friend, and expect them to cooperate. He was just the opposite."

Stevens did some more digging and found the people who contradicted all of the parts of Ira's story. For example, he found Saul Lapidus, who told him about the irate phone calls from Ira to Holly on Fire Island. After the interviews with Saul, Stevens was sure something was wrong. He stayed at it, and soon he found The Leak.

Agnes Johnson, who with her husband managed the apartment building at 3411 Race Street, had never smelled anything like it before. Her husband thought it smelled like a dead animal. The odor was coming from the closet on the screened-in porch in Ira's apartment, a closet he always kept locked.

The months went by, and the smell persisted; by the summer of 1978 Einhorn was lecturing at Harvard University, and although he always sublet the apartment when he traveled before, this time the apartment sat empty. Mr. Johnson wanted to have someone check on the dark brown watery leak in the kitchen of the apartment below, and told Ira that the roofer might need to get into the closet.

Ira refused.

He had little time for these distractions. Ira's public life was accelerating at a rate that even he had never experienced. "In the year after Holly's disappearance, Ira's life really exploded on the public scene," remembers his friend Samuels. "He was lecturing at Harvard, he was dealing with parapsychology, he was into computer science before anyone else, he was organizing major exhibitions, he was being respected by people from the highest levels of the corporate ladder to the latest poets and hippie gurus — his life was really taking off in a very respectable way."

But Ira was about to make a new acquaintance.

His name was Michael Chitwood.

He was a detective with the Philadelphia Police Department.

Stevens, the private investigator, had dropped his file on Chitwood's desk. The interviews, the suspicions, all spelled out nice and neatly.

Now it was Chitwood's turn to go to work. He re-interviewed the people that Stevens had talked to. He brought in a forensic specialist. And it all led him to one conclusion.

Reflecting back on it later, Chitwood would tell us, "When you put this whole thing together, it was like an Alfred Hitchcock story. It really was.

"Except it became real life."

A few weeks later, on March 27, 1979, Ira Einhorn and his friend Stuart Samuels — now a film reviewer for an AM station in Philly — went to see a preview of the film *Hair.* Ira thought it was too simplistic, that it didn't capture the times; Stuart found it entertaining. They grabbed some dinner afterward, and then went up to Ira's apartment. Ira had just been to Yugoslavia and wanted to show Stuart copies of some papers he'd brought back. They talked late into the night, about Einstein, about Nicola Tesla — the Yugoslavian discoverer of alternating current, a favorite of Ira's — about mind-altering phenomena, parallel lines, space, matter, and mass, mind force and its relation to Einstein's theory of relativity.

Stuart sat in a chair near the porch.

A few feet away from the padlocked closet.

The next morning there was a knock at the door just before 9 A.M. Detective Chitwood and a half-dozen other officers stood there. In his hand, Chitwood held a thirty-five-page search warrant.

Ira, as usual, answered the door naked. But for

once, he was speechless.

"He stood back half in amazement," says Chitwood. "How could anybody dare search his apartment?"

Chitwood knew exactly where he wanted to look.

The closet.

"I noticed there was a hasp locked on the door," Chitwood remembers. "I asked Einhorn, did he have a key for this, and he said no he didn't. I asked him what was in the closet. He said he had no idea."

Einhorn's demeanor was as it always was: arrogant, defiant, superior.

Chitwood could have cared less.

He had his men take a crowbar and pry the closet open.

On the floor, inside, was a steamer trunk, with boxes piled high on top of it.

The smell was mostly gone now, just a faint whiff of something that had been rotting for a very, very long time.

As he took down the boxes, looking inside each one, he sensed Einhorn, watching over his shoulder. Chitwood opened one of the boxes and found a woman's small handbag.

He looked inside and was not surprised at what he found. The driver's license, Social Security card, and school identification card of Helen Holly Maddux.

All the boxes were now cleared away. There was nothing left in the closet except the large, green trunk.

"The trunk was locked, and again I asked him, did he have a key, and he said he didn't." He used the crowbar to open the suitcase, again keeping the lock intact.

As he opened the trunk, another whiff of that odor wafted up through the room, a ghost of that remembered smell, drifting out onto the porch, escaping skyward.

Inside, Detective Chitwood found some newspapers, dated September 15, 1977, and under that, some soft Styrofoam, the type you would fill pillows with.

He turned to Ira, looked at him again. Now the defiance was gone from his demeanor; he was nervous, sweaty, shaking.

Chitwood dug down through the Styrofoam and found something hard, but light, almost ephemeral but frozen into a shape, a shape that seemed to be reaching out.

It was a human hand.

He dug a little farther and could see an arm, and a long-sleeve shirt. . . .

He turned to the other officers, then to Ira.

"It looks like we got Holly," he said.

Ira's chin sank to his chest, and he replied, "You got what you got."

And that should be the end of the story.
But that was only the beginning.

Buffy, now twenty, was at nursing school in

Tyler, Texas, on the morning of March 27. She had a teacher who had always had a crush on Holly — as had so many — and he was always asking about her.

For some reason, she had never told him Holly was missing, even though she'd been gone for a year and a half. But this day, something came to her, a whiff of a thought of Holly, and she told him, you know, Holly's been missing for some time. We don't know what happened to her. She saw the shock in his face, and heard him say that he hoped she was all right.

Then Buffy went home.

"I got home and my mom was sitting there crying, and it was one of only two times I saw my momma cry. And she said, 'They found your sister today.' And I said, 'She's dead, isn't she?' And she said, 'Yeah.' And that was the first time we said the *dead* word."

Her older sister Meg, always the thoughtful, precise one, was numbed by the news. "After eighteen months of hoping against hope that maybe she did just take off and go on an extended vacation, then you find out that no, she's dead. Then you find out the details and the ghastly nature of everything, and the suffering that was probably involved — your body, your mind, just go into a kind of numb shock."

After a violent crime, some victims' families crumble, they fall apart, they blame themselves — if only I hadn't let her do this, if only I hadn't let her go there, why did I say this, why didn't I say that — and certainly there was much of that in the Maddux family. The one who felt it worst was Fred Maddux, Holly's dad. Believe me, I know what he went through. The searing, wrenching guilt that wakes you up in the night, wet with sweat and tears, the guilt that tells you, you were the man in the family. You were the father. Your reason for being on earth is to protect those children.

You did not do that. You did not protect them.

You try to push the guilt away, for a time, to go through your day, to eat, to drive, to earn a living, to talk with friends, but like a demon in the shadows it lunges at you, tears at your skin, pounds on your chest. It speaks in the voice of your dead child: you should have protected me. You should have protected me. Where were you?

This is what the guilt did to Fred Maddux. And although he lived for several more years, he would never get over it.

When he died, his family knew, he died of a broken heart.

There is, if you allow it, a channel past that guilt. A way to deal with the unthinkable, unbearable pain of loss. And this is what I tell parents of murdered children, wherever I go: remember the good times you had with that child. Consider yourself lucky that you were together on the earth with that child for the time that you had. This is the message my son, Adam, has left me to pass along, the energy that comes from allowing his sweet spirit to guide me: do not be bitter, do not let anger destroy you. He says, I was a child born of love and nurtured by love, and it is with love that I must be remembered, if you are to go on.

And the sweet, kind spirit of Helen Holly Maddux began to touch the numbed heart of her sister Meg, to warm it. Meg remembers Holly visiting her, in dreams, and says those visits allowed her to feel again, and to feel not anger, but strength, a strength that she would lend to her younger sisters as they went forward.

And believe me, they would need it.

The day of Ira Einhorn's arrest for the murder of Holly Maddux, the front pages of papers across the country were ablaze with the news of the Three Mile Island nuclear disaster. For days, screaming headlines in the Philadelphia papers about the discovery of the body in the closet shared space with the apocalyptic news of the nuclear meltdown.

It was hard to say which event shocked the people of Philadelphia more.

Immediately, Ira's friends rushed to his defense. Some went so far as to say this was a conspiracy — a CIA conspiracy to frame Ira Einhorn to stop his experiments in remote viewing because they knew he had psychics monitoring the Pentagon.

I am not making this up.

On April 3, 1979, a hearing was held to decide Ira's bail. He was defended by one of the most prominent attorneys in town, Arlen Specter — the same Arlen Specter who later became a U.S. senator.

The hearing was being held to determine the likelihood of Einhorn fleeing, and the possible danger to the community if he were let out on bail. But in a bizarre moment, the judge, William Marutani, asked Specter about the facts of the case.

Marutani: "Isn't it a little unusual to have a dead body — I guess it would have to be dead — in a trunk in one's own residence, let alone even a dead cat or a dead dog, but a dead human being? Doesn't that raise some eyebrows?"

Specter: "Judge, there has been no showing of that body being there since 1977 . . . there's an allegation . . . of (it) having been missing since '77."

Marutani: "Even if it were fresh — I guess if it were fresh it's even worse."

Specter: "Well, the allegation is bad, however it's made."

Marutani: "Sure . . . Let me ask you this, Mister Specter . . . I don't know the size of this trunk, but if it contains a body, and I assume it's a normal adult body, it has to be of some size that you couldn't sneak it in at night or sneak it in and out very easily, and therefore, would it be reasonable of me to determine that it didn't get there by pure chance, that somebody just didn't bring it in and forget it there when they went home?"

"I'm not saying," replied Specter, "that it didn't get there by pure chance."

"You know," said Marutani, "I wouldn't want to have someone find my wife's body in a trunk in my home, particularly if I lived alone; I think I'd be in hot water." And so it went, this bizarre exchange, in what has to be one of the most clear-cut cases to ever come before the court — they found the body in his closet, for goodness sakes!

So it seemed clear that they'd throw Einhorn in jail, throw away the key, and keep him there, doesn't it?

Bail is determined by a number of factors. The danger to the community is one of them; the likelihood of him fleeing is another. That likelihood is itself determined by a number of factors, among them the nature of the crime, the chance of conviction, and the potential sentence. On that matter, the judge was clear: "I must say, the most troubling aspect of the entire matter is a possible likelihood of conviction. It's not a good picture, as we all, I'm sure, can easily recognize; and if it's not a good picture, that the possible consequences thereof — namely, the possible penalty, may very well be life."

So clearly, the right thing to do is to deny bail, wouldn't you say?

Especially when you consider who Einhorn is, and what his experience would be. In a prescient moment, the judge asked Specter: "Would it be unreasonable to say that a defendant faced with that kind of a possibility, that he's going to face life, that he might not, as they say in the street jargon, split for parts unknown; and in this case, if he has a familiarity with, is it Norway and Scandinavian countries, Europe, et cetera, that he might just do that?"

Not unreasonable at all, I'd say.

And yet . . . there is the matter of Friends in High Places.

Because Ira, for all his posturing and preening and hogging of the spotlight, did have friends in high places.

And in between the batterings he was taking from the judge, Specter paraded Ira's Friends in High Places before the court, a veritable Who's Who of Philadelphia: A vice president with Bell Atlantic. A prominent lawyer. A priest. An economist. A top businessman. A fancy restaurateur. Thomas Bessinger, theatrical producer. Curtis Kubiak, architect. Ralph Moore, director of the Christian Association, University of Pennsylvania.

One after another, they extolled Einhorn's virtues, they sang his praises, they told of what a nonviolent person he was.

(It should be noted that testimony in the next hearing would show that Holly was beaten brutally about the head, suffering at least a half-dozen blows, before she died; but that was not the focus of this hearing.)

They told of what an upstanding member of the community he was. What a good friend. What an important figure.

And finally, Arlen Specter asked for pity for poor Ira Einhorn, because he had so little money and needed to save what little he had for his defense.

And somehow, in a courtroom of honor, where all are supposedly equal before the law, and where the rich and poor, the mighty and the meek, the obscure and the locally famous, are all supposed to receive equal treatment, the judge decided to let Ira Einhorn free, on just $40,000 bail.

One of his rich friends, the heir to the Seagram's liquor fortune, posted the bail, and in a matter of minutes, Einhorn was walking free, strutting down the streets that Holly Maddux would never walk again.

It still amazes me that, despite all the evidence against him, all of these intelligent and powerful people continued to support Ira Einhorn. Especially after the second hearing, which for Ira did not go as well as the first — instead of the parade of Ira lovers, there was the parade of evidence, to show that there was reason for a trial. And it was extremely persuasive.

And yet, the Ira cadre stood behind him. The going theory — one that Ira did his best to promulgate — was that he was the victim of a mass government conspiracy, that secret government operatives had killed Holly and put her in Einhorn's closet to frame him and stop him from whatever global work he thought he was doing.

The fact that this was just after Watergate, when anti-government sentiment and conspiracy theories abounded, doesn't excuse the fact that they were helping a man get away with murder.

And yet, that's exactly what this rich and powerful and privileged cadre did. It's shameful. But it's true.

Levy, the author, unearthed a letter that Einhorn wrote to a friend in Europe: "What you could work on is a place where I could disappear for a few years — a country house, a room in a large estate, a cottage in some safe far-off place. I prefer Northern Europe and I'm open to anything. I should have enough $ to live quietly for two to four years and friends will add to that." And apparently, that's just what happened.

Because Ira Einhorn was indeed charged with murder. And on January 13, 1981, a pretrial hearing was held.

But Ira's chair was empty.

He had fled to Europe.

And he wasn't coming back.

The fact that Holly's killer was not going to answer for his crime — not right away, anyway — began to wear on Holly's family. As the days turned into weeks, then months, and then years, a stolid, world-weary weight descended on their shoulders.

And somehow, through that weight, a strength was born.

People always ask me about this — why is it that some crime victims' families fall apart, become buried by an avalanche of blame and anger and life-paralyzing frustration, fall victim to depression and alcoholism and divorce and suicide, and others become steeled and determined, forceful agents for change, for justice? I can tell you, after dealing with thousands of victims' families, that there is no determining factor. There's no right and wrong, no way to prepare for the devastation that crime can bring to a family. It's not that the members of one family love one another more, or loved their murdered sister or daughter more, than another family. You cannot blame the families who do not have the strength to bear up under the incredible weight of a situation like this; you can only honor the families who do, and try to help them in any way you can.

And that's how we got involved.

Marilyn Beery had been at *America's Most Wanted* for about a year. We've always had an esoteric mix of people at the show — some with print backgrounds, some with TV backgrounds, some real razzle-dazzle producers, some quiet, plodding reporters. Marilyn, almost from the day she showed up, took on the role of the quiet, studious investigative reporter. She took on the hardest cases, the most complicated ones, as a sort of mission: she liked the fact that the show was always stretching the boundaries, trying to do different kinds of stories, and saw that as a chance to effect some positive change. She was the one who took on the case of Virgilio Paz — accused of the car-bombing murder of a former Chilean ambassador in Washington, D.C.; he'd been on the run for eighteen years, and everyone told us there wasn't the slightest chance of solving the case.

We found him in five days.

By the time Marilyn heard about the Holly Maddux case, in the spring of 1991, Einhorn had been on the run for ten years. There was a lot of ground to cover.

In the intervening years, not only had Holly's dad died, but Holly's mom as well, and so now it was up to the four remaining children to carry on.

After Marilyn did the telephone interviews, we sent a producer to do the on-camera interviews. Of Holly's four siblings, two of the sisters wound up speaking in our first story — Meg, the oldest surviving child, and Buffy, now in her early thirties, with two children of her own.

As I noted earlier, most television programs ask their producers to remain "objective" — if that's possible — which often translates into an unfeeling, hurtful stance toward crime victims; not only do we allow our reporters to get emotionally involved with their subjects, we encourage it. Because of the way the media hounded me when my son was killed, I made a promise that we would never revictimize a victim, that we would treat victims with dignity and respect. And when you tear down that "objective" wall, and allow yourself to really hear their stories, you can't help but become emotionally attached to them.

And that's what started happening, right from the start, with the Maddux family. Every producer they came in contact with started becoming emotionally attached.

We only hoped our viewers would feel the same way, and want to reach out, and help them find justice.

"I don t know how they could ignore a body in a closet for eighteen months," Buffy was saying. "I don't know how they could believe a person of Ira's intelligence would keep a closet locked for eighteen months, with that smell coming out of it, and that he would not look in the closet, and not let anyone look in the closet. I don't know how anyone could not believe that he knew she was in there, but that they would believe there was a CIA conspiracy to kill Holly to silence Ira.

"It doesn't speak very well of their intelligence, does it?"

This was a woman who had lived through terrible pain: she had lost her older sister, just as they were beginning to really get to know each other. She had seen her parents' hearts broken. And she had seen her family tortured by the cruel games of her sister's killer.

And without self-pity, without anger, she conveyed a power, a fury, that we were sure would propel some viewer, somewhere, into action, into making the call we needed.

The hardest part, for Buffy, was talking about the effect of the crime on her family.

"About a year before my dad died, one night we were sitting around the dinner table at two in the morning, saving the world and solving all the world's political problems, and he said, 'I wish Holly and I could have talked like this.' He didn't cry, but he was about to."

The producer continued to ask quiet, simple questions, and Buffy continued to pour out her feelings until he asked one final question:

If you could speak directly to Ira right now, what would you say?

Buffy smiled a sad smile, and leaned back, and let out a long, deep breath, and thought for a while. She looked the producer straight in the eye.

But she saw Ira Einhorn.

"We're very angry," she said.

"We don't hate you.

"But we want justice."

She paused for a long moment, then continued.

"If you think you're going to get away from all four of us, you're not going to.

"We have the odds on you on longevity. We are going to outlive you.

"We're not going to let this die.

"It is not going to go away.

"As long as there's an avenue to pursue, we're going to pursue it.

"You may never be caught, but I hope you're never happy. I hope you're never secure. I hope you're never safe. I hope you never sleep well at night.

"That is our revenge."

That's the only revenge we have."

She paused, then added:

"For now."

The night we aired the re-enactment, a slightly frumpy guy with a big bushy mustache and a thick Philadelphia accent was on our set, helping us take calls. Rich DiBenedetto was the head of the fugitive unit for the Philadelphia D.A.'s office, and had inherited the case back in 1982. It was not a case he was unfamiliar with.

"Everybody here in law enforcement knew that when he got out on bail he was gonna flee, because he had traveled to Europe before, had contacts all over Europe, there were rumors that his bail money had been put up by this wealthy Canadian woman, so there was every indication that this guy was gonna flee," he told us.

Rich was the kind of cop we loved to work with: he was a no-nonsense, straight-talking cop's cop and he had a passion for his work.

And the fact that he had already been on the case for nearly ten years told us that he was not the kind of cop who gives up easily.

I found out later that Rich took this case very personally — to this day, he still keeps a picture of Holly's dad in his den. "For me, I felt that for Fred and Elizabeth Maddux, that the system had never come through for them. He was a paratrooper at D-Day, a World War II veteran. But he never had any bitterness toward the system — and I never really heard him say anything wishing Einhorn ill will. He was a gentleman — like another generation, you know, they grew up differently." After Fred and Elizabeth died, Rich made a promise to them that he would catch their daughter's killer.

The night we aired the story, I made the same promise.

There were some interesting tips that came in that night — a woman who said she'd seen him in a bar in France, others pointing elsewhere in Europe — but nothing solid enough to move on. It was disappointing, but Rich assured us that it was only a matter of time. "I was determined to find the guy. Even with all the resources he had available to him, I knew he could still be found."

We just had no idea how long it would take.

DiBenedetto began at the beginning, back in 1981. After Einhorn fled the United States through Canada, DiBenedetto learned that he had gone to London and then to Dublin with a new girlfriend, Jeanne Marie Morrison. Einhorn, that arrogant, cocksure son of a bitch, was so unconcerned about the hunt for him that he was going by his real name. He was clearly not hurting for money: he was seen with currency from several different countries — deutsche marks, dollars, Canadian dollars, even some yen — although he never worked. He was living comfortably in an area near the U.S. embassy, a fairly high-rent district for Dublin at the time; it was not unusual for him, say, to spend $100 on a book he wanted. Again, while no one was ever charged, it certainly appeared that his cadre of benefactors was still keeping him afloat.

Einhorn rang the bell next to the glass-paned, ivy-framed door of a professor of physics at Dublin University, Dennis Weaire. Weaire agreed to rent Ira a small apartment in the house, what the Irish call a "granny flat."

The professor found Ira to be extraordinarily smart and extraordinarily odd.

"I'm a physicist, and many of Einhorn's ideas concerned the interaction of science and the world of psychic phenomena. And to me the greater part of his ideas are simply crackpot."

Strangest of all, though — although the professor would not realize it until later — was the fact that he had introduced himself using his real name. There was, of course, no way for the professor to know that Ira was wanted for murder.

He certainly didn't keep a low profile — joining discussion groups on James Joyce, and espousing his "planetary enzyme" concepts.

And around Jeanne Marie, several years his junior, he made no point of hiding his true nature, either.

"Certainly with the passing of time, one became aware that she was completely dominated by him, that she did not really have any opinions of her own. Einhorn was always in the foreground, and he would do all the talking. She just listened and admired what he said."

Even when Ira made remarks about his past, saying he was in trouble with the authorities because of his counterculture activities in the sixties — "He claimed that he had come to Ireland to write a book and clear his name because he had some political problems in the United States," DiBenedetto said — the professor wasn't unduly concerned. But soon the professor and his wife, Collette, would have their suspicions. They started as the couple announced they were planning a trip to the States, to Chicago, to visit some relatives.

"When we mentioned this to Einhorn, he immediately became agitated, and during the days leading up to this visit he tried to persuade us not to tell the authorities about his presence in Ireland. It was a strange thing to do, because this wasn't exactly on our minds in the first place, and in fact, it had the opposite effect of persuading us that he had a serious problem and not something trivial in his background, and that we should look into it. And we did."

As soon as the Weaires got to the States, they started asking about him. They quickly found out his true, sordid past — and made a beeline for the FBI office in Chicago. They reported Ira's whereabouts, and they figured that was that, and that Ira would be arrested before they got home.

When the professor and his wife returned to Dublin, they assumed Einhorn was already in custody. But they called their home just to make sure.

And Jeanne Morrison answered.

Flustered, the couple went to the police, to find out why the killer and his girlfriend were still living in their home.

They were told that there was no extradition treaty between the United States and Ireland.

And there was nothing anyone could do about it.

So there was Ira, hiding in plain sight, and all DiBenedetto could do was cool his heels. Still, he kept his composure: "It's pretty frustrating, but I always think that there's a way to do things," said DiBenedetto. "I was trying to explore some possible other options."

The Weaires, for their part, decided not to return home that night. But the next morning, accompanied by the police, they confronted Ira and told him they were throwing him out of their home.

"I know what they've been telling you," said

Einhorn. "It's not true. Can't we talk about this?"

"No," replied Dennis. "We are not having any discussion whatsoever. I don't care whether it's true or not. I only know what the authorities have told me. You will leave in thirty minutes."

And with that, Einhorn was in the wind again.

The last conversation DiBenedetto had with the Weaires was: if you ever see Ira again, call me. Well, it took five years, but he did get that call.

In May of 1986, Professor Weaire was now teaching at Trinity University. His wife, Collette, was with him in the lunchroom, and she spotted a familiar face.

"I literally bumped into him face-to-face," said Weaire. Startled to see Einhorn after all these years — and assuming that Einhorn was just as startled — Weaire decided to stare the bully down.

"Because we had made this dramatic encounter, I decided there was no point in walking away and pretending it didn't happen. So I confronted him and insisted he leave the college immediately. At first, he didn't want to do so. He just wanted me to leave him alone — rather like the first encounter. But I said, 'I'm not arguing about this.' I was going to fling him out, and if he did not agree I would just simply get the security staff to do this. So he laughed. But then he agreed to go, and I escorted him to the door."

Weaire remembered the policeman from the States he had talked to all those years ago and called him immediately.

The extradition treaty between the United States and Ireland had now been reinstated; DiBenedetto was excited to have his first fresh lead after five years, and to know that now Ira could be arrested and deported.

But the game of cat-and-mouse that DiBenedetto and Einhorn had been playing for five years was far from over. DiBenedetto knew that Einhorn was smart enough to realize that Weaire would call the cops, and smart enough not to hang around Trinity.

And now that Weaire had thrown Ira off campus, where exactly was DiBenedetto supposed to look?

It's so infuriating to know that this smug, self-centered, sell important coward kept getting so lucky. But, as DiBenedetto expected, by the time he was able to get the Irish authorities to check the area around Trinity, Ira was long gone.

But, like any good cop, DiBenedetto took a deep breath, picked up the phone, and went to work developing his latest lead.

His first call was to Weaire, to ask if there was anyone with Ira at the time of their encounter. In fact, there was — a professor of German. DiBenedetto had done his homework, many times over, and knew that as smart as Ira was, he always had trouble with other languages. So he asked Weaire to look up this German professor and see if he'd been teaching Ira.

The answer was yes — and no.

He had been teaching the man Weaire knew as Ira Einhorn.

But the German professor knew him by another name.

Ben Moore.

Okay, thought DiBenedetto.

I don't have my mouse yet.

But at least I have his new alias.

And the world just got a little smaller for him today.

"Ben Moore was based on Benjamin Moore paint — paint that covers the world. At one point he was also going to call himself Sherwin Williams."

Professor Hank Harrison, another expatriate American, met Ben Moore when Harrison was in Dublin writing a book about the archaeology research he was doing. He had actually met Ira Einhorn many years before, back in Marin County: "Ira was pitching the Grateful Dead to give money for Earth Day. He was a disheveled, scraggly kind of guy. He didn't look like he had much going for him. By the time I met him ten years later in Ireland, he had lost a lot of weight, wore his hair back in a ponytail, had a suntan, and was very much more fluid in his motions and his actions, much more clever and facile with language. There's no doubt about it: he took me in that second time. I didn't recognize him between the two times. I didn't remember him — but he was the same guy."

In fact, he started living his old lifestyle. Jonathan Philbin Bowman, now a game show host in Dublin, was a neighbor then. After getting kicked out of the Weaires's home, Ira had moved into a flat near the U.S. embassy, and Bowman says he was once again surrounding himself with groupies who thought him a guru. "We're talking about slightly fringy alternative people who thought that smoking dope on a Tuesday evening and discussing dead German philosophers was almost the height of existence," said Bowman.

Harrison brought his daughter — later to become known as the singer/actress Courtney Love — into Einhorn's circle. He remembers a series of philosophy sessions/spaghetti feasts. "Some of these spaghetti feasts turned into sex parties," Harrison says. "I didn't stay for those, incidentally, I want to make that very clear."

And, according to Harrison, Ira resumed what I maintain is his true identity: an abuser of women.

"With men, he was very charming. With women, he was very demanding and very demoralizing. I saw him glare and grab and do things to women that I thought were inappropriate. I actually saw him slap a woman in front of me. I saw him commandeer a car and take a car away from a woman. I've seen him yell at women."

This is what I say to all those people who supported Ira over the years: you were fooled by his con game. Because guys like Ira get through life by fooling people. Of course he was able to attract women: he made a science of telling them what they wanted to hear. If they were interested in dance, he would talk about learning the rhumba; if they were interested in art, he was an expert on Miró. This is how he lured them in, before he shut the trap and began the torture. And all those wealthy, supposedly intellectual friends got snookered by the same con game. Anyone who thinks even for a moment that the murder of Holly Maddux was a crime of passion caused by a moment of rage need only look at how many times, over the course of many, many years, people said the same things about Ira: he hits, he demeans, he abuses. This is a disgusting coward, nothing more and nothing less.

But fortunately, the bulldog on his tail had picked up his malodorous scent.

Now that DiBenedetto knew the alias Ben Moore, he also knew he had to move fast. He got the Irish police to go to the German professor's home and found out that he did, indeed, have Ben Moore's address.

In fact, Ben Moore had called him one night earlier — saying he was about to go on a long vacation.

The cops staked out Einhorn/Moore's new

apartment — but there was no sign of life. He had slipped through their fingers again.

DiBenedetto did learn that Ira and Jeanne Marie Morrison had broken up, but the detective had lost her trail. He picked it up early the next year, when he found out that she had returned to the States. He tracked her down but found her to be a reluctant source. Clearly, Einhorn had prepped her on what to say and what not to.

She didn't give up much, but she did admit she'd received a few postcards from Ira, describing wonderful little bed-and-breakfasts he was staying in up and down the coast of England. This was starting to rankle DiBenedetto more and more.

He had to squeeze something out of this Jeanne Marie Morrison.

He did.

He got her to offer up a few names of Einhorn acquaintances, including the name of a bookseller friend of Ira's, Eugene Mallon. A source in Ireland checked out the store quietly and indeed found books in the store belonging to Ira. So he knew there was in fact some kind of relationship between Ira and Mallon; the question was, what kind.

That summer, two detectives from Philly were headed to Ireland on vacation — one was marrying an Irish police officer — and DiBenedetto asked them to mix a little business with pleasure.

"I asked them to check on this guy Mallon, to see if he knows anything about Einhorn, right? So they went into the guy's bookstore and they just showed him a photo and said look, we want you to know that this guy is wanted for murder in the States. He's not wanted for any political crime or anything, he's wanted for murder.

"And this guy Mallon got real nasty with them, tried to throw them out of the store, called the Irish police on them, wanted to file a complaint."

It was one of those insignificant moments that an entire case turns on. Because, had the shopkeeper been polite, said yes, I knew this man, he bought books here, then DiBenedetto would have never given him a second thought. Instead, because he became belligerent, DiBenedetto figured there was something unusual about his relationship with Ira. The name Eugene Mallon stuck in the detective's head.

And that tiny little fact is what would finally bring Ira Einhorn's run to an end.

The name of Barbara Bronfman, the liquor heiress from Canada, kept coming up; she'd always denied being in contact with Ira after he left the country, but DiBenedetto thought that if he could talk to her directly, he could get more out of her.

In November of 1988, he did.

"We finally get to go to Canada; we did get to speak to her, and she admitted that she had been

338

sending him money, that she had actually gone over to meet him in 1982 in Dublin."

She said that the last place she had heard of him living was Sweden — but she claimed that just five months earlier, she had cut off contact with him, right after Steven Levy's book came out and she became convinced of Ira's guilt. Still, she seemed sad to the detective: "She said that he had met a wonderful woman in Sweden, and she seemed somewhat emotionally upset about having to tell us all this, like this guy had found some kind of happiness in his life and now she was going to be responsible for his ruination."

Tough.

Here's a woman who police believe has been helping to keep a killer on the run for seven years; now she comes to the startling realization that the man who kept a dead body in his closet for a year and a half might have actually committed the crime — and instead of calling up Holly Maddux's family in tears and begging their forgiveness, she feels sorry for *him?* Myself, I don't get how someone can be so cold and so callous. It's a good thing I wasn't there conducting that investigation.

DiBenedetto, of course, did keep his cool, just kept Bronfman talking. He got the name of the new girlfriend — Annika Flodin. He got her address — she and Einhorn were living just four blocks from a police station. (We later asked Interpol Stockholm whether they were embarrassed that he was living right under their noses. "Yes," they replied. "In a sense he was too close to be seen.")

But none of that mattered right now.

All that mattered was that finally, after all these years, DiBenedetto was ready to spring the trap for the Unicorn.

He got Interpol Stockholm on the case, ready to investigate.

They started the surveillance of her apartment.

And what they found out could not have upset DiBenedetto more.

They found out that Einhorn was gone again.

"We found out that, the day after we interviewed Bronfman, someone close to Bronfman had called over and spoken to Einhorn on the phone," said a crestfallen DiBenedetto. "We determined who it was. We had a hard time determining exactly what took place and what was said. They tried to make it sound like they tipped him off inadvertently. But it was our belief that it was done purposely."

Einhorn seemed to be thumbing his nose at the authorities, hiding in plain sight, daring them to try to catch him. "One of his friends once told me, 'You'll never catch him because he's too smart,' " said DiBenedetto. "I have to thank that friend, because it helped motivate me even more."

But he would need the motivation, because

now the prey had escaped again. And now all the hunter had left was a very pretty Swedish redhead named Annika. Annika fit the profile of Einhorn's women: she was pretty, slim, and she had money. The authorities in Sweden could get no more information out of her. And DiBenedetto decided he would have to wait for a while.

"I thought the best thing to do was to lay off her for a while," he said. "First of all, if she was his lover, I figured she's not going to get back together with him for a while, because she figures we'll be watching her. Second, I figured that if this is the first time she's finding out that he's wanted for murder, then he's got some explaining to do, and that's going to take a while. Meanwhile, I figured Einhorn would go back to England, because that seemed to be his base of operations."

Right again.

We learned later that Einhorn did go to England and called rock star Peter Gabriel; they'd known each other in Einhorn's 1970s heyday, and Einhorn still had Gabriel's private number. They arranged a clandestine meeting at a restaurant; Gabriel said Einhorn seemed to be down on his luck, but — tabloid reports to the contrary — there's never been any indication that Gabriel gave Einhorn any money.

Back in the States, prosecutors were fearing that the case was getting too old, and that can be death for the prosecution: witnesses move away, their memories fade, stories get jangled in the passing of years. So they decided to go ahead and try Einhorn in absentia. It didn't take the jury long to figure this one out: after just a few hours, they came back with their verdict: guilty. Einhorn was sentenced to life in prison.

Now all we had to do was figure out a way to make him serve it.

It was at this point that *America's Most Wanted* joined the hunt. We aired the reenactment, and the interviews with the Maddux sisters, several times in the next year and a half, but kept coming up empty. We had one of our forensic artists create an age-enhanced bust of Einhorn, to show our viewers what he might look like today. But we couldn't turn up a single solid lead.

You might think it impossible for us to catch a fugitive in Europe anyway — but that's not the case. Believe it or not, we've caught more than two dozen fugitives in other countries — mostly in countries where we're not aired. There's always some odd twist — we once caught a fugitive in the remote jungles of Guyana because his uncle had visited him there, unaware that he was wanted for murder, then saw his nephew on our show the night he got home.

But we weren't catching that kind of break in this case. So we brainstormed with DiBenedetto to find another source of tips.

There's a Swedish TV show called *Efterlyst*, that country's version of *America's Most Wanted*.

He contacted them, we supplied them with some video, and they aired the case.

And still nothing.

I was thinking, this has to be the luckiest son of a bitch we have ever chased. Three times he's been within a hair's breadth of being captured, but slipped away. We have an international manhunt going on, and we can't find him. The police have located his source of funding and couldn't use it to close the noose.

I also knew that sooner or later, we would catch a break.

In July of 1996, we finally did.

That summer, Rich DiBenedetto, who had now been hunting Ira Einhorn for fourteen long years, got a call from a Swedish woman who lived in Long Beach, California. She was an avid *AMW* viewer and had seen the Einhorn segment years earlier. She had recently been traveling in Italy and read an article in the paper there about an American who went on vacation to Italy with his wife and killed her. There was a picture of the man in the paper. She had a hunch it might be Einhorn.

"I saw the feature about Ira Einhorn on the TV show *America's Most Wanted*, which I watch every Saturday, and if I don't, I'm not home, I tape it," the woman, Hjordis Reichel, told us later. "I particularly remember the story when she was going out and meet this other man on the boat and try to get away from Ira Einhorn. That stuck in my mind, but I saw it many times, and I said, 'Oh, how I wish they could catch this guy.' "

She had saved the newspaper in her luggage until she got home. DiBenedetto knew this woman was probably dead wrong about it being Einhorn in the picture in the paper, but he did keep her on the phone chatting, and later started corresponding with her. He confided in her that he was having trouble with the Swedish police — and she dropped a bombshell.

I have a cousin in the Swedish police, she said.

I will call him.

He will help you.

"After I talked to Rich DiBenedetto," said Hjordis, "I got a brainstorm and I started to think that luckily I have relatives in the police department in Stockholm. I called him at home and I said, 'You have to help me on this one. This is a serious matter. I want names. I want to see what can be done.' "

So when this real-life Agatha Christie, working from Los Angeles, teamed up with the hard-boiled, long-suffering detective in Philadelphia, they began turning the tide in Sweden. It was a major turning point: suddenly, new doors were open. The Swedish authorities, to this point standoffish at best, were suddenly returning phone calls promptly, helping to follow up on leads, brainstorming with DiBenedetto.

"I got Jan Eklinder, the superintendent of Interpol in Stockholm, Sweden, together with

Rich DiBenedetto," Hjordis said. "They had a good rapport. After that it was smooth sailing."

Ecklinder and DiBenedetto, along with other Swedish authorities now suddenly very interested in the case, formulated a battle plan. They agreed that it would not be a good idea to contact Annika Flodin's family in Sweden — they would just call Annika and warn her. DiBenedetto was not going to give Einhorn another heads-up.

But the Swedish authorities did come up with an intriguing new clue.

It seems that Annika Flodin had had her Swedish driver's license changed to a French driver's license, under the name Annika Flodin Mallon.

Mallon . . . Mallon . . . DiBenedetto knew that name! It was the jerk bookseller from Ireland, the one whose name he would have forgotten if he hadn't been such a pain in the butt. Could this web be getting so tangled that Annika was now married to the bookseller, and living in France?

No, thought DiBenedetto. Go for the simplest explanation. The simplest explanation is almost always the right one.

And the simplest explanation was this:

Ira Einhorn had borrowed papers from his friend in order to change his identity. He was now using the alias Eugene Mallon.

Married to Annika Flodin.

And living in France.

The driver's license information led to the small French town of Champagne-Mouton, a beautiful Bordeaux village of rolling hills, brilliant sunshine, lovely châteaus, and endless vineyards. DiBenedetto was not the kind of guy to get very excited, but now he felt he was so close to Einhorn he could smell him. Everything had to go right this time. We cannot tip him off. We cannot let him get away again. I owe it to the memory of Holly's father, Fred Maddux. I owe it to his daughters, who have waited so long for justice.

It's time.

Guy Sapata, of the French Judicial police, a compact, soft-spoken man with a tough set to his jaw, spoke a little English and became the next man to pick up the baton in this manhunt marathon. He and DiBenedetto, on opposite sides of the ocean, plotted the play.

First, DiBenedetto faxed Sapata pictures of Einhorn and asked that the French authorities conduct a surveillance to make sure his hunch was correct. "We knew it would be a difficult thing because he escaped from two or three countries in Europe and in your States," Sapata told us later, "so we had to work with secret, with discretion."

Quietly, armed with pictures of an overweight hippie taken in the late 1970s, he staked out the house. "We make surveillance about him, and about his house. That's our job, to see and not be seen," Sapata said.

What he saw was a heavyset man, graying now, with a messy beard, tending to the garden.

A unique character, no doubt about that.

As unique as a unicorn.

Through Interpol, Sapata contacted DiBenedetto and let him know that he had confirmed the sighting. DiBenedetto sent word back:

Nail him.

On the morning of Friday, June 13, 1997, a bunch of French policemen dressed as fishermen drove through a lovely, warm morning up to a small château in Champagne-Mouton.

They wander slowly up to the door. Then, much more quickly, they enter the house. There, in his pajamas, is the man they are looking for.

They tell him they are the police. They call him by the name Ira Einhorn. And they tell him he is under arrest. The man is so surprised, he cannot move.

The man, known for his great intelligence, has nevertheless never been very good with languages. He has been relying on the woman he is living with to translate for him. But in what little French he has, he tells them, no, no, my name is Eugene Mallon. You have the wrong man.

But they did not have the wrong man.

Sixteen years after he failed to show up in a Philadelphia courtroom, Ira Einhorn finally, finally had nowhere to run.

DiBenedetto couldn't believe it. He was staring at a Teletype from France, a terse message stating that Einhorn was in custody.

His mood was quiet elation, tempered with a tiny fear that maybe it wasn't true. He wanted fingerprints checked, he wanted verbal communication, he wanted some assurance. But by the time he got through to the authorities in France it was 9 P.M. on a Friday night, and the Interpol contacts said they couldn't confirm anything until Monday morning. So the news he had waited sixteen years to give to the Maddux family would have to wait three more days.

On his way home from work, DiBenedetto bought a small bottle of French wine — specifically, a Bordeaux. "I just thought it was more of a symbolic thing than anything, the fact that he had been caught in Bordeaux, the fact that the French police had done such good job on it. It was my way of toasting them."

Over the weekend, DiBenedetto pretty much kept the news to himself. He wanted to make absolutely certain it was Einhorn. But that Sunday, Father's Day, he shared the news with his wife and daughter. "I told them what had been going on — my poor wife had to listen to this for years and years, and she would say, 'Are you ever going to catch him?' — so I was talking to my wife and daughter and I just got up and let out a few yells."

Then, it being Father's Day, he went into his

den, and looked at the photo sitting there, and shared the news with an old friend, long gone.

His thoughts were of Fred Maddux.

It is his honoring of the victims and their families — along with his dogged determination — that made Rich DiBenedetto the kind of cop he is. "His last name means 'the blessed,' " Mary Maddux once told me, "and that's exactly who and what he is, regardless of what job he happens to have, and that's what he'll always be."

Rich DiBenedetto thought of opening the Bordeaux and toasting his old friend, but a cop is a cop, and everything must be done in order. First came Monday morning and the confirmation of Ira's identity. Then came the phone calls to the family.

DiBenedetto's first call was to John Maddux, Holly's only brother. He had become close to John — John had even stayed at DiBenedetto's house during a visit to Philadelphia. John, hearing the news, was stunned.

Rich gave Joel Rosen, who had tried the case in absentia — and who had felt heartbroken seeing the family sit through the pain of a trial that ended with a verdict but no justice — the pleasure of letting Holly's oldest sister, Meg, in on the capture.

"I have some good news for you," Joel told her.

Oh great, thought Meg. They've figured out what continent Ira is on.

But Joel said, "They captured him in a little

town in the middle of nowhere in the middle of France," and Meg let out a Texas cheer.

"It was a feeling of relief, more than anything else," Meg told us later. "I think there's always going to be a sense of vindication with anyone who goes through something like this. However, no amount of vindication, or anger, is ever going to bring back my sister. So it's more relief that we have an answer."

The word spread through the family, to the younger sisters Buffy and Mary, and later that afternoon DiBenedetto and the other Philadelphia authorities held a press conference, and the world exploded with the news that the long strange trip of Ira Einhorn was over.

"It just proves that life is very long and the road is very tortuous," said Lynn Abraham, the district attorney, "but there is a sort of roundness to it. There is a beginning, a middle, and an end, and we're getting close to the end."

And that night, DiBenedetto opened the bottle of Bordeaux and drank a toast to the French police and to auld lang syne, old friends long gone.

"This is a case that cried for justice," he said later. "Yeah, justice can be tardy, but eventually it triumphs."

He drank one glassful from the small bottle and then carefully sealed it. He would drink the rest when Ira was brought back to the States.

He didn't figure it would take too long to have that second drink.

This time, he figured wrong.

Because we all thought that this story was over.

But there was one more brutally painful chapter to write.

We sent Lena Nozizwe, our number one correspondent, to Europe to cover the story. As I've said before, we're not like the big network magazine shows with gobs of money to waste; we're a small show on a tight budget, and Lena knew we had to make every penny count. So on the economy plan, she packed her bags and got on a plane to retrace Ira's steps.

Lena, like a lot of the *America's Most Wanted* team, grew up in "straight" news — she was a well-known TV anchor in San Diego — but was not your typical anchor. The daughter of African royalty, Lena was a stunning presence — strikingly tall, graceful, and good looking, she had the appearance and bearing of a network star; but behind the straight-backed, elegant facade was the heart and soul of a street reporter. She loved to be "on the ground," digging out the truth, and equally important to me, she had the pure passion and caring for crime victims that I always feel is essential to succeed at *AMW*. Lena would be the one crawling under overpasses in downtown L.A. at three in the morning to talk to teenage runaways; and she was the one that they wanted to talk to. She'd produced some of our most poignant crime victim stories, as well as some of our most tough-as-nails fugitive pieces, and now she was headed out to unravel our biggest case of the year.

She began by following Ira's footsteps — through the pubs of Ireland, the universities of England, the streets of Sweden, finally the beautiful French countryside. Immediately, things started going strangely. For one thing, she couldn't understand why everyone seemed so sympathetic to Einhorn. Everywhere she went, she felt like she was the bad guy, and Ira was the hero. We always knew that even though the *America's Most Wanted* concept found its roots in England — with a program called *Crimewatch UK* — most of the continent was less than enamored with our work. Europeans tend to value privacy over all else — a value cultivated in the prewar era, when millions feared a knock on the door would be followed by the sound of the boots of storm troopers, when Nazi sympathizers curried favor with the Third Reich by turning in their neighbors who were secretly Jewish.

I understand the roots of this deeply ingrained worship of privacy. But I also know it was not just that.

What we were starting to realize is that in parts of Europe — particularly in France — there is a disdain for American justice. They think of us as wild, reckless cowboys, an image fed by the countless westerns that played incessantly on French TV when the current adult population was growing up. And *America's Most Wanted* was, for them, typical of what they saw as American vigilante justice.

Despite the disdain, Lena persevered, finding all the key players. (When she sent back pictures of Annika Flodin, Marilyn Beery, the original reporter on the case, blanched: "She looks," said Marilyn, "exactly like Holly.")

Lena's reporting was fast and detailed. A lot of the information you've just read about Ira's travels came from Lena's reporting. But there were more strange twists to come: when she found Eugene Mallon, he actually hit her, then ran away. The day after she interviewed the Swedish Interpol officer on the case, the officer committed suicide. (We later learned that he had apparently been planning this for some time and actually delayed the act to complete the *AMW* interview before he died.)

But the strangest turn of all, the one none of us expected, came on September 2 of that year, when a French court decided to delay extraditing Einhorn to the United States. I couldn't fathom this — why would they want a convicted killer roaming the streets of Champagne-Mouton? But anti-American sentiment was high, and Ira's lawyer successfully argued that Ira's case was tainted because he was tried and convicted in absentia. You see, in France, a convicted killer gets a new trial once he's captured; Ira's lawyer argued that therefore, sending Ira back to the States — where he would not get a new trial — would violate his civil rights.

He also lied. Or at least gave the court bad information. He said that if sent home, Ira would be put to death. We already knew he was sentenced to life, not death, but this pronouncement in the French courtroom fueled the vigilante American image, and the court started tilting in Ira's favor.

Ira almost screwed up the deal for himself when he tried to testify in his own behalf, delivering one of his crazy, ranting, rambling speeches until his own attorney politely told him to shut up.

While Ira sat in Prison Gradigana, deliberations over his fate continued. On December 4, 1997, he was released from prison and allowed to go back to his beautiful home, his beautiful wife, his beautiful life, just checking in once a week with the local gendarmes, while Holly's family sat five thousand miles away, infuriated, astonished, hurt beyond hurt.

Because, for the moment, for all intents and purposes, Ira Einhorn had gotten away with murder.

Steele Bennett was the producer assigned to keep contact with the Maddux family through this period, which he calls the time "when the hunt for Ira Einhorn changed to the frustration with Ira Einhorn." Steele was a good-natured young producer with a no-nonsense work ethic — a get-it-done kind of guy. "I stayed in touch with Holly's sisters," Steele said, "specifically Meg and Buffy, and also covered the bullshit legal stuff — getting random grab shots when Ira would make his weekly check-in at the police station."

I hated seeing Einhorn in those court appearances — sitting there, hands folded across his chest, grinning from ear to ear, like this was some big game that he knew he would keep winning.

In January of 1998, Pennsylvania Governor Tom Ridge signed into law a new bill that would grant Einhorn a new trial if extradition was approved. The U.S. government again pressured the French for extradition. It took several months, but in September Ira was rearrested. He stayed locked up only a week this time, but at least the French courts scheduled a new extradition hearing.

Einhorn, free as a bird, gave an interview to ABC, in which he spouted his theory that he was framed for the murder of Holly Maddux because he had discovered the secret mind-control projects of the CIA. I think he played as a liar or an idiot to American audiences — take your pick — but I was afraid that that sort of conspiracy theory would play well in France.

We also managed to get hold of one interview with Einhorn during this period and aired parts of it — although, I have to tell you, the idea of giving this murderer any air time for his self-serving pronouncements made me sick. Lance

Heflin, the executive producer, kept calmly explaining to me that the interview was news, that it helped us keep this case in the foreground, in the public consciousness; he argued, John, aren't you the one who's always telling parents of missing children that you have to do whatever it takes to keep the case alive? And of course, he was right — but I still hated letting that self-righteous windbag spout off on our program.

Here's what he had to say for himself:

"I was one of the best known people of my time, in the United States. A figure in the sixties who continued social activism for over fifteen years. But . . . I attracted an enormous amount of attention from the intelligence communities . . . I was under great threat."

He said that when Holly "disappeared," he didn't know where she was. "Two years later, she was found in a trunk in my apartment. I did not kill her, I insisted I did not kill her, but my reputation, which at the time had been totally positive through an enormous range of people in the United States, suddenly was blackened. The media jumped on me, and I suffered a media barrage that is really hard to explain to anyone in Europe. When we show people the amount of media that was directed against me, almost totally negative, most people, they shrug their shoulders, they can't believe it, they say, 'Why?' "

Excuse me. But, why?

Why, when a man with a history of violence

against women, who has a mysterious liquid dripping from his closet a week after his girlfriend's disappearance which turns out to be the fluid remains of a decomposing body, who would not let anyone look in that closet for a year and a half, who has the only key to that closet, who professes to be a man of peace and turns out to be guilty of murder, why would the press suddenly become negative?

Oh, I don't know, Ira. Could it be because you're a cold-blooded maniacal killer who is so crazy you've convinced yourself that no one with your reputation is capable of violence, and therefore you must be innocent? Have you actually convinced yourself of that? Are you that far gone?

"The greatest stress [when I was in jail] was being cut off from my source of nourishment. I'm constantly reading, and constantly studying."

My heart bleeds for the mind of Ira Einhorn.

"I'd rather be in the French judicial system than in the American judicial system," he said. "In France, I was treated like a human being. I have very little but praise for the French judicial system. I also want to add that I have been given enormous support in the community, here around Champagne-Mouton, and in Bordeaux. The people seem to understand that it is possible for somebody to be involved in a conspiracy."

He went on to compare his case, if you can believe this, to the murders of Martin Luther

King Jr., John Kennedy, and Bobby Kennedy, implying that there were vast conspiracies in all these cases, and that Ira Einhorn was so important and so dangerous that this conspiracy was launched against him as well, although for some reason in Ira's case the conspirators decided not to kill him, but to kill an innocent woman instead and pin the death on him.

My teeth hurt from watching this bum spew this claptrap on *America's Most Wanted*, but it did have exactly the effect Lance hoped it would: dozens of people called the hotline, incensed that the killer of Holly Maddux was thumbing his nose at the American judicial system, and that the French were not only allowing it but condoning and supporting it. The producers always used the Grateful Dead line to promote this as "the long strange trip" of Ira Einhorn, but to me, his was just a long, aggravating, heartbreaking, lucky trip. No mysticism to it, no great conspiracy, no brilliant fugitive, just a guy who was lucky enough to stay one step ahead of it all.

The appearances on ABC and *AMW* helped keep Ira in the public eye and helped keep the pressure on the American government to keep trying for extradition.

In December, for the first time — but sadly, not the last — the Maddux family ventured to France for a hearing on Ira's case. They knew that Holly's name had never been mentioned in the French courtrooms, and they didn't want Ira's ability to cast an image of the poor conspiracy victim to go unchallenged. There was a real victim in this case, and they wanted all of France to know it.

Someone was paying Ira's expenses, but rarely does anyone help out the family of the victim. So at their own expense, all four of Holly's siblings — eldest sister Meg, only brother John, younger sisters Buffy and Mary — made the long journey to France. They brought pictures of Holly, they talked to reporters. They started to get some sympathetic responses — but the question was, would they get any sympathy from the judge?

On the morning of December 1, 1998, the four of them sat in the courtroom, and saw Ira Einhorn walk in — not in chains, not in handcuffs, just a free man fresh from his morning croissant. It was the first time in two decades that they had sat in the same room with him.

In one of the more disgusting turns of the case, and one that shows the distorted image of Americans that exists in France, Einhorn's lawyers had prepared an image of the Maddux girls as these cowgirls from Texas who had to be treated as dangerous lawless barbaric creatures. It apparently worked, because the Maddux sisters were patted down for weapons before they entered the courtroom.

Ira Einhorn was not.

A convicted killer, he can come and go as he pleases. But three sisters and a brother of the victim — what did they think they were going to do, pull out a couple of six-shooters and take Ira down right there in the courtroom?

Still, they kept their composure.

"Surprisingly, I didn't really feel much of anything when he came through the doors," said Buffy. "It was the first time I really saw him in twenty-one years and the first thing that crossed my mind was, he's not as tall as I remember."

The family struggled to make eye contact with him, to tell him that they were there, that he could not hide from Holly's memory any more.

Einhorn would not look at them.

"He wriggled and fidgeted and kept looking away," said Buffy. "He even put his hand up [next to his face] at one point because we were staring at him. He looked nervous and uncomfortable with the four of us looking at him."

"He looked like a caged animal, from his behavior," said Mary. "Initially, after going into the courtroom, after being patted down for weapons, I walked in expecting to feel some sort of rage or something, or the hopelessness I'd been feeling for twenty-one years. Instead, I didn't feel anything, other than watching him fidget back and forth, feeling so uncomfortable at our being there. It was pretty disgusting, but it was also interesting to sit back and watch this accused murderer be such a coward."

The one who had the hardest time in the courtroom was John, the only surviving male family member. I know what he was going through; as the man, it's a natural tendency to want to be the protector. That's not a sexist stereotype, it's just hardwired into our central nervous system that we're supposed to be the protector, and try as you might to get beyond that, you can't, and when you're sitting a few feet away from the man who murdered your sister, a sister you were powerless to protect, it takes every ounce of strength you have to keep from jumping up and strangling him.

Which is just what Ira tried to goad the family into doing.

Toward the end of the hearing, he was allowed to make a statement.

"One thing," he said. "I did not kill Holly Maddux. *C'est tout* (that's all)." With that he let out a nervous laugh, and turned, and for the first time looked directly at the Maddux family members, and grinned.

"He was trying to provoke one of us into an outburst to make us look bad in front of the judges, and it was just so amazing, he really miscalculated, because we were all just amazed that he was that stupid."

The judge set January 12, 1998, as a date for his ruling on the case — meaning the family would have to return to France after the holidays — and as they left the courtroom, John told the other sisters he would not be journeying back. "I don't need to come back and be in the courtroom with him again," he told them. "I don't trust myself."

Believe me, unless you've walked in that man's shoes, you can't imagine how tough that had been for him.

A month later, the three sisters returned, this time accompanied by Lena, for what they hoped would be the final verdict. Lena could tell how tense they were, pushed by the adrenaline of making every moment of these visits count, pouring all their energy into keeping Holly's name and memory alive in the press — especially Meg, who spoke French and had developed a good rapport with the media.

Lena had developed a lot of "victim savvy" in her years at *AMW*, and she knew she had to help them keep from burning out, so when she could, she got them to take a moment off to enjoy themselves, to sit in a café, have a hot chocolate, do a little shopping, reflect on their surroundings.

On the morning of January 12, the three sisters, along with a lawyer they had retained as a legal and linguistic translator, stood in front of the courtroom, granting interviews to the gathered media, until the doors opened. Meg got swept into the courtroom with the crush of media; Mary and Buffy followed closely behind.

But as they approached the door, a gendarme stopped them.

"They need to go in," the lawyer said in French. "They are the sisters."

"I don't care who they are," he spat back. "You're not going in."

It was a crushing moment — to come all these thousands of miles and be denied access — but a more crushing blow came a few minutes later.

The sisters' lawyer was still arguing with the gendarme when the media horde, with Meg in tow, came rushing out.

"They've put it off," Meg told her crestfallen sisters. "They're not going to give a decision today. Without explanation, they put off the hearing for another month. Until February eighteenth."

"It was just another slap in the face," said Buffy. "I was extremely pissed off. We weren't expecting this. We had behaved very well. We were very calm, very deliberate, we had cooperated in every way, and we expected the same courtesy. And we were hit with this double whammy of, you can't go in there, I don't care who you are, and come back in a month."

There had been no prior hint that either of these were possibilities before they'd spent all their time and money to get to this hearing. The sisters felt like Dorothy and crew being turned away at the gates of Oz, trying to look behind the curtain for the phony prophet pulling all the levers and strings, but there was only more smoke and mirrors, more disappointments, more waiting.

Mary looked over her shoulder and said to no one in particular, "See you in a month."

Sometime after the holidays, I ran into Lena Nozizwe in the newsroom, and told her what a great job I thought she was doing covering the Einhorn case, and asked her how things were going with the Maddux family.

"When you hear this, John," she told me, "you're going to be very upset."

So we stood there and talked for nearly an hour; she told me about the sisters, and how strong they were being, and Einhorn, and how smug he seemed; and the more she talked, the madder I got.

First, I asked Lena for the sisters' numbers. I wanted to talk to them, to hear their story first-hand. I knew how hard this was for them, longing for justice and going years without hope, then having their hopes built up and dashed again and again. I knew how hard it was to fight a fight like this when your opponent has rich friends to help him, and you're counting the dimes to make your plane fare. I remember all the times I had to borrow money to come up to Washington for hearings on the missing child bill, and look around at all the people I was fighting against and know they didn't have to spend one dime to get there, how so much is done to preserve the rights of criminals, and nothing to preserve the rights of victims.

When I did make that phone call the next day — it was a conference call with all three sisters — I was struck by two things: how calm the family had remained, and how deeply they loved their sister. I've met ten thousand crime victims' families over the years, and I don't know many who could endure the twenty years of torture that these people had endured. They poured their hearts out to me, told me all about Holly, and their parents' deaths, and their brother's anguish, and the humiliation they had suffered in France.

And I knew what I had to do.

I made them a promise.

I told them that *America's Most Wanted* is the court of last resort, and that if they weren't giving up on finding justice in this case, then neither were we.

That afternoon, back at the office, Lance was holding a planning meeting with the executive staff, trying to figure out what to do for the February "sweeps," the time when the networks watch the ratings the most closely because they determine the advertising rates for the next three months. For us, it means there's a little more money available — and I knew exactly how I wanted to spend it.

The staff was planning a "world's most wanted" special, where we cover cases of fugitives from all over the globe who might be hiding in the United States. In connection with that, Interpol had agreed to grant us rare access for a feature story — at least not everybody in Europe was against us. Also, the producers were talking about sending a reporter over to do a short update on Ira Einhorn.

I said no, I want to go myself.

Immediately, I could tell the staff was nervous. Sweeps is a very busy time, and it makes it tough on everybody if I'm not easily available.

But this was too important.

I told Lance, here's how we can justify it: let me go over to Lyon and do the world's most wanted with Interpol. Nobody ever gets to show the inner workings of Interpol, so this will give us your exciting sweeps show.

And while I'm there, let me confront Ira Einhorn.

I'll track him down.

I'll find his quiet little garden, where he's sipping his lovely little wine, and I'll get right up in his face; I'll track down every last member of the French media and tell them the truth about this story; I will create such a ruckus that when I'm done the whole world will know what a liar and a coward Ira Einhorn is, and his little game will be blown.

And one more thing.

I want to bring the Maddux sisters with me.

The producers in the room began breaking down the details: logistics, cost, and how we get the tape back, who's going to produce and who's going to edit, and can we do this. But I glanced over at my partner, Lance, and I noticed that he wasn't saying a word, and I've worked with him long enough to know what that meant.

He'd give everybody a few minutes to catch up, but he had already made his decision.

He had heard how passionate I was.

And he was going for it.

We spread the word as fast as we could to all the media: come to France. Ira Einhorn is getting away with murder. John Walsh and Ira Einhorn are going to have a showdown on the streets of Bordeaux. The Maddux family is going to continue their intercontinental vigil to bring the name and the spirit of Holly Maddux before the French courts. We did everything we could think of to drum up some publicity for the case.

When I told the Maddux sisters that we were going to Europe to do two shows — one on the world's most wanted, and one devoted just to their case — they were beside themselves. But I also detected in their voices a note of guarded caution. Yes, the big cannon of *America's Most Wanted* was going to be pointed squarely at Ira Einhorn. But they'd been let down so many times, they'd learned not to get too excited.

Good, I thought.

Smart.

Keep it calm.

Because nobody knows what's going to happen over there.

Especially me.

We were traveling with a big crew and picked up some local camera and sound people in Paris, so by the time we got to work there were about twenty of us. Our first stop was Paris, to get the show done on the world's most wanted. We shot at all the recognizable landmarks — the Arc de

Triomphe, the Eiffel Tower — and knocked the show off in one day. Then it was on to Bordeaux for the showdown with Ira.

But on the train, somehow, the tapes for the Paris show were stolen. I didn't learn about it until I hooked back up with the crew in Bordeaux; you've never seen such a room of long faces. It meant that we'd have to reshoot the Paris stand-ups when we were done in Bordeaux. The staff was pretty morose about it, but Neal Freundlich, the producer in charge of the shoot, is an experienced veteran who knows how to use a little humor to keep his team loose. On the production sheet for the next day, he wrote:

"We'll always have Paris.

We just can't prove it."

In Bordeaux, I was finally going to get to meet the Maddux sisters. Meg, the oldest, wasn't able to make this third trip, and brother John had already decided that he just couldn't trust himself in the same room with Ira Einhorn anymore. But Buffy and Mary were there to represent the family, and I couldn't wait to meet them.

There is something that happens when I meet people who have lost a close family member to murder. It is a terrible club we all belong to, those who have lost children and siblings to violent crime. There is something that binds us, something no one else can understand — my wife, Revé, always tells me it's like trying to describe a color to someone who's never seen it.

But sometimes, when I meet other members of this terrible club, it is like we've known one another for years. Maybe part of it is because they've seen me on TV, and they treat me like they know me, so I start to feel the same way about them — but more of it, I know, is just that our shared pain, not the immediate pain of loss but the long, long pain that stretches out over the years of regret and sorrow, becomes such a part of your personality, such a part of your mind, that you recognize it instantly in others the way someone might recognize a long-lost relative or an old friend after many, many years.

And so, from the minute I sat down at the café on a Bordeau street corner with the two sisters, we were like family. This wasn't our TV interview moment; this was a moment for me, and for Mary, and for Buffy, a moment for three veterans of the nation's saddest war to raise a glass of wine, to toast those who were no longer with us, and to talk about the battle looming in front of us.

It was a cold, damp, dreary February day, so we moved inside and ordered some tea and desserts, and began talking about the logistics of the case. The French law is so full of twists and dodges, we really didn't know what to expect.

After the café, we went to a beautiful château in the hills, to sit by a fire and do a more formal two-camera interview. Again, there must have been twenty people in the room — producers, camera people, sound people; my wife, Revé, had joined us, and she was there, too. It was an amazing conversation: we went on for hours, the sisters pouring their hearts out: talking about Holly, how she would take them trick-or-treating and how she made a great stick horse; about their parents, and how they never recovered from Holly's death; about the toll this ordeal has taken on the remaining family — Buffy reminded me that she had been dealing with this for half of her entire life; Mary brought me to tears when she said, "I grew up overnight when I was nineteen years old, and I've felt a hundred ever since then." They told me how this has bound the four children so tightly together, they talked about their frustrations with the French judicial system — and all the while, they still maintained that air of quiet dignity.

But as they talked about the day, so many years ago, when they learned their beloved sister was found in a trunk in Ira's closet, something changed. Mary, who spoke in a very quiet voice, said she focused on the fact that Holly's purse, her belongings, her papers, were also found in the closet.

Suddenly, from this quiet woman, a shriek flew out:

"He kept her things as TROPHIES!!"

No one in the room moved a muscle. No one breathed. This quiet, deferential woman had loosened her fury, just for a moment, had let us see the terrible pain behind the dignified facade, had for just a moment let herself wail at the pain, at the sorrow, at the injustice.

I thought, what an amazing woman.

I thought, what a painful moment.

I thought, I can't wait to get this guy.

I did not sleep that night, going over the next day again and again in my head, worrying that Ira would slip past me, wondering if I was going to be arrested, knowing that this was not going to be some objective journalistic moment, this was going to be revenge for a beautiful young woman's family, this was going to be me, confronting a killer, man to man. That evening I had seen a quiet woman let down her guard and let her anger out, and how powerful that was. I wondered, here I am, the angriest guy in town on a good day — what's going to happen when I let my own guard down?

The morning of the showdown dawned crisp, clear, and cold, and the crew was up at 5 A.M., mapping out our battle strategy.

We had word that Einhorn was most likely going to be at his lawyer's office, two blocks from the courtroom, from which he could exit, walk the two blocks, turn right into a small alleyway, and enter the court through a rear door. We also knew that the courts, the lawyer, and Ira were totally unpredictable, and we had to be ready for anything. There was no way I wanted to let this guy get to court without a chance, for once, to confront him, to wipe that smug smile off his face.

The production team had staked out the area, a five-block radius around the courthouse, and had five cameras posted and ready at key points. Everyone was on walkie-talkie.

I walked to the front of the courthouse to check out the scene. As I've mentioned, there hadn't been a lot of attention paid to the case, so I was stunned at what I saw.

There was a sea of reporters out there, print people, cameramen, TV crews, radio. *Good Morning America*, Fox News Channel, *Prime Time Live* — everyone. It was a beautiful sight. There was no way that punk Einhorn was going to hide in the shadows anymore.

It was approaching 9 A.M., and I was starting to worry about Einhorn slipping past me. The silence on the walkie-talkies was deafening. No one had spotted anything. Then, suddenly, someone started talking, very excitedly, in French. Neal, the producer in charge, was succinct: "No fucking French on the walkies!" Another sputtering, staticky voice came back, in English this time, saying a heavyset man in a blue shirt and white hair, accompanied by a red-haired woman, entered a door a few blocks away.

I hightailed it to the block behind the courthouse. Steele, the producer who'd kept contact with the family, was outside the lawyer's door. We weren't sure he was in there. I was sweating bullets: what if he went out another door from this office, and walks into the courtroom from a front door?

We were virtually alone. Me, Steele, our camera crew, a few French papparazi who had followed me. It was quiet in the alley.

Then the door opened.

And down the three steps came two lawyers, followed by Annika Flodin clutching the arm of a pudgy, bloated, smirking, white-haired Ira Einhorn.

Time for the showdown.

I can't tell you exactly what possessed me in that moment. I just knew I wanted at him. I wanted at him bad. I knew I couldn't touch him, but I knew I could get in his face. I just wanted him to look at me, to look at another man, for one moment, to look into the eyes of someone who knew he was guilty, and who hated him. I wanted him to feel threatened, the way Holly must have been threatened. I wanted to shatter his protected, pampered little world for just a moment.

The blood rushed to my face. My heart was pounding. The temple-pulsing feeling of adrenaline filled my body, my senses all felt heightened — I could see, hear, smell intensely well, and all this energy centered in my throat, and I took one deep fast inhale and then let it all out.

"Einhorn! Einhorn! Why aren't you going back?" I was pushing my way through his entourage, trying to put my face an inch from his face.

One of the lawyers put his hands on my chest and shoved me away, shouting something in

French. I had no idea what he said, but I shouted out, "Too bad. Too bad."

Now I flanked Einhorn on his right, the lawyer between us, Annika holding Einhorn's left arm, pretending to ignore me. She seemed quite shaken; I felt bad about that — but there was no turning back.

"If you're innocent, why are you such a coward and you don't go back to face justice?" The lawyer kept trying to push me away. I jumped ahead and now walked backward, shoving a finger in Einhorn's face and shouting. "Why don't you go back? You're going to get a fair trial. They're going to give you another trial. Why don't you go back?"

The pit bull of a lawyer shoved me again, hard this time, trying to pin me to the wall. He was like a little gnat, buzzing around and trying to run interference.

I noticed out of the corner of my eye that the cameraman had stopped rolling for a second, running to get to a better position. Up to this point, I was being furious but not physical, and I was using no profanity, although the lawyer was cursing a blue streak. But in this moment when the camera was off, I leaned into him and said, "You push me one more fucking time and I'm going to break your jaw."

Suddenly, the pit bull lawyer steps aside and I'm in front of Einhorn again, walking backward, not impeding him, not touching him — I just didn't want to get arrested in this moment —

and I noticed for just a moment that the smug smile had dropped from his face, and he looked frightened, like the coward that he is. He looked back and saw that I had caught him, and he put the frozen smile back on his face and walked on. A crowd had started to gather around us, and Ira tried to look unconcerned.

"You're a coward! You're a coward! Go back! Go back! You're going to get a new trial, you coward!" It poured out of me, with fury and a vengeance.

I knew I only had a few moments left. I turned my attention to Annika. "Ma'am, how can you sleep next to him? Don't you know he killed his girlfriend? You could be next! Ma'am, I'm begging you!"

Then I noticed a strange thing. Ira had his left arm cocked, the way a man offers his arm to a woman, as though he were escorting Annika through the turmoil. But when they reached a tight spot where they had to squeeze through a crowd, he shook her off and pushed on alone, totally unconcerned about his wife, concerned only about himself, and I thought, well, that's what we always knew about Ira Einhorn, wasn't it.

They turned the corner to the back door of the courthouse, Ira holding Annika's hand now. He was rattled. He was shaken. I was behind him now, yelling, "You are going to face justice!" as I saw his pudgy back disappear up the narrow staircase.

I stood there for a moment, drained, breathless, feeling what few victims ever get to feel.

I felt, well, for whatever it's worth, someone finally said it to his face. For a moment, we ripped away the polite treatment, the kid-gloves reverence that surrounds this murderer, and we threw the truth in his face and forced him to look at it.

It may not seem like much, but when you're a victim of crime, sometimes there's nothing sweeter in the whole damn universe.

There wasn't much time to savor the feeling. I had to run around to the front of the courthouse. I was about to try to get inside when the crush of media spotted me, especially the French press, and I decided to hold a little impromptu press conference.

They're expecting the American Cowboy to spout some vigilante justice, but they weren't at all prepared for what I had to tell them.

I just told them to go get their facts straight.

You've got it wrong, I told them. Ira Einhorn has bamboozled you. He does not, and cannot, face the death penalty. I gave them a quick rundown of the facts of the case — how impossible it would have been for that body to be there and Ira not to know it — and they looked stunned. Clearly, Ira and his lawyers had been their only source of information.

The adrenaline was pumping like crazy now. This was what I had come here for. To confront

Ira. To shine a light on the facts of the case.

Then I felt a tug on my sleeve. It was Neal, our producer. It was time to go into the extradition hearing, to get the final decision.

Now there was a mad rush to the door. I noticed, by a side gate, my wife Revé and the Maddux sisters, standing together, pointing toward me.

The sisters are not forward people — but Revé is not shy. She told the gendarme guarding the gate that I was a member of the immediate family.

And in we went.

Outside the courthouse, after this mad rush of activity, things were quiet. Neal Freundlich sat down on a bench with Tony Zanelotti, a long-time member of our team, the man directing this shoot. The producer and director work hand in hand to pull off something like this, and they had done a fantastic job. Now they had a moment to relax.

Tony pulled out a pack of cigarettes.

"Do you think we can smoke here?" he asked Neal.

"What are they going to do," Neal replied, "extradite us?"

The courtroom was packed. Somehow, our interpreter had managed to work his way in and sat next to me. Einhorn's lawyers spotted me and tried to have me thrown out of the court-room; the bailiff came over, but my interpreter convinced him I was not going to be a disruptive force, and the bailiff walked away. Einhorn's lawyers were fuming, chattering away at the bailiff and pointing at me, but the judge, sitting on a high bench, looked down unconcerned.

I looked up at the judge, and out at the press of media in the room, and realized that for the first time, the judge has got to make his decision in the sunshine, not quietly in the shadows, and I let myself, for the first time, have a little hope that he would finally, finally do the right thing, and kick Ira Einhorn the hell out of France.

It all happens very quickly. The interpreter is whispering in my ear, trying to stay even with what's going on.

I hear a lot of legalistic mumbo jumbo, but then I hear the word we've been waiting for. The interpreter, whispering in my ear, in the middle of all this chaos, this intimate little voice telling me:

The judge is reversing his previous decision.
Einhorn is going back.

I don't know what came over me as I ran out of that courthouse. I was jumping up and down like one of my kids. Here I am, supposedly doing a courthouse stand-up like any normal reporter would do, and I'm giggling and bouncing like I just got out of school.

So while the other reporters were doing their stand-ups in front of their cameras, I was shouting at ours: "Yes! He's extradited! The best news! The best news! The French judge says in the courtroom if he gets a new trial and he doesn't face the death penalty, he's extradited. He can appeal. It'll be a long process. But justice has been served today! The French criminal justice system has done the right thing! It may be years before he goes back but the message was sent: Ira Einhorn, you can run, but you can't hide. You're going back to face justice. Great day. Great day."

I spun around, looking for Mary and Buffy. We hugged, and laughed, and cried. We got out the cell phones and called everyone who was hanging on the verdict: sister Meg, and brother John, and a special call went to Detective DiBenedetto, the true author of this day. We asked him if he was going to drink the rest of that bottle of wine now.

"No," he said. "That's for when he comes back here."

But on our end, we decided to allow ourselves a little celebration. Somebody came up with a bottle of wine, and some glasses, and we raised another toast, and took a moment to chat.

"You know what I'm thinking?" Buffy said. "I'm thinking, we got you cornered, you s.o.b., we got you cornered."

A little later, Buffy was more introspective. "It still makes me sad that my mom and dad never got to feel what I'm feeling now. I don't know if I'll ever be able to forgive him for that. But this is

God's way. I think they know. And I think they're happy."

We went back to meet the media horde out on the court house steps. Suddenly, they couldn't get enough from the sisters. Can we get some more pictures of Holly? Is it true that Ira was abusive to her? Can you tell us what else was found in that closet?

I stood on the side, and watched, and smiled as these two noble women finally, finally had their moment in the sun, and I realize that in a very real way, the sun shone brightest for Holly this day as well.

It's not over till it's over. While Ira Einhorn's appeals snake their way through the system, he still walks the streets of Bordeaux a free man. Einhorn lives just a hundred kilometers from the Spanish border, and there's always the chance he'll flee again. Still, the tide has turned against him. We hear that Champagne-Mouton has tired of him, that he was kicked out of his card club, that they're fed up with this pompous ass parading around their town like he owns the joint. The French press have soured on him as well; Mary's and Buffy's performance that afternoon turned the tide, brought the press around to realize that Holly is the victim here, not Ira Einhorn.

I found it ironic to note that, after all the fuss the French made about Einhorn being tried in absentia, a French judge last fall declared that a Nazi war criminal living in Syria would be tried in France for crimes against humanity — tried, of course, in absentia.

Around the time of that announcement last fall, while an extradition order for Einhorn languished on the prime minister's desk, a reporter from *Enquire* spent a few days with Einhorn. He did a big article, complete with pictures of a cheerful Einhorn romping around his villa; the Philadelphia D.A.'s office included this information in a plea to then Secretary of State Madeline Albright to intervene. "There is really no earthly reason why Mr. Einhorn should be able to cavort in the nude while the extradition order sits unsigned," D.A. Lynn Abraham wrote to Albright, who acted on the letter, expressing her concerns to authorities in France.

So slowly, slowly, the wheels of justice are turning. Holly's family, as always, remains patient and cautiously hopeful — "I am certainly not going to tap-dance on the prime minister's desk and say, 'Sign the paper,' " said Meg. "It's tempting, but I can't tap-dance."

Shortly afterward, the prime minister did sign the extradition order, leaving only the final appeals standing between Einhorn and an American jail cell.

The experience has changed the family in small ways and big ones: Meg, a nurse, works in a clinic, and "if a woman comes into the clinic with a kid with a runny nose or an earache, and has a black eye, I'll deal with the runny nose or earache, but that woman's not going to leave without me finding out about that black eye."

Christmas and Valentine's Day still carry a sad element, as do other random moments. The family still wonders, what would Holly think of this election? How would she like this color on me? How would her hair be graying? And they think about her when they feed Douglas the Parrot, who has been handed down to Mary now; Douglas the Parrot, who still sings, "I love you, I love you," just like Holly taught him, so many years ago.

7

The Angel
in the Windshield

After twelve years of working week in, week out, in the world of crime and violence, you could get a little cynical.

But I see miracles happen every day at *America's Most Wanted*.

They are miracles that lift the soul. Every time we bring a missing child home, safe and alive, you know that it was not just a television show, a viewer, and a telephone that made that happen, but something bigger than all of that.

But as many miracles as I've witnessed, the strangest of all was the story of Christopher Garza.

I don't know if you believe in angels.

I do.

And now Christopher Garza does, too.

Chris Garza, by his own admission, was no angel himself. He grew up in tough circumstances. When he was just two months old his mother, a Mexican immigrant trying to make ends meet by working hard, tiring jobs, decided she couldn't care for him and passed him on to her sister Joaquina to raise. Joaquina had two kids, including a newborn of her own, but she took in baby Chris.

Since they were about the same age, Chris and his cousin Sergio grew up like brothers. They loved to play basketball, and every day after school they'd go down to the community center gym and try to pick up a game. Aunt Joaquina would tell them to stay out of trouble, and the sports helped with that.

Other relatives would help out when they could: whenever Chris had an ear infection, his aunt Paula Garza would be the one who took him to the hospital. Aunt Paula held a special place in Chris's life and in his heart: she lived just eight minutes away on the bus, and she and her husband were his godparents. "She was like my second mom," Chris said. Chris often went to her house to eat something, play a little cards. But Aunt Paula was a diabetic and died of lupus at the age of fifty.

Chris became an exceedingly restless and troubled youth. He bounced around, attending a different school almost every year, and by high school he was partying a lot, and worse: he'd become a gang member and small-time marijuana dealer.

Then something happened that changed his life.

That something was Elizabeth Hernandez.

You'd have to call it puppy love: Chris was sixteen, and Liz just thirteen. But he was bowled over.

Chris met her during a few months he spent back living with his mom.

They'd skip school and go to Fantasia, a video arcade, or they'd spend time with Chris's family, eating and talking around his aunt's table. They were so young.

Liz's mom worked in a factory, and her dad in a bar. It was a big household: besides her and her two brothers and sister, her dad had six daughters from a previous marriage. Her mom's sister and her four children also lived with them — a total of fourteen children.

Her enterprising dad saved enough to buy his own bar and keep his pretty daughter in shiny gold jewelry, looking well-groomed and well-dressed. But he also kept her on a short leash — she always felt he was much stricter with her than with her older brother. She yearned to be free and loved to hang out with her friends and party. When she met Chris, she thought she was in love.

And they made the mistake so many young kids today make.

When Chris was eighteen and Liz not quite sixteen, she got pregnant.

And, like so many teenagers, they thought they could handle it. Liz thought the baby was her ticket out of her house, and the two kids had starry ideas in those first months. Elizabeth moved in with Chris at his aunt's house.

Now, say what you want about how irresponsible Chris had been to this point — and getting a teenage girl pregnant is about as irresponsible as it gets — but an incredible transformation came over him.

He became a man overnight.

He decided to do the right thing — to make the best of the situation and provide for his little family-to-be. Chris got himself a job working as a driver's assistant at a local firm called Globe Furniture Rental. They'd furnish rental apartments and then, when the tenant was done, they'd go and bring everything back to the warehouse. It was hard work, but it was fun, and it was honest. Chris had stopped dealing drugs, had stopped hanging around with his gang friends, and had turned an important corner in life.

He liked the work, he liked the driving, and he liked his partners. He started at $6.75 an hour, and after a month was given a dollar-an-hour raise. It wasn't quite enough for him and Liz to get their own place, and it must have been frustrating to spend his days furnishing the nests of so many other young people and not be able to afford one of his own. So the star-crossed lovers kept moving from relative to relative. Still, when little Jose was born, in August, Chris was ecstatic — although he knows now what a precarious situation he was in.

"I was happy. My sister had a son, and they

looked happy," Chris remembered. "I thought, this was a person I wanted to be with, so why couldn't we have a kid and be together? We thought we were adults once we had children. We were wrong in thinking that way and starting so soon."

I give Chris a lot of credit for at least taking responsibility for his actions, for trying to make a real life for him, for Liz, and for little Jose. But it's also a simple truth that parenthood is as difficult as it is joyous, and kids just aren't equipped, emotionally or financially, to deal with being moms and dads.

And soon the pressures began to take their toll.

The young couple started fighting more and more, and soon Liz moved home, back in with her parents, taking little Jose with her.

Chris felt lost without Liz, but he felt totally adrift without his son. He wanted to be a dad to Jose. His son's birth had changed him, steered him toward a clean, respectable lifestyle. He tried to stay in Jose's life any way he could. He'd give Liz money for Jose and would take care of him on weekends. Liz worked at a Michael's Arts and Crafts store as a cashier, and she and Jose soon moved into an apartment with a friend.

The two youngsters were now young adults, and their lives could not have taken more different paths.

Chris met a nice woman named Michelle who

was a little older than he and a little more stable than his previous girlfriend. Michelle had two girls of her own, and the two of them adored little Jose — who spent a few days a week with Chris — who had grown into a happy, chubby little child. With his soft dark eyes and ready grin, Jose captured their hearts; he was the brother that completed their family. Chris and Michelle, with the three kids in tow, would go to parks and to the playground, and to the swimming pool up the street. Whenever Jose was with Chris, the two little girls always wanted him to sleep over.

Soon Chris asked Michelle to marry him. They fantasized about a real family life together, maybe even including little Jose.

Liz, on the other hand, was partying more and more with her new roommate — and with her new boyfriend, Aaron Borrero, a good-looking young man with a cocky attitude who lived upstairs. Borrero was trouble. He was into small-time drug dealing, say the Seattle cops, and used drugs recreationally himself, as Liz did.

In February of 1997, Liz and Aaron moved to Pasco, Washington, about three hours away from Seattle, across the Snoqualmie Pass. Liz's sisters all lived in the area. Liz was pregnant with Aaron's child, still in the first trimester. And they had Jose, now two and a half years old. They rented room 28 in the Airport Motel in Pasco.

The two made a handsome pair.

Like Bonnie and Clyde, the police would later say.

The relationship between Liz and Chris had deteriorated. They saw each other only to exchange Jose, and were frequently angry with each other. Chris would keep Jose for days on end when he felt Liz was partying too much, and Liz resented it more and more as time went by.

Liz wanted Chris out of her life, and out of Jose's life.

But no one imagined how far she would go to make that happen.

By March, it had been a couple of months since Chris had seen his baby. So when Liz called on March 5, he readily agreed to meet her — even though it was almost eleven, the girls were sleeping, and Chris and Michelle had been settling in with some rented videos.

Liz was calling from a pay phone; she told Chris to meet her there and she'd take him to little Jose. Chris promised Michelle he would take his cell phone and call home later; then he jumped in his '77 Olds Cutlass and drove to meet Liz.

When she got in the car, she was quieter than usual, less argumentative. She directed him through the downtown streets, winding up on a road under the overpass of a major freeway. It was dark beneath, but even if it had been light, all Chris would have seen was dirt and garbage.

He stopped the car, and Liz got out, walking

away from the car and then back again, making this little cycle twice, as though she were trying to make up her mind about something, or perhaps working up the courage to do something she'd already decided to do.

When she came back to the car the second time, she opened the passenger door. He turned toward her and in that split second thought he had been hit by a brick.

It wasn't a brick.

It was a bullet.

Liz Hernandez shot the huge .45 caliber gun four times at the father of her child. At such short range, Chris Garza should have been a goner. But Liz hadn't shot the gun before, and she was a tiny girl, not strong enough to control its power, the recoil pushing her backward, making the gun swerve upward, her overcompensation in trying to correct her aim throwing the gun slightly side to side.

So he looks over at her as she opens the door and *bang:* a bullet grazes his left cheek, and comes out near his ear.

Bang: another bullet, this one to the right side of his face, again, a grazing wound. He goes to put the car in gear, and *bang:* Liz puts a bullet through his right bicep, blowing a rough chunk out of the top of it. He takes his foot off the brake, so he can race away, and *bang:* she hits him in the left leg.

Incredibly, with the car in gear and the brake

off, with blood gushing down his face, from his arm, from his leg, Chris's right foot finds the accelerator pedal, and the car roars away from the scene.

Liz stood, stunned for a moment, like a woman watching a dead man get up from his grave and drive away. She just threw the gun away and started walking up the hill to a bus stop. It took a while for the bus to come, and she stood there in the midnight gloom, contemplating what had just transpired. The bus came, and she got on, headed for a friend's house, where she spent the night. She had no idea whether Chris Garza would survive her calculated, murderous attack.

But there are some things you can't calculate.

"I've been shot! That bitch shot me!"

By an incredible coincidence, Michelle had picked this very moment to call Chris on his cell phone, and couldn't believe the furious, agonized words he was screaming into the small receiver. Bleeding, blind, in incredible pain, Chris drove on into the night, not sure where he was going or if he would ever get there, just driving, away from the woman who had tried to take his life, fearing that at any moment her murderous goal would be realized.

All of a sudden, the 911 operator is on the phone. Chris is scared. He doesn't think he can possibly live.

Stunned and dazed, not realizing what he's

doing, he hangs up.

He drives slowly, honking, in the middle of the road, trying to attract attention. No one stops. His fast-thinking girlfriend had given the police a lead on where Chris might be — he was, understandably, a little unclear on the phone — but they haven't found him. So he drifts slowly to a halt in the middle of the street, feeling like he is going to die then and there.

He sits, motionless, the car idling, his life slipping away.

And then he sees it.

An angel in his windshield.

The image of his aunt, Paula Garza, is above the steering wheel.

"Go ahead baby," she urges, "you'll make it."

The blood is pouring down his face. But she is so clear. His aunt Paula Garza, his mother's sister, the one who took him to the hospital when he was little and had an ear infection. The one who died too young.

And here she was.

Telling him it wasn't his time.

He is blinded by the blood that streams down his face, and yet his vision is clearer than ever, crystal clear, illuminated by a light that is not of this earth. He is wracked with pain, but he feels strangely peaceful, soothed by the grace of a loved one long gone, now suddenly by his side.

He put the car back in gear, and it lurched into motion, and he drove and somehow found his way to a nearby Veterans' Hospital. It had no emergency room or trauma unit. Before they could transport him to Harbor View, which boasts one of the country's top ERs, Michelle showed up, along with Chris's cousin Vicky. It was a bumpy ride to Harbor View, and all his bullet wounds hurt, so he joked with the medic to keep his mind off the pain.

The medics were able to stabilize him, and the next day a surgeon rebuilt his cheekbone.

He is lucky to be alive.

But he will be blind in his left eye.

And he still doesn't have his son back.

And Liz is nowhere to be found.

Dave Ogard was a young detective, just thirty-three, but he had more than nine years' experience with the Seattle police force. A tall, thin man with thin-rimmed glasses and a dry sense of humor, he'd been assigned to domestic violence back around Thanksgiving.

Around nine-thirty on the morning after Chris Garza's life was saved by an angel in the windshield, the case file landed on Ogard's desk. He started to review it: victim shot in the face repeatedly.

Within hours, Ogard got a tip — Liz was at the Airport Motel in Pasco. Room 28.

But when the police went to investigate, room 28 was vacant.

Liz and Aaron were gone.

And so was little Jose.

As in many major cities, the Seattle Police Department, the FBI, and other local law enforcement departments have formed a joint task force to facilitate capturing criminals. At that time, Seattle P.D. detective Chris Wrede was on the task force. Ogard knew Wrede from his patrol days. They also both moonlighted for Metro, Seattle's public transit system, which hires off-duty cops to ride around and throw sleeping drunks off the buses. Over coffee, on breaks, Wrede would tell Ogard that if he ever needed anyone arrested, to just call.

So he did.

Ogard knew the fugitive unit had tools for tracking people down that he just couldn't access. And once the case was in the hands of Wrede and the rest of the fugitive task force, everyone realized just how much danger little Jose was in.

Not just because he was on the run with his mom, who happened to be an attempted killer, who happened to be a fugitive from justice.

But because of the other person on the run with them.

Mom's boyfriend, Aaron Borrero.

When Wrede found out Borrero's back story, he realized there wasn't a second to lose.

Here's how dangerous Aaron Borrero is.

Less than two weeks after Chris Garza was shot, a drug dealer named Les Lemieux was kidnapped in a Seattle suburb. Les Lemieux — sounds elegant, but this guy was no prince. He dealt high-grade marijuana that he purchased from major distributors and sold to street level dealers. On March 19, Lemieux went to the home of a high school friend whom he occasionally dealt to, to make a buy. Aaron Borrero and another punk were there, too. The three ambushed Lemieux, hog-tied him with speaker wire, and put him in a duffel bag. They stowed him in the trunk of his own car and drove him to Yakima, in eastern Washington. On the banks of the Yakima River, Borrero and the other punk dragged him out of the trunk and dumped him from the duffel bag into the fast, cold water.

What happened next, strangely enough, is yet another miracle.

On the way down the river, Lemieux managed to catch a branch hanging over the water.

With his chin.

Then he managed to break the wire binding his wrists to his ankles and shimmied up the side of the river to the road, where he was rescued by some fishermen. It wasn't what they had expected to catch, this soaking, bound man, screaming at them to get away, because men would be back that would kill everyone.

Of course, the men didn't come back.

Aaron Borrero was on his way to California.

To meet up with Liz, who was already there.

With Jose.

Now small Jose is really in trouble. On the run with two violent people who had tried to murder in cold blood, not once, but twice; people who were not murderers only because God had graced each of their victims with a miracle.

When Wrede and his task force colleague Dave Burroughs, an FBI special agent, put this whole story together, they were appalled.

"They were like a little crime wave," says Burroughs, who has relied on *AMW* many times to get the word out about dangerous fugitives. "They had enough money and drugs to keep them going for a while."

Not your typical family vacation: her with a felony warrant for assault, with the caution "armed and dangerous." And him, wanted for kidnapping and "armed with pistol."

And Jose, with the big dimples and soft brown eyes, still young enough to blindly love and trust his mother.

Chris Wrede called Tom Morris, Jr., a reporter at *AMW* whom he'd worked with before. He explained the weird story, and the danger Jose was facing. Morris has four kids of his own, the youngest of whom is a beautiful boy he named Justice. That, and the strong relationship *AMW* has always enjoyed with the Seattle task force, prompted Morris to plead with the show's producers to get the unhappy family on the air immediately.

The show was already in the can for that week,

but Morris was insistent. Little children do not belong on the run with drug-dealing scumbags who throw hog-tied people into the river, with women who settle family disputes with a .45. His eyes were wide, his voice unwavering. "We have to get this little kid back," he said. "There is no telling what these people are going to do."

Now, we have a funny rule at *AMW*. Whenever someone becomes truly passionate about a case, we don't question why. We know that sometimes you just have to put logic aside and let the emotion take over.

So we did.

Fox always airs a very long commercial break about forty-five minutes into the broadcast of *America's Most Wanted*. As I mentioned earlier, they give us back about ten seconds in the middle of that break, to try to hang on to the viewers.

We use the time to sneak one or two more fugitives onto the show; this week, the ten-second "Break Four Tease" was going to be Elizabeth Hernandez and Aaron Borrero.

It wasn't much.

But at least it held out some hope for finding little Jose.

Dave Ogard knew his case was going to be on *AMW* that Saturday night, April 26, 1997. He stretched out in front of the television, and he watched. And he watched. And he watched. Finally, at the very end of the show, still pictures of Liz, Aaron, and baby Jose flashed up on the screen.

"Here's an urgent alert! This couple is wanted for two attempted murders. They're traveling with her little boy, Jose. If you've seen them, call 1-800-CRIME TV."

Ogard thought to himself, that's it?

Turns out, that was all it took.

The tip came into our hotline immediately: it was from three individuals who said they had met with Aaron Borrero in a remote area near a community called Lemon Cove, California. John Zapalac, who was then working for the sheriff's office there, checked out the tip.

The tipsters had given us a description of Borrero's vehicle, and Zapalac decided to cruise around to see if he could find it.

Being a smart cop with a good street sense, he didn't have to go far.

The first place he decided to check out was the home of a known drug user. In these circles, he knew, birds of a feather flock together.

And there, in front of the house, was Aaron's car.

He went into the house and confronted the resident. Yes, the little family had been staying there, but had gone to the abandoned firehouse across the street the night before.

Zapalac called for backup; soon they arrived, and he and his men fanned out, covering all the building's entrances.

It's a tense moment whenever you're making an arrest and there are children involved. You're always worried that something could go wrong, something crazy could happen, a child could get hurt.

Slowly, quietly, he pushed through the door.

There, on a blanket on the floor, lay Aaron and Liz, sleeping, with Jose between them. Aaron had dyed his hair with peroxide. But Liz had done nothing to alter her appearance, and Zapalac had enough information on her tattoos to make a positive ID.

They put up little resistance.

And before Zapalac left the scene, he had headquarters reach out to a terrified dad. They contacted Chris Garza and patched him through to Zapalac's cell phone.

"Is he all right?" he asked the sergeant.

He was assured that little Jose appeared just fine and was going to be placed in Child Protective Services.

For the first time in many a month, Chris let go a relaxed, happy sigh.

Elizabeth Hernandez and Aaron Borrero were immediately extradited to Washington, where Borrero stood trial for the kidnapping of Les Lemieux. He was convicted and sentenced to more than sixteen years in prison. He is now appealing his case.

Liz claimed she was innocent, right up to the day of her trial. But after hearing that the original assault, one charge would be upped to attempted murder, she pleaded guilty. She's in until 2005.

However, because of the guilty plea, she never spoke in court, never testified in any hearing. She never publicly admitted her guilt.

Until now.

This winter, our researcher Lydia Strohl contacted her in prison.

And she said what she has never said before:

Yes, she did it. She shot Christopher Garza.

Liz said that from the time she left Chris, he wanted her back. The arguments were not pleasant: she said that Chris sometimes became physical with her.

That fateful morning in Pasco, "I got up and decided I was going back to Seattle and shoot him. I had tried to make amends with him. I had had it, I wanted him out of my life, not to be bothered by him at all."

When she got to Seattle, "I went and I got a gun and I called him from a pay phone and I told him to come and get me and he came and found me on Beacon Hill. I told him which way to go.

"I had the gun with me the whole time. I opened the car door, the passenger side, and shot at him. I wanted to kill him at that moment. I shot, and he pressed the gas and the car started."

She says when she got back to Pasco, she had to tell Aaron what she had done, since the police had already called the motel.

Liz claims she didn't know then that Aaron was wanted for the kidnapping of Les Lemieux when he joined her in California. But then she says: "We were planning to go to Mexico. Aaron had caught a case, too, and so he was wanted, too.

"The house we got busted in wasn't the house we were staying at," Liz continued. "We were staying with a family living across the street. That night, we noticed cars coming around and that was suspicious. Aaron said get your things together, we're going across the street. Someone was going to bring a motor home and we were going to Mexico the next morning."

When the police came in, Liz didn't put up a struggle. "I was pregnant at the time. I was tired of running and I didn't care if I got caught. I didn't know what to do.

"They arrested all of us and took Jose away. I was extradited back to Washington and I sat in the county jail. I was going to take it to trial because I thought I could get off on it. It was only him saying it. I almost wanted to take the chance to see if I could get off."

She was convinced her lack of criminal history would help her with a jury. "I'm not a violent person. I had stopped being in a gang a long time ago. I had [Aaron's] baby while I was in the county jail. I just wanted to be a mother to my kids."

She seemed to be pleased to have finally admitted her guilt.

"I don't think I ever thought it was okay," she says, accepting her sentence. "I never said I did it, and I know it was wrong."

As you listen to her, you could almost believe Elizabeth Hernandez is sincere. That she just wanted to keep her kid together.

Until you talk to Chuck Lind.

Lind, the lawyer who prosecuted the case, has a simpler explanation for Elizabeth's motive.

He thinks Liz was put up to the hit and provided with the gun.

And that the motive wasn't love, or anger, or custody of Jose.

It was pure and simple greed.

Why?

It turns out that Chris Garza had a $75,000 life insurance policy.

And the beneficiary was one Elizabeth Hernandez.

She told Lydia that she never knew about it.

There are many things people in prison tell us.

I tend not to believe them all.

I do believe that Jose's life was saved by that whole series of miracles — the angel in the windshield who saved his father's life, the man who managed to catch a tree branch with his chin and survive to tell police how dangerous Aaron Borrero was — information that red-flagged this case for all of us — by excellent police cooperation, and, finally, by the tipsters who took their own lives in their hands by letting us know how to find these desperadoes.

But there was one more miracle to come.

The miracle of watching a little five-year-old boy be reunited with his father.

There was a huge crowd at the airport that day: Chris, Michelle, her two girls, Chris's aunt Joaquina, and even his mom. Detective Ogard, the cop who'd kept this case going from the beginning, was there, along with Detective Chaumness. They brought a white stuffed bear and "Welcome Home Jose" signs.

Chris was nervous, fidgeting, pacing.

The time for the flight to arrive came.

And went.

The plane was an hour late.

"Well, you waited this long, what's another hour?" Ogard joked with Chris.

He laughed, nervously. Maybe something was wrong. I know that when your child is taken from you, nothing will make you calm, nothing anyone can say to you, until you see that child in the flesh, wrap your arms tightly around him, hear his giggles in your ear, press his cheek into your neck. Jose had said he wants to go to McDonald's and then see *Jurassic Park*, and at this moment there is nothing else in the world that Chris could imagine wanting to do.

Michelle's little girls snacked nonchalantly on creme-filled cookies and graham crackers.

Finally, someone called out: "Chris, the plane's here." Everyone chimed in, in a singsong: "The plane's here! The plane's here!"

A full planeload of people came through the gate, but no sign of Jose. Chris stayed at the back of the pack of welcome-wishers.

Finally, he heard someone call out, "Here he comes!" Chris instinctively inched forward, and when he saw his little boy, alive and well, toddling along in a puffy Sonics jacket, his heart swelled. Jose looked tired and confused until he saw his father, and then his face shined like the morning itself, and he called out, "Papa!" and ran into his father's arms.

And that is why we make *America's Most Wanted.* To get to see moments like those.

And I'm sure that Chris's angel, Aunt Paula, was looking down on this wonderful moment, as well; looking down, and smiling.

I know Jose and Chris have a tough road ahead. Jose knows that his mom shot his dad and went to prison. And he will have to deal with that. Chris knows that his own past is not pristine. But that afternoon, while Jose was bouncing on his dad's bed, Chris told us, "I have to prove to myself that I can raise him the right way. God has given me a second chance to do it right."

And that, perhaps, is the greatest miracle you can hope for.

8

Terror in the Park

Joann Donnellan stood in the dark outside room 509 of the Cedar Lodge, and screamed.

In all her years as an *America's Most Wanted* producer, she had never been anywhere as creepy as this spot: a spread-out hotel, built on the cusp of a raging river on the edge of California's Yosemite National Park. By daylight, it was hard to imagine a more beautiful display of nature; but at night, it was a different story.

Building Number Five was completely separate from the main office building of the Cedar Lodge, which housed a restaurant and gift shop with employees' rooms above them. There were hardly any lights on the path from the office to Building Five. And room 509 was hidden on the ground floor under a stairwell. It was not visible from the highway. In fact, it was hidden from just about everything.

The camera's bright light suddenly flipped on, bringing the door of the room into harsh focus, illuminating scratch marks and a slight indentation, as though someone might have forced it open. Through the window, Joann could see the carpet had been ripped up, the beds and the rest of the furniture taken away. A stack of bedding lay piled at the back, near the entrance to the bathroom.

This is the room they stayed in — the woman and the two girls who had now been missing nearly two weeks. Joann realized that the furniture and the carpet must have been taken away by law enforcement, as part of the investigation.

But the scratches on the door? She looked at the other doors, none of which had the same marks.

Was it possible something had happened to the women here?

The light flicked off abruptly, and it seemed even darker than before. Some of the other reporters covering this case were actually staying here at the lodge, but Joann couldn't imagine it. The wiry, athletic young woman thought it was too scary, and her camera-and-sound crew — two grown men — were frightened, too. Better to face a two-hour, winding drive through the mountains to a hotel in Modesto than stay here, at this place, on this night.

It is too isolated, Joann thought.

No one would know you were here.

As if to punctuate the point, the manager from the hotel came up to the threesome. Even though they'd been turning their bright lights on and off for more than half an hour, she had just noticed them and had come by to chase them away.

Don't worry, Joann told the unwelcoming clerk.

We're going.

The insistent sound of the Merced river enveloped them as they hurriedly packed their gear, and Joann wondered: what if you screamed; would anyone even hear?

So she let out a yell, just to see if it could be heard. The river swallowed up the sound. Joann could scarcely hear herself; a scream probably wouldn't carry to the parking lot, let alone the hotel office.

As the crew packed up their gear, Joann turned back and looked at room 509.

This is the place, she thought.

This is where the women were attacked.

From an early age Carole Carrington was adventurous. As a student at Montgomery High School in Santa Rosa, California, in the 1970s, she was always on the go. Her mother, also named Carole, and father, Francis Carrington, tried to limit her extracurricular activities — after all, they had four other kids to take care of — but Carole couldn't keep herself from getting involved. Luckily, she had an uncanny knack for planning and organizing that allowed her to keep all of her plates spinning at once.

So it wasn't too surprising when Carole came home from school one day and said she wanted to study abroad. A speaker had come to the school that day from Youth for Understanding and sparked Carole's sense of adventure. A hundred students applied for the chance to join the exchange program; Carole was one of the few accepted. Destination: Argentina.

It was tough leaving her family, and her sweetheart, Jens Sund, too; but she believed that if they were meant to be together, their young relationship would survive the six-month absence.

The trip had a rocky start: the Carringtons had to make a special trip to the Argentine consulate in San Francisco to get a visa. Perón was still in power, and there were occasional shootings. That didn't deter Carole, any more than accidentally leaving her one allowed suitcase at the airport in Los Angeles. It took about six weeks for her parents to get it to her.

Luckily, Carole landed with a wonderful family in Cordoba, Argentina. The Cucco family had two daughters, one of whom, Raquel, was just a year older than Carole and a student in a local college. She shared not just her belongings with her new American "sister" but also her heart; the two would be friends forever.

When she came back to the United States, Carole resumed her relationship with Jens, and in 1978 she did just what her parents had done: she married her high-school sweetheart. The newlyweds spent their honeymoon at scenic Yosemite National Park.

Despite the fact that her family was wealthy, having built a successful real estate enterprise with shopping centers in thirteen states, Carole was determined to make it in life on her own two feet. So she finished a degree in business, got her real estate license, and was well on her way to fulfilling her dream of becoming a successful businesswoman. Carole's parents moved to a ranch outside of Eureka, and a year later Carole and Jens moved there, too, into a small bungalow. They didn't need a big house, they figured, because having kids was just not part of their plan.

But as they say, life is what happens when you're busy making other plans.

"When she got pregnant she was not too happy about it; neither was Jens," her mom, Carole Carrington, told us, chuckling a little at the memory — because once little Julianna Sund came into their lives, in September of 1983, the couple was totally captivated by her. "You'd have thought no one ever had had a child before," Carole Carrington said.

Little Juli was a little adventurer, just like her mom. Jens remembers hearing a thud one night when she was just six months old. It was the baby, who had fallen out of her crib. But instead of lying there and wailing, Juli picked herself up and crawled into her astonished parents' room. They were soon to find it was hard to stop her — her grandmother remembers that once Juli learned to walk, she ran. The two-year-old got a kick out of streaking naked through a roomful of adults. "She loved life," her grandmother remembers. "She just couldn't wait."

Carole and Jens saved up their money to take two-year-old Juli with them to Argentina to visit her soul-sister Raquel, who by now had married, too. She and her husband, Pepe Pellosso, had two daughters, seven-year-old Paula and three-year-old Silvina. The young mothers were so happy to see each other, and they passed their days happily in the Pellosos' tropical, sun-filled courtyard while the little girls played. During the two-month stay, Silvina and Juli became fast friends, just like their moms had so many years before.

Carole and Jens had another reason for going to Argentina. The couple had been discussing the possibility of adoption, and the more she looked into it the more it tore at Carole's heart — she never knew so many children were abused, so needy. Coupled with their newfound love of parenthood, Carole and Jens took passionately to the idea of adoption. They wanted to adopt an Argentine child, and had come to the country armed with letters, documents, and information, ready to go, but all in vain; the Argentine government had recently run into problems with international adoptions and was denying all adoption requests from foreign petitioners.

It didn't stop them for long. When Carole and Jens got back to California, they immediately went to work on adopting a child in Eureka; soon a little boy, Jonah, joined their family. When Jonah's birth mother had another child, the

Sunds traveled to San Francisco and adopted one-week-old Gina, too. They just loved kids, Carole's mom told us, and a few years later they adopted a two-year-old boy named Jimmy.

In the process of adopting all these children, Jens and Carole had to get certified as a foster home. Even after they reluctantly admitted they should adopt no more children and instead focus on the four they had, her big heart was never too full for a child. Throughout the years, the Sunds provided emergency housing to other foster kids, and Carole, convinced that these homeless, abused children were the ones society should pay the most attention to, threw herself into advocacy work. In addition to her job as a loan broker, she volunteered with CASA — Court Appointed Special Advocates — a group that helps make sure children are properly represented in the legal system. She worked with Adoption Horizon and Council for Adoptable Children.

The Sund home was the hub for all these activities and more. Despite the fact that her family was in real estate and so successful, Jens, Carole, and Company lived in the same pale green bungalow in Eureka, close to the kids' schools. The old house had been added onto and added onto until it had five bedrooms, and they added a pool to gather around in the summer. The kids all took piano and other music lessons and were all involved in sports. The house was a hive that buzzed with constant activity. Instruments played, phones rang, dogs barked, kids ran in and out with friends. There was a constant flow of rehearsals and practices and tryouts and lessons and field trips. And somehow, Carole kept it all under control. Carole was the undisputed organizer of everyone's schedules, the leader of the household. When Jens traveled for work, she always knew his schedule, sometimes even better than he — he'd call home at night and she'd say hey, what are you doing there? You're really supposed to be somewhere else.

Carole never missed a beat.

And there was no doubt that Juliana was her mother's child. Inheriting Carole's enthusiasm for joining, Juli took up the violin, dabbled in guitar, wrote poetry, and was on the cheerleading squad. On birthdays, her grandmother would take the birthday child to lunch at the mall, with a budget of $80. After lunch, Juli rushed her grandmother from store to store until, exhausted, they had to stop, because Juli was down to $1.79.

Juli also inherited her mother's can-do attitude and her compassion. She was troubled mightily by the disappearance of Karen Mitchell, a fellow high school student. Juli collected newspaper articles and photos of her in a scrapbook and hoped fervently that she would return. In her freshman year of high school, two of her fellow cheerleaders were raped at knifepoint, so Juli helped found a local support group, Girls Against Violence.

It was important to her that nothing like that ever happen to any of her friends again.

In Argentina, Silvina Pellosso was growing into a beautiful girl, too. She loved science, leaning toward biology and botany: she loved to plant things on the balcony of her family's home. She also loved dancing and roller skating, and put the two talents together, becoming an award- winning roller dancer, lining the shelves of her room with trophies.

When November and December rolled into Argentina, she jumped at the chance to take some time off to go to California and live for a few months with her family's friends, the Sunds.

Silvina arrived in California in early December 1998. Jens Sund was impressed with the quiet and polite girl, who was ecologically astute and, as children from other cultures often are, more aware and thoughtful than the average American high school kid. She dove right into the whirl-wind of activity at the Sund house.

She told her parents that she was having fun but was having a little trouble connecting with some of Juli's friends. She was self-conscious about her English, and that made her a little shy getting to know people. She went to classes and school dances with Juli, though she wrote her mom that the American boys couldn't dance to a Latin beat.

But she felt at home in the Sund household, where pictures hung of her mother and Carole from college, and of her and Juli as babies. And as they were then, the two girls, who even looked alike with their long, brown hair and rangy frames, became fast friends again.

Carole expertly worked Silvina's tourist needs into the jam-packed schedule. They took her to see Fisherman's Wharf in San Francisco. She saw the redwood trees and went to Disneyland. When it snowed, Jens took Silvina up to the Carringtons' ranch to see her first snow. She quickly picked up skiing and snowboarding at nearby Mount Shasta. The family, plus Silvina, spent the Christmas holiday at the ranch. Juli and Silvina made a gingerbread house together. They shot target practice, and Silvina shot better than the boys.

But the big trip would come during the long Presidents' Day vacation. It was to be the highlight of Silvina's trip.

Carole would take the girls to the place where she and Jens had spent their honeymoon.

The most beautiful, and peaceful, place on earth.

Yosemite National Park.

It would be, Carole thought, the trip of a lifetime.

The Sund kids would all have that entire week off from school, so Carole went to work on her computer, scheduling the week down to the hour, making three different drafts of the schedule before deciding on the final plan. On

414

Friday, February 12, Carole, Juli, and Silvina would fly from Eureka to San Francisco, where they would rent a car and drive eighty miles to the University of the Pacific in Stockton, California, so that Juli could participate in a cheerleading competition the next day. On February 14, they would drive more than two hours to El Portal, just outside Yosemite National Park, where they would stay at the Cedar Lodge. After two days of sightseeing at Yosemite, they would stop back in Stockton so Juli could meet up with a neighbor from Eureka and tour the University of the Pacific campus. After the tour, they would go back to San Francisco and meet Jens and the other kids at the airport on the night of Tuesday, February 16. From there, Jens, Silvina, and the three youngest kids would fly to Phoenix to visit Jens's sister and see the Grand Canyon.

It was a daunting schedule. But daunting schedules were Carole's strong point. Everyone knew she could pull it off.

The trip was going great: Juli had a wonderful time at the cheerleading competition that weekend, and on Sunday, they all drove up to the Cedar Lodge in the red Pontiac Grand Prix Carole had rented at San Francisco International Airport. She and the girls were given a room in one of the six guest buildings. It was the off-season in Yosemite and the end of the holiday weekend: not only was there no one in the room next to theirs, there was also no one else staying in the entire building.

Carole, Juli, and Silvina spent Monday in the midst of the stunning beauty of Yosemite. It appeared, on that day, as it had appeared to the young honeymooners twenty years before to be a place of timeless beauty, a place where you can sit quietly and feel that you are in the palm of God's hand.

But sitting quietly was not a big part of the day's schedule. Carole and the girls took pictures, went ice-skating, and bought souvenirs. It was a full day of fun. Francis Carrington, Carole's father, said later, "They were having the time of their lives."

That evening the threesome returned to the lodge and rented a VCR and some movies from the front desk. Carole called Jens and told him that they were going to spend a few more hours at the park in the morning before heading to the University of the Pacific tour. She was a little concerned about staying on schedule because of some construction at the entrance to the park, but she was going to give it a go anyway.

After the phone call, the three ladies walked over to the restaurant building and had dinner in the lodge's old-fashioned diner. Juli and Silvina had hamburgers. Carole had a veggie burger that she didn't finish, so she had it wrapped to go. At about 7:35 P.M. they left the diner and made the walk back to their room to relax and watch the movies. Carole left her doggie bag behind. The waitress held on to the bag, thinking she might come back for it.

She never did.

February 16, 1999, was a stormy day in Northern California. Jens took the youngest kids to the airport to meet Carole, Juli, and Silvina's plane. He had to stand around for five hours, because the flight was delayed. Carole tries to plan for every possibility, he thought, but there's no way she could have planned for this.

Life is what happens when you're busy making other plans.

It was about 10:45 P.M. when the plane landed. The schedule had gotten too tight — Jens was worried about making the last plane to Phoenix, for his part of the vacation, the trip with the three younger kids to Phoenix and the Grand Canyon. A little nervous, Jens and the kids watched the stream of people leaving the plane, waiting for his wife, waiting for his beautiful daughter, waiting for her sweet friend.

But the last of the passengers departed, and the flight attendants, and the pilots.

And the three women weren't on the plane.

Jens took a moment to page Carole, but she didn't answer. He didn't have much time to worry about it — they had ten minutes to take the last plane to Phoenix that night, and he decided to go for it. He took the kids and made the plane. Once the plane was in flight, he used the airphone to call home.

There was still no answer.

When they arrived in Phoenix, there was still no word from Carole. Maybe it was the construction at Yosemite, combined with the winter weather. Jens was puzzled, but not too worried: he knew that Carole would put a backup plan into effect. She could handle anything.

Or maybe he was just mixed up. It had happened before, as it can happen to men who are married to very organized women and who become a little less organized themselves. Jens traveled a lot for work and a few times actually boarded a plane headed for the wrong destination. After that, Carole always left him printed itineraries. He wouldn't have been at all surprised if Carole called him, saying, "What are you doing? How did you get the days mixed up? Why did you go to Phoenix a whole day early?"

That's what he was hoping, anyway.

With no way to get hold of her that night, he went to sleep, sure he'd hear from her on Wednesday.

He didn't.

And in that moment, for the first time, Jens was truly worried.

Sure, Carole would find a way to get back on schedule, but she would have told him her plan by now.

We know this moment all too well at *America's Most Wanted*. Whenever someone disappears for more than a few hours, there are those first moments when your mind starts looking for the logical explanations. You do not want to believe that anything is wrong. Surely there has been some misunderstanding. Surely everything is all right. You keep hearing your loved one's voice in your head and trying to will that voice into a telephone call.

But no call comes.

And you know, in your heart, that something is wrong.

Your head will not accept it, but your heart is beginning to pound, and someplace deep inside, you know.

Something is terribly wrong.

Jens called the Cedar Lodge; they said it appeared the trio had left. They hadn't checked out at the desk, but their car was gone and the room key had been left in the room along with the VCR, the tapes, and some personal items. Jens asked them not to remove anything else from the room.

He called Carole's office. He called Carole's close friends. He called her parents, Francis and Carole Carrington. They had just gotten back from a month-long trip to Brazil, and they hadn't heard from their daughter at all.

Finally, that evening Jens called the California Highway Patrol and told them what he had been so reluctant to accept.

He said the terrible, terrible words, words that, in all the years I've worked with the National Center for Missing and Exploited Children, we know too well, because we hear them over and over again, always from voices choked with panic and fear, voices strained from the burning desire not to speak those words:

My wife.

My daughter.

Her friend.

They are missing.

When Carole Sr.'s father, Francis Carrington, heard the news, he called the local sheriffs' offices in the Yosemite area and told them of the women's disappearance. They all told him the same thing: wait forty-eight hours before you start to worry.

I said it earlier, and I will say it again: if I could will one change into the world, if I could shake every cop and sheriff and state trooper and park ranger in this country by the shoulders and scream into their faces and get them to understand one thing, it is this: when you get a report of a missing person, do not wait! I know that resources are strained, I know that most of the time the so-called missing person shows up a few hours later, with a mouthful of apologies and sad stories of broken-down cars and lost maps and closed roads and snowstorms and bad directions. But all you have lost, if you trouble yourself to investigate these nondisappearances, is some time.

What you risk losing, if you do not investigate right away, is so much greater.

Immeasurably greater.

And besides, Francis said, it had already been forty-eight hours since anyone had heard from his daughter. And Francis knew Carole: "If she is ten minutes late," he said, "she would call."

The park authorities agreed to check into what could have happened to the women, and told him to try to get some sleep, and not to worry. He tried to take the authorities' advice, but he went to bed that night feeling as worried as can be. He knew his daughter. He knew there would be no simple explanation. "You just have this feeling," he said. "Down there."

He finally got up at 3 A.M. and started packing up his truck. He wasn't sure what he was dealing with, so he prepared for every eventuality. He packed a first-aid kit and water. He packed material to start a fire. He packed a heavy rope for towing another vehicle.

Then he started the eight-hour drive from Eureka to Yosemite.

A father, driving through the night, desperately hoping he was being a foolish worrywart, and knowing in a father's heart that he was not.

A father, driving through the night, to rescue his daughter, his granddaughter, and her lovely young friend.

A father, driving through the night, not knowing where his daughter is.

The loneliest drive in the world.

When he got to Yosemite, the first thing Francis did was stop at the Mariposa County sheriff's office. They were going on the assumption that there had been an accident, and deputies were already searching along the river. As Francis continued to Cedar Lodge, planning to make that his base, he spotted a patrol car, driving slowly, taking care to look over the steep hillside for any sign of the women. Francis did the same on his way to the Cedar Lodge, looking out over all the overpasses, from which he could see the river almost continuously.

He couldn't believe they had strayed off into the river.

But then, where were they?

At the Cedar Lodge, Francis rented a room from the desk clerk, then asked if she knew anything about Carole and the girls. She was extremely rude and turned away as he was talking to her. He shrugged, and walked to his hotel room.

As he walked, he noticed two of the maintenance men peeking around the corners at him. It gave him the creeps, but he had to stay there. Jens was on his way, too, along with his brother-in-law Ron; they had dropped the kids off at Jens's sister's, and this was the spot where they planned their rendezvous.

When Jens and Ron arrived, they came in with news of a sighting on a nearby road. Francis, who had the only four-wheel drive vehicle, went to check it out, and asked Jens and Ron to talk to the suspicious maintenance men.

And so it started, the sometimes innocent and

sometimes not-so-innocent web of tips that surrounds any missing-persons investigation.

In this case, a clerk at a nearby motel had reported seeing Juli and Silvina on Wednesday, the day after the disappearance. They were sure these were the same two girls who popped in to inquire about the cost of hotel rooms. When the hotel told them that a room would cost $75, they said it was too much and left.

But Carole had credit cards and plenty of cash. And, thought Francis, $75 wasn't too much.

It was now three days since the women had failed to show up at the airport, four since they were last seen at that restaurant — and finally word was beginning to spread.

Bulletins were broadcast on the radio, and several people throughout the region reported seeing one or more of the missing women driving on the road, shopping in gift shops, filling up at gas stations, getting information at hotels and motels. "Of course, they were all wrong," Francis told us later.

He doesn't blame anyone. "People want to help," he said. "But it set the search in the wrong direction."

Back at the Cedar Lodge, a deputy with Mariposa County did a preliminary search of the room. She found no evidence of foul play or a violent struggle. There was no luggage or clothing in the room, but there was a paper bag with some food and souvenirs from Yosemite. It wasn't like Carole to leave things behind in a hotel room — yet here were the souvenirs, the room key, the videotapes.

Francis and Jens were stumped.

Then on Friday investigators got their first break in the case. A girl walking to school found part of Carole's wallet — the insert containing her identification and credit cards — in the median strip of a street in Modesto.

A street two hours from Yosemite.

The discovery of the wallet elevated the case. Now no one could deny this was more than just a family taking an unannounced extension of a vacation. Something had gone terribly wrong.

With the wallet suggesting the possibility of foul play, the FBI came into the case and set up a command center at the Doubletree Hotel in Modesto. They looked at all the angles. Carole was driving a nice car, so there was always the possibility of a car jacking. The Carrington family had money, too, so even though there hadn't been a request for ransom, it was possible there had been a kidnapping. They advised the family to offer a reward, and Francis did: $200,000 for the safe return of his beloved women.

The world, it seemed, converged on Modesto overnight. Jens and Francis, who had been begging people to talk with them about their family, were now being bombarded by media. It is the double-edged sword that I always talk about. When a family member goes missing, you desperately need the media to pay attention to get the word out, because there is no other way you know to find them. But the media also become a devouring beast, eating up all your precious minutes and seconds, when every part of your heart wants to spend every one of those seconds searching, hoping, praying, walking the streets and combing the woods and screaming your child's name.

All families of missing persons develop this love-hate relationship with the media, and Jens Sund and Francis Carrington were no different. They set up a command center at the Holiday Inn in Modesto and learned the ropes quickly: it was best to hold one press conference a day to answer questions, so they could be out searching the rest of the time. Jens was more attuned to the media's needs, staying up around the clock, doing interviews if asked; anything to get the word out. Francis, at first, didn't see the sense in this and thought the media was intrusive.

So as we jumped into the case, Joann Donnellan, our missing-child coordinator, gave each of her field producers the same charge:

This is *America's Most Wanted.*

Remember that we are not here just to get a story.

We are here to help.

Jens, I think, understood this from the start. He welcomed our crew to come along with him. A family friend who owned a plane had taken to surveying Yosemite from the air, looking for the red car, and he invited Joann's crew to join him.

When the footage came back, Joann was screening it in her office, and I remember how achingly painful it was: staffers would pass by her office and look at the footage of acres and acres of park-land, and they would stop and instinctively start scanning the footage themselves, as though there was something that Jens and the pilot might have missed. Again and again, they stopped the tape and said, look, does that look like a car?

But again and again, there was none.

After the plane search, Jens spent hours traversing the park on every road and path accessible to a four-wheel drive. He was a quiet man, soft-spoken but determined. He seemed to believe that patience and persistence would give him the answers he so desperately sought.

He made a plan and tried to carry it out to the letter. After all, that's what Carole would do.

I called Jens and the Carringtons during that time, just to see how they were, and to offer support. First, I asked how our team was working out. They told me, as they would say often during this ordeal, that Joann and her crew were great at keeping them calm. I was grateful for that.

But I was worried about something else.

Jens and Francis were very upbeat, very excited about the discovery of the wallet, hoping that it would provide them some answers soon.

And I knew I had to warn them.

People tend to be glad when they see the parents of missing children get excited and upbeat. That's the spirit, they tell you. Keep your chin up.

But there is another side, and I thought that Jens and Francis needed to hear it straight, from someone who's been there, and from someone who's been through it with hundreds of other missing-child families.

"You need to know about the other side," I told them. In a case like this, the high that a new lead gives you can be just the peak of a roller-coaster ride. You are going to go through depression and despair like you've never known. It might be followed by bursts of elation and promise. But nobody's gonna tell you this but me: you are going to be miserable and frightened and depressed, and unless you promise yourself that you will keep eating, and keep exercising, and keep your strength up, then you are going to fall apart at the seams. I've seen it a hundred times. It's your job to keep your strength up, I told them. For Carole, and for Juli, and for Silvina.

I knew these were harsh words.

I didn't want to be saying them. I wanted to be offering encouragement, to be saying, don't worry, Jens, we'll find your wife and daughter; leave it to us. Francis, we'll bring your daughter and granddaughter back; call the folks in Argentina, tell them we'll bring Silvina back.

But I knew that in that moment, what I could offer best was the truth: this is going to be the most painful, gut-wrenching, fear-filled time of your life, and the odds are against us, and you should be prepared for yourself, and your loved ones, to fall into the darkest depressions, and all you can try to do is be ready for that so you can, with God's grace, drag yourself out and keep up the search.

I hoped I was doing the right thing by preparing them for these harsh realities. Much later, Francis told one of our researchers that the advice I gave him helped a lot. I'm very, very grateful for that.

But when I hung up the phone, I thought, you know, three women, with a history of accomplishments and self-discipline, do not just disappear off the planet. Molesters do not keep grown women alive for very long.

I didn't think these women were going to show up alive.

It was time to get to work and figure out what happened out there.

The days dragged on without another lead in the case, and the search went on, but something else was happening in Modesto, too, something wonderful, the proverbial silver lining. In those dark days, in the seam between winter and spring, the Carringtons' home base at the Holiday Inn was bombarded not only by the media but also with volunteers. They brought plants, cards, and muffins, which overwhelmed a large table at the entrance to the room. They set up computers and manned phones. They gathered everyone who was willing to help and coordinated their own search efforts to assist the National Park Service, the Mariposa County deputies, and the California Highway Patrol, all of whom were actively searching the areas in and around Yosemite. They printed and distributed fliers in Modesto and near Yosemite.

It was a community, a community of help and healing, that had sprung up in response to a tragedy.

And it was a community that was growing every day.

Francis Carrington was the leader of this strategy room. We followed him as he charted out searches on a large map, and he and Jens flew search missions high above the Yosemite area. Silvina's parents flew in. By February 24 — ten days after anyone had heard from the women — there were more than a hundred searchers joining law enforcement in a meticulous search of Yosemite.

The FBI determined that Carole was the last person to use the credit cards, back on Valentine's Day at the Cedar Lodge. How the wallet insert came to rest at an intersection in Modesto was still anyone's guess, but the investigators did not believe Carole lost it there. There was still no sign of the red Grand Prix; though the license plate was broadcast throughout the region, no one had spotted it. The mountainous area was dense with trees, but there were only so many places that a car like that could go. The searchers had discovered nine abandoned vehicles in their search, two of which were reported stolen.

But not the Grand Prix.

By February 26, the search in the hills was scaled back. "They are gone," was the official word from James Maddock, the FBI agent in charge of the investigation. They had no idea where Carole, Juli, and Silvina were, but they were confident they weren't in Yosemite National Park.

February slipped into March, with no new sightings and no new clues. By this time the volunteers and law enforcement had taken about 1,300 tips, but only a handful were deemed helpful. Francis Carrington offered another $50,000 for anyone who could even just find the cherry red Grand Prix, and the media broadcast the reward far and wide.

Nothing.

The FBI gave polygraph tests to members of the family — standard procedure, just to make sure they weren't involved in the disappearance. All of the family members were happy to get the tests out of the way and passed with no problems.

But when no new facts could be found, the rumors started to surface.

There are lots of people who move to the hills near Yosemite to get lost. The locals call them "runners": running from the law, running from their enemies, running from their friends. They are mostly drifters and druggies. A lot of the runners know one another — but not too well. They may know enough about one another to meet at a local dive and have a few drinks together, maybe score some marijuana or some methamphetamine — meth, also known as crank, a powerful drug, was the local drug of choice — but they were misfits and loners by nature.

Many of these drifters had outstanding warrants or were on probation for some crime or another. It certainly wouldn't be far fetched to think that one of them would carjack a tourist, especially if they were hopped up on crank.

Tips started coming in to the FBI that some of these runners were telling stories. That maybe they knew something. And some names started coming up more often than others. On March 5, the police jailed Billy Strange, a night kitchen janitor at the Cedar Lodge, for parole violations. Another man, a fellow named Eugene "Rufus" Dykes, was arrested after a standoff with deputies. And that was just the beginning of the roundup.

The next day, we decided to air a comprehensive story on the case, filling our viewers in on every detail, seeing if someone could spot something the rest of us missed, or — as I desperately hoped — if someone who knew something would experience the family's anguish and resolve, and be moved to call us. The fact that you can call the *America's Most Wanted* hotline anonymously leads to a lot of information that otherwise wouldn't come out. After thirteen years, I still ask the writers to make sure we mention our guarantee of anonymity at least once in every show.

On that Saturday night, we began at the beginning: showing how the files Carole left on her computer, along with the details of eyewitnesses, gave investigators a minute-by-minute account of where the women were and where they should have been. We showed the FBI's search headquarters and the equally impressive command center that was set up by the family. We showed videotape of Juli and her cheerleading team competing in Stockton.

We followed Jens, flying high above the hills, binoculars in hand, searching desperately for the car. He told us: "What goes through my mind is, the longer it gets, the worse it could be. I'd heard from Mr. Maddock before that it was unlikely that they'd be found alive."

The truth was, though he'd heard Maddock, Jens didn't really believe him. He couldn't. When the piece aired, we could all see in Jens's eyes that the concept of his wife and daughter being killed was still incomprehensible to him. He was working so hard, he was talking with the media on a daily basis to keep the story in the public eye, and he still believed — truly, truly believed — that he could find them alive. The FBI agents had been trying to prepare him for the likelihood of their death, but they knew he still wasn't getting it.

I know this all too well. I remember one time that a member of our staff came to me. He had a missing stepsister — she'd been missing for many years — and still his stepmom refused to believe that she might have met with foul play. She was convinced that her daughter was being held by a cult, and spent every penny she had hiring detectives and psychics to try to penetrate every cult she heard about on the evening news, until the family was broke. Her stepson called her one day, and as gently as he could, told her that maybe she had to consider the fact that her daughter was no longer alive.

Within hours, he got a furious phone call from his father.

"Why did you tell Mom that Jackie is dead!" he screamed. "Now she wants to kill herself. Please, call her back and tell her you didn't mean it!"

The staffer came to me and, tearfully, told me of the experience. Had he done the wrong thing? Should he never have brought up the possibility?

I reassured him that he had done nothing wrong, but he had to understand that for parents of missing children, or husbands of missing wives, the part of your brain that does not want to believe the worst is very, very powerful, and that once a person is forced to face those dark thoughts, they may not be prepared for the torrent of emotions that will inevitably be released.

And that is just what happened to Jens Sund when, on March 10, the FBI sat him down again and, as kindly and gently as they could, tried to prepare him. They told him that, given their experience, they did not think it likely that Carole, that Julie, that Silvina could still be alive. That there was probably a violent crime, and that whatever happened, the women probably didn't survive.

And at that moment Jens finally allowed himself to hear them and to believe them, and a volcano of emotions, the emotions he had been suppressing since the night they didn't show up at the airport, finally began to come to the surface.

And he lost it.

That night, Jens told the press that the FBI had told him something awful. He said he couldn't reveal the details of the briefing, but he told reporters, "I'm devastated. My worst possible fears have come true." The media scrambled, thinking there had been some new discovery. They pressed him for details.

"It doesn't look good for my family," was all he could say.

The next day, an exhausted Jens apologized for his misleading statements. He told reporters that he overreacted. The stress was getting to him, and he "just couldn't hold up every day."

Although it was Francis Carrington who at first disdained the press, leaving it to Jens to handle the crush of interview requests, he could see that his son-in-law's nerves were fried, and it was time for him and his wife, Carole, to step up to the plate.

He told Jens, you've been honoring every request for interviews, from morning till night, and you just can't do it anymore. You've searched every acre of these woods yourself, from the air and on the land.

You need to take a break.

Your other three kids have been with your sister all this time, and they need their daddy now, now more than ever. And Jens, you need them, too.

So Jens passed the torch to Francis and Carole Carrington and went home.

Without his wife and daughter.

Media interest started to lag once Jens left the command center. Francis could tell that even the local law enforcement agencies were starting to give up; searches in El Portal, Modesto, and Yosemite were being scaled back. He knew he had to do something to reenergize the efforts. "The first week, everyone is interested," Francis told us. "Then they say, 'We've driven all the roads. We have other cases.'"

The Carringtons are not flashy people; they are decent, fair, and quiet. I never once saw either of them raise their voices in anger through all their ordeal, though there were a hundred times they could have; they are not overly demonstrative, and not at all the type to be comfortable playing the media hog. Nevertheless, they knew that to solve the case, they needed to keep the public's attention, and the media's attention.

So they decided to do it in their own dignified way, by staging a Vigil of Hope at a local park. They would have other parents — parents of other missing children — come and speak.

The turnout on March 14 was incredible and heartwarming: some 1,500 people came to the Modesto vigil.

Francis spoke first, talking about the terrible question a parent of a missing child must endure, a question for which one answer drives you to tears, and the other drives you insane: do you believe they were victims of foul play, or an accident?

We all knew the answer: as horrible as it sounds, you want to believe they were kidnapped.

Because that possibility holds out a glimmer of hope.

"As a father, I could imagine them rolling off the road, having no water," he told us later. "But we knew as time went on, there was nothing we could do about it if it was an accident." The only way to keep some glimmer of hope alive was to consider it an abduction. Even in that case, they might not still be alive, but it was their only chance.

After Francis spoke, he and his wife, Carole, sat on the stage while nearly twenty other people spoke of their own missing family members. They heard parents whose children had been abducted at six or seven years old, who had been missing for ten or fourteen years, or more. They heard them tell how every day, several times a day, they would take a second look at someone on the street, someone who just happened to be about the age that their loved one would be, just in case. It is the hope that never dies.

Sitting on that stage, listening to the pain of these families, astounded at the number of families living in this kind of suspended grief — the grief you can never really know until you own it — Carole and Francis Carrington were transformed. The grief, and the courage, were so palpable that both she and Francis resolved that day that they would do what they could to make sure these cases weren't ignored. At some point — when they had emerged from this overwhelming eddy of events — they would do something to help. Not just talk, but action — like their daughter would have done — something that would empower these families. They didn't know what, and they didn't know how, but they would make it their business to help these families keep hope alive.

Hope and strength are the lifeblood of the family of a missing child. Everyone in that audience knew that the chances of seeing their loved ones again might be one in a million. But the people in this area were familiar with the local case in which the impossible came true.

Back in 1972, in nearby Merced — in a case I would later get very involved in — a seven-year-old boy named Steven Stayner was on his way home from school when he was kidnapped by a previously convicted pedophile named Kenneth Parnell. For seven years, he kept this young boy, convincing Steven that he was now his new father — enrolling him in school by day, sodomizing him and torturing him by night, convincing him that this was how life was supposed to be. But when Steven turned fourteen, his entrance into puberty ended Parnell's sexual obsession with him. One day, Parnell brought another little boy home, and something snapped in Steven's head; Steven went to the police station and said, I think there's something wrong here. He freed himself and the other kidnapped boy as well, and was able to tell the police what he remembered of his former life. Steven was soon reunited with his family. He came home alive, a hero, back from the dead after seven years.

The case was so miraculous that a book was written about it, followed by a TV movie. It was the stuff that filled the dreams of these parents sitting on the stage at the Vigil of Hope. Carole Carrington, a confirmed true-crime buff, had read the book and knew the story.

But there was no way she would have ever predicted the bizarre way in which Steven Stayner's story would intersect with her own.

That bizarre twist in the case would not come until later.

Right now, there was a more pressing matter at hand.

On March 18, the Carringtons and Pellossos were summoned by Maddock to the FBI command center. Agents wanted to talk with them before a press conference at the Doubletree Hotel.

When they arrived at the strategy room, they were surprised to see everything packed up; computers, supplies, almost everything was boxed and ready to move out.

This was the news: after a month with no sign of the women, the FBI was breaking up the command center and moving back to their offices in Sacramento.

Stoically, Francis Carrington accepted the situation, even though in his heart he felt that the agents were giving up. He offered no argument. "There was nothing to say," he told us later.

The hotline phones were mostly silent during this conversation; now one rang pathetically, as if to punctuate the disappointment of the two families.

Then the families noticed the agent who answered that phone call getting excited.

They moved closer to him, instinctively, and became aware, through his side of the conversation, of what the person on the other end of the line was saying:

Someone had found the car.

Retired carpenter Jim Powers was target-shooting in the woods about a quarter mile from his cabin near Long Barn, California — more than a three-hour drive from Yosemite, two hours from Modesto — when he stumbled across the burned-out car. It looked like just one of the many cars that were trashed and abandoned in the local woods, completely torched, and for a moment he thought about using it for target practice. Then he noticed a smudge of red paint near a rear door handle.

He had heard about the red Grand Prix that everyone had been looking for down near Yosemite. He took a look inside. The backseats had burned clear through to the trunk; he couldn't see anything inside. He decided he should report the vehicle, so he went looking for the license plate. One of the license plates had been burned to a crisp; the other had melted but was legible. Having nothing to write on, he took the license plate itself back to his cabin and called the California Highway Patrol.

Now when three women are missing, and their car has disappeared, and some guy shows up with the car's license plate, any cop is going to be a little suspicious. Jim Powers was questioned for three hours. The FBI even gave him a lie detector test. Finally they were assured that he was not complicit in any way — he was just the guy who found the car.

And God bless him for that.

The FBI blocked off the scene so that they could do a thorough examination of the car and the site the next day. They announced the discovery of the car to the media, but all they knew at the time was that it hadn't gone off the road accidentally, and there were no bodies found in the car. The Carringtons and Pelossos held hands during the press conference, holding on for dear life.

The FBI had some unpacking to do.

The search was back on.

Joann Donnellan had covered well over a hundred missing-child cases, and had developed a keen understanding of the pain of the parents: a kind, empathic ear, she was willing to talk to them on end, listen to their problems, and offer advice when asked, and they came to trust her. It is the most difficult job at *America's Most Wanted*, that of missing-child coordinator, because of the enormous well of emotions you encounter. The only way to deal with it is to try to keep a healthy professional distance; despite that, you can't help being drawn deeply into some of the families you're working with.

Such was the case with the Carringtons. When she was done producing any given story on the case and the cameras went away, she stayed behind, helping in any way she could. She was living at the Holiday Inn, where the Carringtons and Pellosos were staying, and it was the first time she was involved with the families of a missing child twenty-four hours a day, seven days a week, experiencing their grief every day and night.

Almost from the start, trading witticisms with Francis Carrington, having coffee and taking walks with Carole Carrington, Joann discovered strong connections with the family.

Carole Sund had adopted three children; Joann was herself adopted. Carole Sund served on the board of her retarded sister's home; Joann did volunteer work with Special Olympics. Joann felt passionately how wrong it all was: Carole Sund was a woman taken away before her time. And the two young girls — Joann was not so far past her teens that she could not remember the sense of immense hope and possibility that surrounds an eighteen-year-old, and now she felt deeply the pain of their disappearance.

So when the Carringtons and Pellossos got up at four-thirty in the morning to continue operations, Joann was there. When they stayed up late to review tips and give interviews, Joann stayed up, too. She brought the camera crews when everyone wanted her to, to keep publicity about the case alive; and she left the crews behind when the families felt they needed their privacy.

And back home, no one dared mention going a week without updating this story: the rest of the media might have given up on this family, she would say, but *America's Most Wanted* will not.

I know that she was just doing her job. But I also know that it was much more than that. The position of missing-child coordinator requires an ocean of compassion, an infinite ability to help someone in pain muster a slight smile; I know that Joann was doing her best to be a comfort, not a pain, to the families, and I thank her for that.

Joann also sent a team to Eureka to follow Jens and see how he was dealing with day-to-day life without his lifelong sweetheart, the Great Organizer. Jens was doing all he could to provide stability for Jimmy, Jonah, and Gina, and his sister Vicki was still chipping in to help. Every man is a hero to his children, but Jimmy, Jonah, and Gina have no idea just how courageous Jens had to be. "I fall apart periodically," Jens told us. "People have asked me how I can do this and hold up so well, but I have three children to take care of, I do have a business to run. I want my family back, but I have to continue."

But even with the combined efforts of Jens and Vicki, it was hard to keep the family's plates spinning as Carole had done so effortlessly. One day, a chagrined Jens turned to our crew, who had followed the family to one of the boys' basketball practice. "I just realized something," Jens admitted. "I forgot to bring Jimmy to practice. I brought Jonah, but I didn't bring Jimmy."

Jens looked absolutely lost without his wife. We were with Jens and the kids when the first footage of the discovered rental car hit the local news. The helicopter shot revealed the devastation. He was inconsolable: "Just look at that, it's burned . . . wow," was all he could say, shaking his head, unable to continue.

"She did everything for me," he told us later. "She could have organized the search much better than me."

Joann stayed with the Carringtons during this terrible turn of events and was stunned to see them responding optimistically to the discovery of the burned car. They were determined to find Carole and the girls, and the Carringtons were now convinced the three had been kidnapped and were being held somewhere.

It is a belief that comes from that eternal wellspring of hope that every parent of a missing child holds dear: this was no accident. Therefore it was a kidnapping. Therefore, they might still be alive.

But by the next morning, we learned the truth.

At breakfast, Joann heard there was going to be another press conference, at eleven o'clock in Tuolumne County, where the car was found. When she went to meet up with the families, she was unable to find them: they were behind closed doors, meeting with the FBI.

She was told that crying could be heard coming from the room.

The night before, all the investigators had been able to do was look through the shell of the car and secure the site before night fell. They had announced what they saw: no bodies were in the car. But when they opened the trunk the next day, they found something. They thought they might be mistaken. They weren't sure what they were dealing with. The heat had burned the car so badly they couldn't tell.

At first, they couldn't tell if they were looking at the remains of three bodies, or two, or one.

In Modesto, the remaining volunteers crowded into Joann's hotel room to watch the press conference live on television. The FBI announced they had found two bodies in the trunk of the car. The volunteers started to cry. Reporters started to scramble. Joann was in a daze.

I have seen some amazing things happen to survivors. I have seen people find unbelievable courage and grace, despite the pain they were going through. And this was a moment when the Carringtons and Pellosos showed the most amazing grace you can imagine.

After all this time, all this hope, and then after hearing this worst of all possible news, when a normal and acceptable reaction would be to rage, to scream, or to bury your face in a pillow and cry until there are no more tears, these families came into the volunteer center and thanked everyone for their work.

They hugged everyone who needed a hug.

And then Francis spoke.

There was a mad scramble, photographers and videographers trying to get his reaction. Probably because he is so composed, normally so stoic, it made sense for Francis Carrington to speak for the families. But this wasn't the Francis anyone had come to know. The emotions of the past month had finally broken through the dam he had constructed. He wept openly, saying simply, "I'm supposed to die before my daughter and my granddaughter." Then he apologized for getting emotional and excused himself.

Carole explained that they just wanted to thank the volunteers for their hard work, and that this would probably be their last interview for a while.

And then the families turned away, for a private moment of unbearable grief.

By the end of the day, investigators felt confident enough to tell us the bodies were probably those of Carole and one of the girls. The third body had not been found.

On March 20, Joann had to leave, to fly back to Washington and edit her story on the case. The Carringtons walked Joann to her car and helped her with her bags. As they loaded up Joann's rental, she wondered if they noticed: it was a silver Grand Prix, the same model car that their daughter had been driving. It was all so surreal. Joann thanked them for sharing so much of themselves. She told them she knew it was hard, but at least now the wondering is over. With eyes welling up, Carole agreed.

Then Joann got on the plane and began to cry.

The FBI announced that another body had

been found, on a scenic overlook about halfway between Modesto and the Cedar Lodge in El Portal. By the time of our Friday night taping, they had not sorted out whether it was Juli or Silvina whose body had been discovered in the car with Carole, so Joann and I had to go through a grisly ritual of writing and reading the copy over and over, for each of the possibilities, including the possibility that the FBI would not be able to determine the answer to this morbid question.

Joann was caught in the whirlwind of producing on deadline: exhausted from jet lag, emotionally spent from the entire ordeal, she was running on instinct and adrenaline now, trying to keep up with the ever-changing events, going quickly from rewrite to reedit and back to rewrite again. At 8 P.M. that Friday night, which is usually when we are wrapping up Saturday's show, the FBI announced it was Juli's body that had been found on the scenic overlook, which meant it was Carole and Silvina who had been in the trunk of the car.

A grim-faced Joann told her editor to rescue the tape, for it was time for one more edit: they placed the correct voice-over and started matching to it the still pictures of the women, the three women who had died too soon.

Pepe Pellosso flew back to Argentina; his older daughter, Paula, flew to California to join her mother. When she arrived, the Carrington and

Pellosso families made their first trip to the site where they found Juli's body. James Maddock led the families to the location. Dozens of people had turned out from the community. They brought hugs and kisses, they bore cards and homemade angels. People who had worked so hard in the volunteer command center came out to bid Juli farewell. They held hands and prayed. "This is the time to cry," Carole told us. "This was harder than the car, but I'm glad I came."

Joann had flown back out for the memorial service, by this time every bit as much a grieving friend as a television producer. A news crew wanted to get a one-on-one interview with Carole, and the reporter balked about our crew being nearby, concerned that the interview wouldn't be exclusive. "Don't mind them," Carole consoled the reporter. "That's just *America's Most Wanted*. They've been here from the beginning. They're like family."

Families shouldn't have to do what these families did. Raquel Pelloso and Paula went to Eureka to get Silvina's belongings. Raquel had never been to the Sund's house, and she saw for the first time pictures of herself on the walls: pictures of her and Carole, young mothers together, smiling.

Juli and Silvina together as babies.

Silvina was supposed to be back home by now. That's the way it should have been. Instead, Raquel and Paula gathered her things and packed her suitcase.

The FBI's investigation heated up with the discovery of Juli's body. At the time, they said only that a "source" gave them the location of the body. The next day, the FBI rounded up about ten more local parole violators. The press went nuts, digging even harder to get information from some of these losers, even though the FBI was adamant about not naming any one of these drifters as an official suspect.

First there was a report that Michael Larwick, the half-brother of Eugene Dykes — one of those first people arrested, what seemed now like a million years ago — was the most likely suspect. Larwick gave an interview to a Fresno television station and said he had nothing to do with it. Then Jeffery Keeney, one of the men who was rounded up after Juli's body was found, denied in a Modesto paper that he had any involvement.

So by April 7, California prosecutors went to work with a grand jury to force some of these runners to testify, in hopes of sorting through the morass of conflicting stories. Witnesses came in and out telling their stories. Each day the papers would reveal the details of the "secret" grand jury proceedings of the day before.

It was the ultimate media circus. A tabloid-style TV show reported that they had a recording of a phone conversation between a young man and woman, revealing details about the murders. A rumor circulated that there was a box somewhere containing some of the women's possessions. There was another story about some of their jewelry. A Fresno TV station reported that a relative of Larwick and Eugene Dykes gave the FBI a complete account of the attack. A Modesto paper printed a scenario of what happened to the women based on "unnamed sources." Agents said that some of the details of the story (although they wouldn't say which) were completely inaccurate.

It got more ridiculous. A man who happened to know some of the "unofficial suspects" drowned in the Tuolumne River, and the rumor mill whispered that he was killed because he knew something about the Sund case. Later, his own relatives told newspapers that he had walked in on one of the girls being raped in a room in Modesto. Once the story was completely blown out of proportion, another relative came forward and said the family had just been repeating a rumor they had heard somewhere else. About a week later, an autopsy showed there was no sign that the man had been murdered at all.

He had simply drowned while swimming.

It was hard to sort out the truth. We got a tip from a caller who said he'd heard the whole story of the abduction and murder from his friends. The people implicated were some of the "unofficial suspects"; he was willing to tell us everything he knew. But when we went out to interview him, we found that most of his story floated on the conjecture and crap that had already billowed to the surface. The only usable part of his story was the fact that the area was ripe with methamphetamines. Crank.

But even our informant was a former crank-head.

And that was really at the heart of all the problems the FBI had with the investigation: almost all of the people they had picked up were strung out on drugs that had fried their brains. One day they would relate all sorts of gruesome details about who did what to whom and where and how. The next day the story would be completely different, and they'd probably believe it just as much as the first story they told. The day after that, they'd be lucky to tell you what they had for dinner the night before. And then it would start all over again. One guy told the Associated Press, "If I was involved, it wasn't through my knowledge," a statement only a drug addict could make with a straight face.

Still, the FBI slogged on. By the middle of June, they told the families that it might take a while to sort out what really happened, but they assured them that everyone connected to the killings was behind bars.

They were dead wrong.

Joie Armstrong, a twenty-six-year-old naturalist at the Yosemite Institute just a few miles up the road from the Cedar Lodge, didn't show up to meet friends in Sausalito, as planned. They became worried. Joie, an energetic Orlando native who loved to lead kids on educational hikes through the majestic park, had apparently expressed anxiety at being alone in the park since the news of the triple murder.

So the next day, a small search squad went to Armstrong's rustic pine cabin in Foresta, where they found her truck, still in the driveway, packed with bags for her trip. The search team spread out to survey the immediate area. Minutes later, just a few yards from the cabin, they found Joie.

She had been decapitated.

Upon investigating, a park employee recalled seeing a blue and white truck in the area on the evening prior. That afternoon, park rangers spotted the same truck on the shoulder of a road running along the Merced river. The rangers walked down to the riverbank and found a man smoking a joint in the nude. The man told them he was an employee at the Cedar Lodge, just a few miles down the road from Foresta, but he said he hadn't been anywhere near Joie's cabin. He let the rangers confiscate his marijuana and search his car, but he did not let them search the backpack he was carrying. The truck had four different tires, and investigators photographed them all.

Then the man was allowed to go on his way.

The next day, though, the rangers had a few more questions for him — because the unique tire pattern on his International Scout truck had matched tracks left at Joie's home.

But the man, who hadn't missed a day of work

in more than a year, didn't show up at Cedar Lodge.

And so they began quickly to investigate him.

His name was Cary Stayner.

It was a last name that everyone in the region knew.

Because it was the younger brother of the one-in-a-million Steven Stayner, who had so famously disappeared in 1972, only to reappear seven years later.

It turned out no one really knew too much about Cary Anthony Stayner. The thirty-seven-year-old was rather good-looking but a loner, like many who lived in Yosemite. Some say it was the disappearance of little Steven that had derailed his potential. Cary Stayner, who had suffered a drought of attention when Steven disappeared and a larger one when he returned, grew up lonely and disturbed.

After graduating from high school, Stayner worked for many years in a company that made windows and mirrors. In 1997, he took a job as a maintenance man at Cedar Lodge. During the time that Carole, Juli, and Silvina went missing, Stayner was laid off for the slow winter.

But he still lived at the Cedar Lodge.

Stayner had been questioned by the FBI twice during the initial investigation at Cedar Lodge. He was more than helpful, opening rooms for evidence technicians, gathering sheets and blankets so forensic scientists could do fiber comparisons.

But now that they had to question him about the matching tire tread, he was nowhere to be found. So they put out a news bulletin and, acting on a tip from someone who saw the bulletin, found him that Saturday — at a nudist camp near Sacramento. Back in Sacramento, Stayner waived his right to remain silent. He wanted to talk.

In fact, he seemed thrilled to talk.

He was still on a high from killing Joie Armstrong.

And the sick bastard had been waiting five months to tell everyone his story.

A story that turned out to be 100 percent true.

The story of how he killed Carole Sund, Juli Sund, and Silvina Pellosso.

Here is the confession Stayner made to the Mariposa County sheriff:

A little after ten o'clock on February 15, Stayner knocked on the door of Cedar Lodge room 509.

When Carole asked who it was, he replied, "Maintenance. I need to fix a leak in the bathroom." Carole didn't know of any leak, but there was this clean-cut hotel maintenance man with his toolbox in hand, telling her the leak was behind the bathroom wall. She let him in.

Stayner proceeded past Carole and the girls and went to the bathroom. He poked around at the fan where he said he thought the problem was. A few moments later, Stayner emerged from the bathroom with the .22 caliber pistol he had stashed in the toolbox.

"This is just a robbery," he told them. "I just want your money and your car."

He convinced the women that if they only did what he said — exactly what he said, and without a lot of noise — they wouldn't be hurt. Not that anyone could have heard them anyway, as Joann's little experiment would later prove.

Stayner bound the women's hands behind their backs with duct tape. He made Juli and Silvina lie down on the floor. He then went back to the bed where Carole lay and put a rope around her neck.

He smiled to see the terror in her eyes as he pulled the rope tighter and tighter, strangling the woman, until the struggling and tension left her body and she lay limp, breathless, dead.

Then he hefted her body out into the parking lot and placed her in the trunk of her rental car.

The girls, terrified and bound with duct tape, were unable to escape. Stayner returned, and brought them back into the bedroom. He says he started to sexually assault Juli while Silvina watched. But he changed his mind.

He first took Silvina into the bathroom, where he placed her in the tub, and strangled her as well.

Then he says, he came back into the room, and as her mother lay dead in a car trunk out-side, as her best friend lay dead in the bathtub, he began to sexually assault Juli, again and again.

It was somewhere between 4 and 5 A.M. when Juli asked to go to the bathroom. It was then that he took Silvina's body and put it in the trunk with Carole's. He then took nearly all of their belongings and threw them in the back of the car. He told Juli he needed to take her somewhere, bundled her up in a pink blanket, wrapped duct tape around her hands in front of her, and drove off with her to Lake Don Pedro Reservoir.

He drove to a scenic point, took Juli out of the car, and carried her up to a more secluded area.

After assaulting her one last time, he took out a knife, slit her throat, and left her to bleed to death.

In the woods, Stayner ditched the knife and duct tape. He went back to the car and drove toward Long Barn, looking for a place to hide the car.

When he found a secluded spot, he went off the road and backed the car into the brush about a hundred yards until he got stuck on a tree stump and couldn't go any farther. He wiped down the car for prints, and walked a mile and a half to a restaurant, where he ate breakfast.

Then he went to a pay phone and called a cab to take him back to Yosemite.

It cost him $165.

Back at Cedar Lodge, he changed the sheets and cleaned the bathtub of room 509. He even wet down the towels to make it look like the women had gotten up, taken showers, packed, and left.

Two days later, before the search was in full swing, Stayner took some gasoline, drove back to where he had stashed the car, and set the car on fire. He took Carole's wallet and threw it out at the intersection at Modesto, to confuse the search.

For a while, Stayner had gotten away with murder.

A month later, when they found the car, Stayner wrote an anonymous letter to the FBI, telling them exactly where to find Juli's body. In the letter he referred to himself as "we." He wrote random names on a sheet he placed on top of the letter, so the imprints would show through, just to confuse things. He even got someone else to lick the envelope. So there would be someone else's saliva should they test for DNA.

The feds knew Stayner wasn't making this up. He knew too much about the case, too many details that had been kept secret.

But they weren't convinced that he acted alone.

They still aren't. Too much doesn't make sense. Even with a gun, it defies logic that he was able to subdue and kill three grown women without one of them getting away or putting up more of a struggle. To do all he did in one evening by himself would have required uncanny speed and forethought. Stayner is the only person charged with the murder at this time, but investigators are still not ruling out the possibility of other accomplices.

A reporter snuck in to talk to Cary Stayner in jail, and the first words out of this cold-hearted bastard's mouth were: How much do you think I'll get for the movie rights to my story?

That's sick enough — he knew they had made a movie about his little brother's miraculous story and so now he was going to get his — but it gets worse. He tried to blame the problems of his entire worthless life on little Steven — he was jealous of Steven, he said, and that sent him on a wrong road. Well, I gotta say, you're jealous of a seven-year-old who is kidnapped and then spent seven years being sodomized and tortured? What is that to be jealous of? As far as I'm concerned, it's just a pathetic excuse from a pathetic individual, and I'm just sorry that, if he grew up so miserable, he didn't have the decency to take his own rotten life before he got a chance to take the lives of those three wonderful women.

But he did roam the streets of this world, and now he would pay for his terrible deeds.

Francis Carrington believes that Stayner is one of the maintenance men who stared him down when he first arrived at the Cedar Lodge. And he and Carole are both unconvinced that Stayner acted alone. Francis thinks there's no way he could have handled all three of them by himself. They were too strong-willed to let him take advantage of them.

In December of 2000, Stayner was sentenced to life for the murder of Joie Armstrong. The fact that she was killed in a national park made hers a federal case and gave it precedence. He could still face the death penalty for the murders of Carole and Juli Sund and Silvina Pelloso.

After the bodies were discovered, the Carringtons and Jens Sund had gone home to Eureka and tried to keep life as normal as possible. They did it for the three younger children — Jonah, Jimmy, and Gina; and they did it for Carole Sund, who would have wanted things to keep moving on schedule. They had Easter and even organized the traditional Easter egg hunt.

But life just couldn't get back to normal. First there were the memorial services, one in Eureka, and one in Modesto. Our cameraman Jim Meyers became so close to Jens that Jens asked us to cover the Eureka memorial service. They did not want a media circus there; would we cover the event and feed it to all the others?

Normally, we wouldn't be the ones to cover a live event, since we're not on the air when it's going on, but Lance, our executive producer, agreed to do it for the families; so Joann and a field producer flew out to coordinate the three-camera shoot and subsequent feed.

After the service, Joann hopped on a plane to San Francisco and arrived there at 8 P.M. The next day was the Modesto memorial service, and the Modesto police had asked Joann to make a tape for that service.

In Eureka, people knew Juli and Carole and Silvina as friends, school chums, and neighbors; but here in Modesto, they were only known as the victims of a horrible crime. The police wanted to give these hardworking volunteers more to remember them by.

She worked all night, interspersing video from the Eureka memorial service with footage of majestic Yosemite, interviews with Raquel and friends of Carole and Juli, shots from a videotape found in the women's camera after their death.

It also included bits of a poem that Gina Sund had written while her mother was missing, a poem that to this day none of us can forget. It begins:

Late at night, I await for your return
But deep in my heart I know something my mind
   doesn't want to learn.

The life of a missing-child producer is a mixture of tears and total deadline panic. Joann finished at 3 P.M. the next day, then got in the car and drove like crazy to Modesto. She got there at 7 P.M. — "one of those *Broadcast News* moments," she later said — and the tape went up in front of the thousand mourners gathered to grieve for the three women.

It was a painful and powerful tribute. At that

moment, the reality of the loss hit home for all those volunteers.

Joann looked up at the screen, and one more time, said a tearful good-bye to three women whom she never knew, but who now, she realized, she could never forget.

I talked to Francis and Carole a lot over the next few days. Those of us who have lost children to violent crime have no one to turn to but each other, and so I tried to offer what help I could.

I remember Francis saying to me, John, this was my daughter, this was my granddaughter, how can I get over this — will I ever get over this?

I told him, quite honestly, and as gently as I could, you will never get over this. It is a wound that heals over but leaves an eternal scar; holidays and birthdays make it bleed all over again.

We talked about preparing for the trial, for the brutality of a criminal justice system that treats victims' families as though they were the criminals.

And I told him to be prepared for one other thing: everyone will ask you, for the rest of your life, why do you think Cary Stayner killed your daughter, and your granddaughter, and her friend? And you will never know the answer to that question, and you will go insane if you allow yourself to try to understand it.

You will never find that answer.

But I do have another answer:

461

You can make sure they did not die in vain.

You did what I did, when Adam died, I said to Francis: I launched the biggest search anyone had ever seen, and did things no one had done before, and you have done the same.

You also went up against something I never went up against: the fact that nobody really wants to spring into action when adults go missing. Your daughter was gone, your grand-daughter was gone, and people told you, don't worry.

In Adam's memory, I did everything I could to try to help all the other children who would go missing. I have made it my life's work, and it is how I make sure that Adam did not die in vain.

In the memory of Carole and Juli, and in the memory of Silvina, if there is something you can do for missing adults, then they will not have died in vain.

And shortly after we talked, the Sund/ Carrington Foundation was born.

True to the promise they made to themselves at that Vigil of Hope, they started a foundation to try to help all those other families, and to help crime victims yet to come. They called it the Sund/ Carrington Memorial Reward Foundation.

The Carringtons knew that their ability to offer big rewards had made a big difference in their case. They paid the $50,000 they had offered for the discovery of the car. But there was still the matter of the $200,000 they had offered for the safe return of their loved ones.

So they decided to turn their loss into a benefit for crime victims everywhere. They decided that the money would go to other families who didn't have the resources to offer rewards in their own cases.

The foundation would become involved in, but not limit itself to, cases in which an adult had gone missing. The criteria were strict: the victims had to be totally innocent, like Juli, Silvina, and Carole had been. The families had to be unable to post a significant reward on their own. And law enforcement had to believe that the reward would make a significant difference in the case.

Today, the garden of hope that Carole and Francis planted by starting the Sund/Carrington Foundation is in full bloom. As of this writing, the fund has posted $311,000 in reward money for missing persons and murder cases in sixteen states — numbers that are growing every day.

And the foundation's executives go far beyond just the rewards — helping to organize press conferences, sometimes taking the tips themselves to assure the tipsters they will remain anonymous, helping families learn to coordinate efforts with police, helping them rally the media.

All the skills the Carringtons wish they had never had to learn. Carole Carrington gives her time and her heart, calling mothers whose children are missing, attending barbecues and concerts as fund-raisers.

It is the next best thing the parent of a murdered child can do. You can never bring your precious loved ones back alive, but you can try to help the next person find some answers, find some justice. It is what has kept me sane all these years, and what keeps Carole and Francis going, and now it is what I would like to ask you to do.

Here are three cases that the foundation has posted rewards on, three cases where families are crying out for justice.

Maybe you can answer those prayers today.

Fugitive: Javier Vasquez
Reward: $8,000

On January 19, 1999, at almost 3 A.M., police responded to a call from a Denny's restaurant in Fresno, California, where a small child had been wandering unattended. The Fresno police found no report of a missing child and couldn't figure out the child's identity. They called a news conference asking the public for help.

Acting on tips from callers who recognized the child as two-year-old Dannon Credo, the police went to his mother's home at the Casa De Paz Apartments.

They found the body of his mother, Mona Credo.

Investigators compiled evidence and issued a warrant for the arrest of her estranged boyfriend, Javier Zurita Vasquez.

Vasquez is known to have family members living in the Visalia, Farmersville, and Pixley areas of California and may be working as a farm laborer in the San Joaquin Valley. The Sund/Carrington Foundation has offered a $5,000 reward for information leading to his arrest and conviction; there is an additional $1,000 reward available through Fresno Crimestoppers, and the father of the victim has added $2,000.

Missing: Dorien Deon Thomas
Reward: $5,000

Dorien Thomas was last seen on October 26, 1998, in Amarillo, Texas. He was last seen near NW Ninth and Lipscomb on his bicycle. He was wearing a red T-shirt with blue or black jeans, and white sneakers with blue eyelets and white laces. His bicycle, which is a girl's style aqua bike with small white tires and a rusty chain, is also missing.

He would be eleven today, and stood four feet tall and weighed sixty pounds when he disappeared. He had an arrow shaved into his black hair, and had a scar on his knee and a round scar on each elbow.

Fugitive: Courtney Sconce's Killer
Reward: $15,000

On November 8, 2000, fishermen found the body of twelve-year-old Courtney Sconce along the Feather River in Sutter County, California. Courtney, a dark-haired, energetic tomboy, had been missing only a few hours from her home in the Rancho Cordova neighborhood of Sacramento. She is believed to have been abducted while walking alone to Harry's Liquor & Food convenience store at the corner of Folsom Boulevard and Cordova Lane to buy candy.

The fishermen who found Courtney reported seeing a white male fleeing naked from the scene. Police are looking for a white male in his early twenties, about six feet tall and weighing 145 to 165 pounds, with shoulder-length dark hair. He was driving a dark sedan, perhaps a mid-1980s BMW 300 series, and left a pair of silver wraparound Oakley sunglasses and a black T-shirt with a yellow skull and tribal design at the scene.

The Sund/Carrington Memorial Foundation has offered a $15,000 reward for information leading to the arrest and conviction of Courtney Sconce's killer.

Anyone with information about any of these three cases, please call: 1-800-CRIME-TV

I know that someone who is reading this book, or someone who has seen these cases on *America's Most Wanted*, can help solve them, can help bring answers and healing and, just possibly, justice to the families of the victims.

At *America's Most Wanted*, we have formed a

unique partnership, a partnership among the public, the media, and law enforcement. Sometimes, through the worst of circumstances, people are thrust into that partnership.

The Carringtons are part of that partnership now, and they are doing all they can to help others who are lost, and hoping, and praying for answers.

Now you are part of that partnership as well.

And I welcome you aboard.

Because I truly believe, with all my heart and soul, that together we can make a difference.